AGENDA

FOR

REFORM

AGENDA
FOR
REFORM

WINTHROP ROCKEFELLER AS GOVERNOR OF ARKANSAS, 1967–71

CATHY KUNZINGER URWIN

THE UNIVERSITY OF ARKANSAS PRESS
FAYETTEVILLE   1991

95   94   93   92   91   5   4   3   2   1

Designer: Lisa Heggestad
Typeface: Janson

The paper used in this publication meets the minimum requirements of the American National Standard for Permanence of Paper for Printed Library Materials Z39.48-1984. ∞

Photos courtesy of the Winthrop Rockefeller Collection, University of Arkansas at Little Rock Archives, University of Arkansas at Little Rock Library.

Library of Congress Cataloging-in-Publication Data

Urwin, Cathy Kunzinger, 1954–
    Agenda for reform : Winthrop Rockefeller as governor of Arkansas, 1967–71 / Cathy Kunzinger Urwin.
        p.   cm.
    Includes bibliographical references and index.
    ISBN 1-55728-200-5 (c)
    1. Arkansas—Politics and government—1951–   2. Rockefeller, Winthrop, 1912–1973. I. Title.
    F415.U78 1991
    976.7'053'092—dc20   90-48340
                                                                          CIP

For my parents,
Frederick William and Joan Catherine Kunzinger
with love, gratitude and respect.

Contents

Illustrations

(Following page 86)

The Rockefellers, circa 1916.

The Rockefeller brothers, 1958.

Aerial view of Winrock Farm, August 1960.

Ten Years in Arkansas appreciation dinner, Little Rock, August 7, 1963.

The beginning of the 1964 gubernatorial campaign.

Campaigning in 1964.

Rockefeller's inauguration as governor, January 10, 1967.

After the inauguration, January 10, 1967.

The memorial service for Dr. Martin Luther King, Jr.

Portrait taken during the 1970 campaign.

Winthrop Paul and Winthrop Rockefeller with Spiro Agnew in 1972.

Winthrop Rockefeller at Petit Jean Mountain.

Acknowledgments

There are a number of people without whose help this work would not have been finished.

I am very grateful to the staffs of the various archives used. In particular, I am indebted to Thomas E. Rosenbaum at the Rockefeller Archive Center in North Tarrytown, New York, Betty Austin at the University of Arkansas, and Martin M. Teasley at the Dwight D. Eisenhower Library. I owe a special debt to the staff at the University of Arkansas at Little Rock. Dr. Bobby Roberts, Linda Pine, and Joy Geisler gave unfailingly of their time and expertise. Their patience made the many hours of research a pleasure, and the grant I received from the University of Arkansas at Little Rock's Winthrop Rockefeller Endowment helped to defray my expenses.

I would like to thank those participants in the events that unfold here who gave their time to answer my many questions. I am grateful to Maurice "Footsie" Britt, Dale Bumpers, Marion Burton, Sterling Cockrill, G. Thomas Eisele, Orval E. Faubus, Robert Faulkner, Everett A. Ham, Jr., Cal Ledbetter, Jr., and John L. Ward for their invaluable insights.

My dissertation director at the University of Notre Dame, the Reverend Thomas E. Blantz, C.S.C., gave me patient and learned guidance. I cannot thank him enough for both his editing and his support. Mrs. Catherine Box, secretary of the history department at Notre Dame, gave me encouragement and made sure I met all deadlines. I would also like to thank the readers, Dr. Philip Gleason, Dr. Robert L. Kerby, and Dr. Walter Nugent, for their comments and suggestions.

I am grateful to Dr. Foy Lisenby and Dr. Harry Readnour, past and present chairmen of the department of history at the University of Central Arkansas, for allowing me to use the department's word processor. And this book would still be half-finished if not for the knowledge and patience of Mrs. Carol Griffith, secretary of the history department at the University of Central Arkansas. She taught me how to use the word processor and helped fight my battles with it. She was there whenever I needed her, and I will be forever grateful. Dr. Gary Wekkin, of the University of Central Arkansas's political science department, provided insights on the legislative process that were of great assistance.

I would like to thank my editor, Sandra Frierson, and all her colleagues at the University of Arkansas Press for their expert assistance in the preparation and publication of this book.

Finally, my deepest gratitude goes to my parents, Frederick and Joan Kunzinger, and my husband, Gregory J. W. Urwin. From my parents I received the encouragement and support I needed to attend graduate school. My husband gave me the encouragement and support to finish the book, as well as his time as an invaluable editor and proofreader.

Anything of merit found in the pages that follow is due largely to the people listed above. Any errors of fact or judgment are mine.

AGENDA

FOR

REFORM

Introduction

The decade of the 1960s saw massive social and political upheaval. Civil rights and the Vietnam conflict were but two of the causes of political realignment on both the state and national levels. The South, in particular, experienced drastic change, as sit-ins, freedom rides, demonstrations, federal legislation, and court orders brought down one of the main pillars of its society—segregation. Not since Reconstruction had the structure of Southern life been so disrupted. This disruption resulted in a dissolution of traditional voting patterns. The previously "Solid [Democratic] South" turned to Independent George Wallace and Republicans Barry Goldwater and Richard Nixon as presidential choices. At the state level, record numbers of GOP candidates were elected, in most instances because they repudiated the national Democratic party's civil rights actions.

Thanks to the 1957 Little Rock Central High School crisis, the rest of the nation saw Arkansas as a prime example of a Southern state dragged kicking and screaming into the twentieth century. But, during the latter half of the sixties, Arkansas saw little of the violence plaguing much of the nation. Political upheaval, namely the election of the state's first Republican governor in over ninety years, resulted in social, political, and governmental progress.

That pioneering Republican, Winthrop Rockefeller, served two terms as governor of Arkansas. After an unsuccessful bid in 1964, he won election to his first two-year term in 1966 and was re-elected in 1968. The grandson of John D. Rockefeller, the United States' first billionaire and founder of Standard Oil,

Winthrop was an anomaly in Arkansas politics. Raised in sheltered affluence in New York City, he became the first Republican since Reconstruction to be governor of the South's smallest state. His immediate predecessor in the governor's office was Orval Faubus, who had stepped down in 1966 after serving six terms, longer than any other governor in Arkansas's history except Bill Clinton. Faubus had dominated both the state's government and its Democratic party for the previous decade. But the public had tired of allegations of cronyism and corruption as well as continued racial tensions. The voters perceived Rockefeller as a fresh start, an opportunity to cleanse state government and start over.

Rockefeller's governorship was sandwiched between two very distinct eras in Arkansas political history. He followed the Faubus machine and preceded a succession of young, reform-minded Democrats. But to what extent can responsibility for this change be attributed to Rockefeller? Was he the catalyst that triggered the change, or merely the recipient of a propitious shift in voter preferences? In the February 14, 1988, *Arkansas Gazette*, "Forum" editor Robert McCord wrote:

> Until the advent of George Wallace, Arkansas was the most loyal state in the union for the Democratic Party. Democrats always won because the good old boys in the Party kept a firm grip on the State Capitol and the courthouses where the election laws were made and the votes counted.
> But it's been different ever since Winthrop Rockefeller produced the courage and the millions to bust up political machines like the one in Conway County. . . .
> . . . Chances are we wouldn't even be talking about a political code of ethics and Bill Clinton would never have been elected governor if Rockefeller hadn't brought political reform to Arkansas.

This book will examine the nature of the Rockefeller legacy.

When Winthrop Rockefeller became governor, he had already been successful in business, philanthropy and public service. Upon his move to Arkansas, he founded Winrock Farms, a Santa Gertrudis cattle-breeding operation. Both in New York and later in Arkansas, he was actively involved in a number of charitable organizations dedicated to improving education, health care, and civil rights. And he served, from 1955 to 1964, as the first chairman of the Arkansas Industrial Development Commission. Appointed by Faubus, Rockefeller's job was to convince new industries to locate in the state. These varied experiences made him well qualified to assume the governorship.

Once in office, he worked hard for reform in education and the prisons. His administration successfully passed Arkansas's first minimum wage law. He brought blacks into the political process and into state government. Due largely to Rockefeller's efforts, Arkansas did not experience the level of racial violence other states saw in 1968 and 1969. He took steps to streamline state government and to eliminate corruption in government agencies and in the voting process.

In addition to examining Rockefeller's governorship and its impact on Arkansas, this book will attempt to place his governorship in a proper perspective by comparing his experiences with those of other Republicans in the South. Was he unique, or was his election part of a trend? Did Rockefeller represent the mainstream of growing Republicanism, or was he an exception to that growth? What was his impact on the Republican party, both within and outside the state?

ONE

Heir to a Legacy of Wealth and Public Service

Winthrop Rockefeller belonged to the third generation of a financial dynasty built by John D. Rockefeller, Sr. Born in 1839, the son of a traveling medicine man, John D. Rockefeller began amassing his fortune in Cleveland, Ohio, as a produce commission salesman in 1859, but in 1865 went into the oil business. On January 10, 1870, he and his partners incorporated the Standard Oil Company. Standard Oil became one of the largest corporate empires of the late nineteenth century, expanding both horizontally and vertically. By the end of the decade, Standard Oil refined nearly 95 percent of the oil produced in the United States.[1] Rockefeller retired in 1896, at the age of fifty-seven.

John D. had four children, but only one son, John D., Jr. In 1884, when his son was ten, Rockefeller moved from Cleveland to New York City, and the heir grew up in a large townhouse on West Fifty-fourth Street. While in Cleveland, the children had been tutored at home, but in New York, the son went to a private school. He then attended Brown University, graduating in 1897.

At the time of John D., Jr.'s, college commencement, Standard Oil was under increasing attacks as a trust and as a monopoly. But despite this and his father's retirement, there was never any question as to whether or not the son would join the business. He commented later in his life: "My one thought from the time I was a boy was to help my father. I knew from the beginning I was going into his office."[2] At first, John D., Jr., was involved in helping to manage a wide range of family investments. But he gradually disassociated himself from active participation in these businesses, resigning as a director of Standard Oil in 1910. He eventually turned his attention full-time to his father's post-retirement occupation—philanthropy.

The Rockefeller Foundation, designed to act as a clearing-house for the family's philanthropic activities, was incorporated in May 1913. John D., Jr., was president. While the foundation contributed to a wide range of causes—medical research, conservation, education, the arts—it was the restoration of Colonial Williamsburg in Virginia that became the younger Rockefeller's favorite project.

John D. Rockefeller, Jr., married Abby Aldrich, the daughter of Rhode Island senator Nelson Aldrich, in 1901. The couple lived in a nine-story town home on the same block as his father. Weekends were spent in Abeyton Lodge on the family's thirty-five-hundred-acre estate at Pocantico Hills in North Tarrytown, New York, about thirty miles north of the city. They spent their summer vacations at another large estate at Seal Harbor, Maine.[3]

Winthrop, born on May 1, 1912, was the fifth of John D. Rockefeller, Jr., and Abby Aldrich Rockefeller's six children. Winthrop's siblings were Abby, born in 1903; John D. III, born in 1906; Nelson, born in 1908; Laurance, born in 1910; and David, born in 1915. Growing up, Winthrop faced problems endemic to his position in the family. He suffered frequent bullying and teasing by his older brothers, Nelson and Laurance, while lacking the special status that David held as the baby of the family.[4] When Winthrop was ten, his mother wrote in a letter to Nelson and Laurance: "It seems cruel to me that you big boys should make Winthrop the goat all the time. I realize that he is often trying, but you know very well that the only way to help him is by being kind to him. Abuse only makes him angry and much worse, while for love and kind treatment he will do anything."[5] Biographers of the Rockefeller family have made much of this sibling rivalry, pointing to it as proof of their descriptions of Winthrop as the outsider, the "black sheep,"[6] the "odd man out of the family, the fumbler."[7] However, in "A Letter to My Son," while he acknowledged that the teasing did take place, Winthrop saw it as beneficial in the long run, saying that Laurance and Nelson

> were always teasing me. . . .
> . . . but as I look back on it now, I am sure that I was a normally annoying younger brother, and had most of it coming to me. . . .
> . . . the teasing I got from Laurance and Nelson—and their very direct methods of curbing me when I lost control of my temper—did help me to keep it under control in later years. . . . Losing one's temper . . . is a luxury that no one can afford.[8]

Little of the correspondence between Winthrop and his brothers in their adult years is open to researchers. The letters that are available deal almost exclusively with political and business matters, but they are open and warm and show no indication of a lasting sibling rivalry.[9]

Winthrop, his brothers, and his sister grew up the children of one of the richest men in the United States. After federal inheritance taxes were raised sharply in 1917, John D. Rockefeller, Sr., began transferring his fortune to his son. By 1921 the father had given his son close to $465 million.[10] But surprisingly, money was a source of tension between Winthrop and his father. The elder Rockefeller required all his children to keep strict accounts of how they spent their allowance. This accounting continued throughout their college years and until each began earning his own income. Winthrop was almost always the worst at keeping these accounts.[11] For a number of years, the sore subject of financial records set up a block between Winthrop and his father. The son was uncomfortable whenever he was alone with his father, fearful that the subject would be brought up. Winthrop later said that this problem helped give him "great sympathy" for anyone with financial problems, as well as an understanding of the value of money and its use.[12] Winthrop's problems with his accounts, the teasing he took from Nelson and Laurance, and his repeated failures in school probably all contributed to the compassion that he exhibited toward the underdog throughout his adult life.

Winthrop started his education at the Lincoln School, established in 1917 by the Teachers College of Columbia University. It was an experimental school based on the educational theories of John Dewey.[13] Nelson, Laurance, and David attended the same school, and it gave the Rockefeller brothers exposure to children of different races and from all walks of life. The curriculum emphasized a student's freedom of choice, public speaking, and coeducational shop and home economic courses rather than the competitive aspects of traditional schooling.[14] While the Lincoln School certainly helped to broaden Winthrop's perspective and remove some of the insulation that growing up as a Rockefeller must have entailed, the lack of emphasis on the basics may not have been best for him. He did so poorly there that in the tenth grade he was transferred to the Loomis School, a formal prep boarding school in Windsor, Connecticut, which his brother John had attended. The Loomis philosophy stood in sharp contrast to Lincoln. Scholastic standards at Loomis were strict, and on his first report card Winthrop failed every subject.[15] With the help of a tutoring camp that he attended over two consecutive summers, he graduated from Loomis in June 1931, earning a coveted school prize for "industry, loyalty, and manliness."[16]

Rockefeller entered Yale in the fall of 1931. He went, despite his lack of attraction to the academic world, because it was expected of him. He later wrote, "I went to Yale without enthusiasm or purpose."[17] His grades reflected this lack of interest.

During the summer between his second and third years at Yale, he went to work for the company his grandfather had founded—Standard Oil of New Jersey. He spent the summer becoming acquainted with various phases of the business in New Jersey, Massachusetts, and Texas. It was in Texas, in the production end of the oil industry, that he found a niche. Of this experience in Texas he later wrote: "From the lowest roustabout to the highest executive, men were working with their hands and their minds, producing something real, something of value. I was fascinated by everything I saw—I wanted to become a part of it."[18] This theme of enjoying working with his hands, of being a producer rather than a financier, recurs throughout Rockefeller's life and may account for some of his motivation in leaving New York to take up residence in Arkansas in 1953.

Rockefeller returned to Yale in the fall of 1933, but he did not finish out the school year. Having found something that he genuinely enjoyed, he could no longer endure struggling through college. In February 1934 he resigned from Yale to return to work in the oil industry.[19] He apparently did so with his father's blessings, and the elder Rockefeller was pleased that one of his sons had shown an interest in the oil business.[20]

Winthrop spent the next three years in Texas learning the oil business from the ground up. He followed a set program, going from one phase of production to the next, spending several months in each job. The first eighteen months involved manual labor, after which he worked in the executive offices of the Humble Oil and Refining Company in Houston.[21]

It was in Texas that Rockefeller first became actively involved in attempting to improve race relations and the living conditions of blacks. His interest was aroused when his black maid had an appendicitis attack and he learned first hand of the problems of health care in the segregated South. Most blacks did not get medical attention on a regular basis. They could receive free treatment for medical emergencies at white hospitals, but Houston's "Negro Hospital," built by a white philanthropist, had to charge its patients in order to stay open. As a result, the forty-bed hospital had an average occupancy rate of between seven and twelve. Rockefeller's maid, despite the financial hardship it would entail, had insisted on going to the Negro Hospital, "because the care given Colored people in the white hospital was so inferior."[22] Through a letter to his father, Rockefeller and his maid's black doctor enlisted the assistance of the Rockefeller Foundation and the Rosenwald Foundation in Chicago. They attempted to establish a local community health organization that would be run by blacks for blacks.

Unfortunately, the attempt failed at the time, due to lack of support for the idea by the white trustees of the black hospital. Rockefeller later recalled what happened when a black doctor from the Rosenwald Foundation came to Houston to explain the idea to the trustees.

> We went to my apartment, where the trustees of the Negro hospital were waiting. The meeting was rather painful. Some of the trustees showed that they were not at all interested in the problem of the Negro—that they were interested only in building a reputation as good and philanthropic people. Certainly they were not prepared to sit down with a Negro—no matter how well qualified he was—and discuss anything.
>
> ... Nothing was done about Dr. Bowsfield's intelligent suggestions—but I do not think the luncheon was entirely wasted. ... Dr. Bowsfield's visit did open the eyes of some people to what should and could be done, and a seed was sown which later brought improvement in the problem I was attacking.[23]

In January 1937 Rockefeller returned to New York to continue his training. He spent a year at the Chase National Bank learning the financial end of the oil industry.[24] This phase of the business bored him, and halfway through his year there he left the bank to become vice-chairman of the brand-new Greater New York Fund, a municipal fund-raising agency.[25] In January 1939 he took a permanent job in the oil industry as Near East liaison in the foreign trade department of the Socony-Vacuum Oil Company.[26] The job did not turn out to be as permanent as was anticipated, but it did have one significant effect on Rockefeller's life. Shortly after Hitler marched into Poland in September 1939, thus triggering World War II, Winthrop went on a ten-week business trip to Italy and the Middle East. The trip helped to convince him that American involvement in the war was inevitable.[27] In July 1940 he participated in a business and professional men's special Citizens Military Training Camp at Plattsburg, New York, and the following January he enlisted as a private in the Army.[28]

At his request, Rockefeller was assigned to the infantry. He became a sergeant in August 1941, and in October of that year entered the Officers Infantry Training School at Fort Benning,

Georgia, graduating as a second lieutenant on January 24, 1942. He went overseas in late 1943, fought in Guam and the Philippines, and won promotion to the rank of major in January 1944. In April 1945 he was injured in a kamikaze attack on a troop transport ship off Okinawa. He returned to duty and shortly afterward contracted a severe case of hepatitis and was sent back to the States. Before leaving the Army as a lieutenant colonel in October 1946, Rockefeller toured the United States, surveying veterans' readjustment problems for the secretary of war.[29]

Upon his discharge, Rockefeller resumed working for Socony-Vacuum. He also resumed his numerous activities on behalf of various philanthropic organizations. These give interesting insight into the ideals and beliefs that were an important influence on him in seeking and holding the governorship of Arkansas.

At the age of twenty-five, Winthrop Rockefeller had first become involved in a fund-raising drive. In early 1938 he was appointed vice-chairman of the campaign committee for the Greater New York Fund in its initial year. The fund was a united appeal for donations from corporate and employee groups by some 450 charitable organizations. The 1938 drive raised over four million dollars[30] and was a huge personal success for Rockefeller, particularly in winning high praise from his family. After a fund dinner, Nelson sent Winthrop a telegram: "You can't imagine how proud of you Mother and Father were last night. I never saw them so enthusiastic and to tell you the truth I was rather glad to be your brother myself."[31] Their father wrote, "We are going away rejoicing in the splendid piece of public service which you are rendering so efficiently and so whole-heartedly."[32] Winthrop remained active, though not on as grand a scale, in the Greater New York Fund throughout his remaining years in New York.

During Rockefeller's years in the political spotlight in Arkansas, a great deal of debate went on in the press and among politicians concerning the degree of his commitment to racial equality and civil rights. This interest had been manifested in his effort to establish a black medical facility in Houston in 1938 and in the various causes and organizations he supported: the National Urban League, the United Negro College Fund, and the Riverdale Children's Association.

In 1921 the Rockefeller family began supporting the National Urban League, an organization dedicated to improving the living conditions of urban blacks. Winthrop became personally involved in 1940 as a member of the executive board.[33] As one of the principal speakers at a postwar league conference, he denounced the firing of blacks from wartime jobs in favor of now-plentiful white laborers as "un-American." In 1947 he was appointed chairman of the Urban League Service Fund's corporate division.[34] In addition to working as a fund-raising speaker for the league, Rockefeller donated approximately $100,000 worth of Standard Oil of California stock in 1952, for the purpose of purchasing a league headquarters building. Rockefeller's connection to the league, actively and financially, continued into the 1960s.[35]

James "Jimmy" Hudson was a black private detective from Harlem who began working for Rockefeller in 1937. With the exception of World War II, when he was employed by other family members, he served Winthrop until 1960, when Hudson left Arkansas to accept a position with Nelson's New York State Labor Commission. Hudson accompanied Winthrop on his post-war tour of the United States, and he gathered information in each city on the problems of black veterans. This fieldwork was incorporated into the final report, in which Rockefeller stated that the black veteran had encountered the most difficulty in reverting to civilian life because "his color nullifies the fact that he is a veteran." He called on leaders in the armed forces to take on the task of combating racial prejudice at home.[36]

In a 1973 interview, Hudson spoke of Rockefeller's "great empathy" for the problems of blacks. Hudson worked for Winthrop on behalf of the Greater New York Fund in Harlem, and stated, "Winthrop was one of the few men, after his exposure there, who could walk through Harlem, or go anywhere in Harlem, and be greeted and welcome."[37]

Throughout the late 1940s and early 1950s, Rockefeller championed the cause of fair employment practice legislation both in federal employment and in American industry. For this he was honored by the Urban League and was one of seventeen named to the honor roll of a Chicago black-run newspaper in 1949. In a 1952 speech to the National Urban League Conference, Rockefeller called fair employment practice legislation a "very useful tool" against discrimination. He called for an educational campaign to awaken people to the immorality and economic waste of racial discrimination.[38]

Rockefeller maintained his affiliation with the National Urban League for the rest of his life. But in the years prior to his move to Arkansas, he gave money and time to many other philanthropic organizations. He was a contributor for over a decade to the Colored Orphan Asylum, later known as the Riverdale Children's Association, a counseling and foster care agency for black children in New York City.[39] He was also on the board of trustees of the Industrial Relations Counselors, Inc., an organization that his father helped establish in 1926.[40]

Improving education in the New York City public school system was another major concern of Rockefeller's. As chairman of the Public Education Association's committee on school administration and legislation, he lobbied unsuccessfully in Albany for additional state aid for school districts, in order to help free school financing from local politics.[41]

Rockefeller spent considerable time coordinating fundraising efforts for the new New York University–Bellevue Medical Center. When the center was completed in 1949, he was named chairman of its board of trustees. In 1950 he was named to the newly created New York City Board of Hospitals, a policy-making agency for the Department of Hospitals.[42]

In 1951 Rockefeller resigned from the Socony-Vacuum Oil Company to devote himself full time to his philanthropic activities with Rockefeller Brothers, Inc., and to head the IBEC Housing Corporation, a division of the International Basic Economy Corporation, which had been founded by his brother Nelson in 1947. The goal of the Housing Corporation was to build prefabricated low-cost housing in Central and South America.[43]

The public acclaim that Winthrop was receiving for his

philanthropic activity at this time was unfortunately matched by negative comments concerning his private life. He had married Mrs. Barbara "Bobo" Sears on February 14, 1948, in Palm Beach, Florida, and they had a son, Winthrop Paul, later that year. They were separated on October 1, 1949,[44] though they were not divorced until 1954.

On June 7, 1953, the *New York Times* reported that Winthrop Rockefeller had established a residence in Arkansas but apparently for the purpose of obtaining a quick divorce.[45] This made it appear that the move was a temporary one, but Rockefeller intended it to be permanent. He had made several investigative trips to Arkansas earlier that year at the invitation of an old Army buddy, Frank Newell, a resident of Little Rock.[46] According to Jimmy Hudson, who accompanied Rockefeller to Arkansas, Newell sold Winthrop on the state with a visit to Petit Jean Mountain, an almost virgin wilderness with a breathtaking view forty miles from Little Rock.[47] Here, Rockefeller saw the opportunity to use his money to create something of his own, to build from the ground up rather than on the foundations of family tradition.

Intending the move to be permanent, Rockefeller cut his ties with New York. He ceased contributing to the Greater New York Fund, citing as explanation that he was now a resident of Arkansas.[48] He resigned from the New York State Chamber of Commerce, but was later persuaded to continue as a nonresident member in order not to disrupt a three-generation tradition of Rockefeller family membership.[49] He also resigned from the New York State Society for Medical Research, the New York City Public Education Association, the board of trustees of the New York University–Bellevue Medical Center, the governing council of New York University, and the Historical Society of the Tarrytowns. "Most significantly," one historian notes, "he resigned from the executive committee of Hills Realty, the company in which he shared ownership with his brothers in the Pocantico Hills estate. Nothing could be clearer than that to indicate that Winthrop had no intention of ever returning to New York."[50]

Every biographer of the Rockefeller family has speculated

on the reasons for Winthrop's move to Arkansas. Peter Collier and David Horowitz, in *The Rockefellers: An American Dynasty*, claimed that Rockefeller went south in an attempt to be one in a million instead of merely one of five brothers. Ferdinand Lundberg, in *The Rockefeller Syndrome*, alleged that Winthrop "departed more or less in exile in Arkansas" following the breakup of his marriage. And in *The Rockefeller Inheritance*, Alvin Moscow concluded that Winthrop realized that he was not a New Yorker in the sense that his brothers were, and decided to make a new life for himself.[51] To a degree, all of these explanations appear valid. Twenty years after the move, Jimmy Hudson stated that Winthrop went to Arkansas because he wanted a fresh start. Rockefeller felt that he "couldn't achieve anything in life in New York City," and that his "domestic problems got to a point that he felt that he had to leave the area."[52] His early life indicates that Winthrop had always enjoyed being a producer, a builder, rather than an administrator. Starting fresh in Arkansas, rather than stepping into an already established family enterprise, gave Winthrop the opportunity to produce something. Working as a roustabout was fine for a young man learning the oil business but was totally unacceptable for a mature, third-generation Rockefeller. Moving to Arkansas, Winthrop was able to work with his hands and build on a grand scale, as befitted his name and resources.

While Rockefeller cut his ties to New York in 1953, this did not mean that he also cut ties with his family. On the contrary, he maintained close ties to the family, using the resources of the family offices in Rockefeller Center whenever necessary. He also maintained his seat on the boards of Rockefeller Center and the Rockefeller Brothers Fund.[53] Shortly before the actual move to Arkansas, he was named chairman of the board of Colonial Williamsburg, succeeding his brother John, who had served since 1939. Colonial Williamsburg was John D. Rockefeller, Jr.'s, special project, and handing direction of it over to Winthrop was a symbol of continued family support.[54]

Upon his arrival in Arkansas, Rockefeller bought more than nine hundred acres of land atop Petit Jean Mountain and proceeded to build a cattle ranch, which he named Winrock.

With a seemingly total disregard for the costs involved, Rockefeller simply decided what he wanted to do, and then did it, insisting on the best of everything. First of all, he chose to live on top of the mountain, not at its base. Furthermore, he wanted his cattle up there with him. This involved bulldozing hilltops to provide grazing land and laying pipe to pump water 850 feet up the mountain from the Petit Jean River. At the top, six lakes were dug to store the water. Roads had to be built that could handle trucks and farm machinery. An airstrip was constructed to provide quick access to Little Rock. And a home and farm buildings were erected. The farm was constantly under construction. Eventually, the main house had dining and cooking facilities to accommodate a hundred people. Smaller houses were built for guests and employees. There was an employee cafeteria, separate shop buildings for painting, carpentry, and auto repair, and a reception center. In all, the original architect built twenty-four separate structures. On the ranch, Rockefeller raised Santa Gertrudis cattle, an all-American breed developed on the Texan King Ranch in the 1920s. Winrock was a breeding ranch, and Rockefeller's cattle were sold all over the world.[55]

Rockefeller was able to build the farm as he wanted, regardless of costs, because he was a Rockefeller. His father had begun turning his fortune over to his children in 1934, when six trusts were established. The three eldest children each received stock worth approximately $12 million. Laurance, Winthrop, and David each received fifty thousand dollars worth of stock. Their father explained the disparity on the basis that they had not yet had "that longer period of training in the handling of gradually increasing sums of money which has been so helpful to the three older children."[56] However, the threat of an increase in gift and estate taxes the following year prompted Junior to add $16 million worth of stocks to each of the three younger sons' trusts. The terms of these six trusts stipulated that only the income from them could be used without the permission of a committee of advisors at the Chase Bank in New York. The trusts were irrevocable and generation-skipping—the principal would be distributed to John D. Rockefeller, Jr.'s, great-grandchildren upon the death of their inheriting parent. After the

1934 trusts, Junior continued to transfer his wealth to his children in varying amounts dependent on their worthiness. When Winthrop married in 1948, his father added $6 million to his 1934 trust. Additional trusts were established for each of the five brothers in 1952. Winthrop's was valued at approximately $4.3 million.[57]

The Arkansas Rockefeller found was a long way from New York City. Its 1950 population was 1,909,511, making it the smallest state in the South. Furthermore, that figure was constantly falling. Thus, a relatively large impact could be made with investments that might have appeared small elsewhere. It was soon after work began on Winrock that Rockefeller became involved in other activities in Arkansas, activities that reflected many of his long-standing interests. In 1954 he proposed and financed a rural health clinic in Perry County, one of many Arkansas counties with no doctors. In that same year, he gave $100,000 in Standard Oil of California stock to four Arkansas colleges, two white and two black, to establish scholarship funds. In February 1956 the Rockwin Fund was established by Rockefeller to coordinate his philanthropic activities in Arkansas in the same way that the Rockefeller Brothers Fund coordinated the joint activities of him and his brothers in New York. In Morrilton, a town near Winrock, Rockefeller donated approximately $1.5 million to build a model school system, on the condition that the school be integrated.[58]

Following family tradition, these gifts were made with the understanding that the projects would find other sources of financing at the end of five years. Rockefeller would pay the initial costs of the Morrilton school, for instance, but the community was expected eventually to maintain the school system. The Morrilton school experience illustrates a fact of life in Arkansas that Winthrop Rockefeller never understood or accepted. Arkansans seemed unwilling to pay for services that necessitated higher taxes. In 1960 Morrilton voters soundly defeated a tax increase required to continue the model school system when Rockefeller's funding expired. This despite the fact that tests showed that in the four years the program had been in effect, Morrilton students had dramatically improved their performance, raising their scores from below the national average to above it in basic subjects.[59] Even as governor, Rockefeller apparently never understood that Arkansans simply were not interested in many improvements if it meant they had to pay the cost. Maybe his vast wealth prevented him from understanding the priorities of the average citizen. But if Rockefeller's attitude was at one end of the spectrum, Arkansas's was at the other. Even in 1986, Arkansas had the lowest per capita tax burden in the nation, and a corresponding lack of services.[60]

Rockefeller continued his interest in improving race relations and creating better opportunities for blacks. One of his first steps upon becoming chairman of Colonial Williamsburg in 1953 was to desegregate all inns and restaurants there.[61] At a National Urban League Conference in 1958, he criticized the slow pace and tokenism of school desegregation in the South in the four years that had passed since the *Brown* v. *Board of Education* Supreme Court decision.[62]

In the years following his move to Arkansas, Rockefeller's personal life seemed to straighten out. Following lengthy, well-publicized wrangling over a property settlement and Winthrop's visitation rights to their son, Winthrop and Bobo Rockefeller were divorced on August 3, 1954, in Reno, Nevada. On June 11, 1956, Rockefeller married Jeannette Edris of New York. This was her fourth marriage, and she brought two children, Anne and Bruce Bartley, with her to Arkansas.[63] It then appeared that Winthrop Rockefeller had settled into the relatively quiet life of a wealthy rancher and philanthropist, but this was not the case.

Orval Faubus had been elected governor of Arkansas in November 1954. In March 1955 he convinced the legislature to create the Arkansas Industrial Development Commission (AIDC) to attract new industry to the state, and on April 1 Faubus named Rockefeller chairman of the commission.[64] Faubus did so, he later claimed, "because of the magic of the name."[65]

In assuming chairmanship of the AIDC, Rockefeller was taking on a tremendous challenge. In the post-depression South, industrialization was essential in order to absorb the thousands of rural workers displaced by new farming techniques. Prior to the creation of the AIDC, Arkansas had no organized efforts to lure industry to the state, the result being that between 1940 and 1960 Arkansas lost 8.4 percent of its population.[66]

Rockefeller brought two big advantages to his job as head of the AIDC: his name and his wealth. As a member of one of America's first industrial dynasties, Rockefeller had connections that most Arkansans could only dream about. Secondly, Rockefeller used his wealth to attract top staff members from out of state by supplementing out of his own pocket the low salaries set up by the state legislature. As executive director of the AIDC, Rockefeller recruited William Pennell Rock of Baltimore, raising his state salary of seventy-five hundred dollars to approximately twenty thousand dollars.[67] This supplementing of state salaries was a controversial practice that Rockefeller continued during his governorship, much to the chagrin of many state legislators. The practice, however, apparently had the governor's blessing. More than thirty years later, Faubus recalled: "I knew about it. [Rockefeller] discussed it with me and I agreed to it."[68]

The years 1955 to 1957 were the honeymoon period of Rockefeller's chairmanship of the AIDC. In 1956 the AIDC claimed that 12,521 new jobs in 194 new or expanded industries had been created as a result of its recruiting efforts. Faubus wrote Rockefeller that "the entire people of this state are not only mindful of the good that has been accomplished but are as well grateful and appreciative."[69]

Winthrop Rockefeller prophesied the end of this honeymoon between the AIDC and the Faubus administration in two speeches he gave in 1956. Before both the Little Rock Women's Republican Club and the Arkansas State Society in Washington, Rockefeller warned that the South's attitude toward court-ordered integration was a roadblock to the movement of industry into the area. He told GOP women, at a luncheon in Little Rock, that "big industry is shying away from Southern states which think they are above federal control" and that "it was time for all persons to realize that the United States is run by law and not emotion."[70] His warnings would be borne out the following year when the South's most well-known showdown over integration took place in Little Rock, Arkansas—the Central High crisis.

Prior to 1957, Little Rock appeared an unlikely place to become a symbol for violent opposition to integration. After *Brown v. Board of Education* in 1954, "a number of interracial groups in Little Rock actively supported integration." One prominent forum for interracial cooperation "was the Urban League . . . in the mid-1950's headed by Winthrop Rockefeller."[71]

The Little Rock school board drafted a plan for limited desegregation in the schools starting from the top down. This plan delayed integration until 1957 to allow time for completion of the new Hall High School in the more affluent western part of the city. The existing white high school, Central, attended by predominantly lower and middle class whites, would be desegregated while Hall would remain all white since there were no black neighborhoods in its vicinity. The plan contained a provision allowing any student who was in the minority in a particular school to transfer. This provision insured that white students could not be forced to attend the black school, Horace Mann High.[72]

While this plan was justifiably attacked by the NAACP as tokenism, it had the support of the business community fearful of the dislocations that would result if the Supreme Court ruling were defied. Until late 1955, it appeared that moderates, favoring minimum compliance with the law, would dominate in Little Rock. However, before the end of the year, two events showed the precariousness of this moderate domination. The NAACP challenged the integration plan in court on the basis that the program was too gradual. They lost the suit, but it was evidence of growing dissatisfaction among blacks—the children's parents had contributed to the legal costs. On the other end of the spectrum, desegregation of the public schools in Hoxie, Arkansas, proceeded without incident until segregationists started inciting opposition. The leader of these segregationists was Jim Johnson. Hoxie brought him to the forefront of Arkansas politics, making him a rival of Faubus and, later, of Rockefeller.[73]

In 1956 Johnson opposed Faubus in the gubernatorial race. While Faubus easily won, the voters approved Amendment 44 to the Arkansas state constitution, instructing the attorney general to resist desegregation. Passage of this amendment showed the changing tide of racial attitudes in the state, and while, up to this point, Faubus had tried to steer clear of taking a stand on integration, he now jumped into the debate firmly on the side of the segregationists. As one journalist later recalled, "Faubus made prejudice respectable," creating "an atmosphere of hate that hovered over Little Rock like a toxic cloud."[74] Historians agree that Faubus's part in the Little Rock crisis was a direct result of his desire for a third term in the governor's office.[75]

In February 1957 the legislature considered a bill supported by Faubus to create a State Sovereignty Commission with broad investigative and police powers. The purpose of the commission was to prevent integration, and it was one of four segregationist bills that became law in 1957 by wide margins. Rockefeller spoke out publicly against the bill, stating the commission would be an "Arkansas gestapo," and called it the most "flagrant violation of civil rights" he had ever seen.[76]

The Little Rock school board's desegregation plan was scheduled to begin on September 3, 1957, when nine carefully chosen blacks were to enter Central High School. After failing to persuade the school board to go to court to delay integration, Faubus appeared in chancery court on behalf of the segregationist Mothers League of Little Rock. He testified that he had information that violence would result if the blacks were allowed to enroll. The appeal failed.[77]

On September 1 Faubus met with Rockefeller and a staff member of the AIDC, William R. Ewald, Jr., at the Albert Pike Hotel in Little Rock to discuss the integration situation. Ewald later told the FBI that, at this meeting, Rockefeller tried to persuade Faubus to take a public stand that, as governor, he would obey and enforce the law, in this way lessening the possibility of violence. According to Ewald, Faubus told them that he was against forced integration and did not want to "elect rabid segregationist opponents" by complying with the law. Ewald suggested to Faubus that by voicing opposition to integration while stating that he had no choice but to obey the law, he could avoid being branded an integrationist. The governor made no commitment to Rockefeller at this meeting, remarking, "I can't make you any promises."[78]

In recalling the same meeting in his 1980 autobiography, Faubus alleged that he told Rockefeller that, as governor, he had sworn to uphold state law and the state constitution, which was in conflict with the "mere order of a federal district judge." Faubus agreed with Ewald's statement that Rockefeller left the meeting not knowing what the governor's next move would be. Faubus claims that he himself did not know. However, the National Guard and state police had already been alerted and a proclamation for use of the guard written.[79]

The night before school was scheduled to open, Faubus ordered the Arkansas National Guard to seize Central High and prevent integration. Faubus's allegation that he called out the Guard to prevent violence overlooks the fact that he could have legally used the Guard to maintain the federal court ruling by ensuring that the black students were allowed to enter Central High.[80] On September 4 a federal judge issued a court order that black students be admitted, and on September 5 Faubus's troops prevented those same students from entering the school. The National Guard remained on duty at Central High, preventing integration, until September 20, when the federal court ordered Faubus to withdraw the troops. This time, Faubus complied. In the midst of this standoff, a meeting was held between Faubus and Eisenhower, but no suitable compromise was reached.[81]

On September 23 integration was attempted by the school board with the help of the Little Rock police. It was on this day that the mob Faubus had been predicting for three weeks finally arrived. About a thousand whites stood outside the school, demonstrating against integration and menacing the journalists and photographers covering the incident. The black students were sent home. Two days later, Central High was integrated when President Eisenhower took over the Arkansas National Guard and ordered a detachment of the 101st Airborne Infantry Division to the school to protect the black students. Federal troops occupied the school grounds for the remainder of the academic year, while the president worked to change the climate of public opinion in Little Rock to the extent that integration could continue peacefully once the troops were withdrawn.[82] This attempt failed. A special session of the legislature in August 1958 passed a Faubus-supported bill that established a "legal basis to close schools forced to integrate and transfer public funds to private schools."[83] On September 27, 1958, the people of Little Rock voted to close the city's high schools, and they remained closed for the entire 1958–59 school year. Closing the schools shocked the city's business elite into taking action, and in May 1959 desegregation forces swept the school board election.[84] In the fall of 1959, the Little Rock schools reopened, and both Central and Hall high schools were integrated on a limited scale.

On October 5, 1957, a month after the crisis began, Winthrop Rockefeller finally issued a statement to the press that the crisis was damaging industry.[85] Rockefeller had already received a letter from one firm that had previously committed itself to establishing a plant in Ratcliff, Arkansas. Seamprufe Inc., a garment industry firm based in New York, stated that Faubus's actions would "undo much of the good your office has done in promoting Arkansas" and urged Rockefeller to "exert every effort to do the right thing towards all people regardless of race, color or creed." In a similar letter to Faubus, the company pressed the governor to "see to it that the law of the land is obeyed."[86]

There is evidence that the Little Rock crisis did damage the state's industrial and economic growth. After the crisis, not one major firm moved into Little Rock for the next three years.[87] Those in Arkansas who opposed Faubus's stand suffered the consequences. The *Arkansas Gazette*, as a result of a boycott launched by the segregationist Citizens Council, lost 18 percent of its circulation and more than a million dollars in net income. The Urban League withdrew from the Community Chest fund-raising effort in October 1957 because of threats of a boycott against the entire Chest. And seven-term Congressman Brooks Hays, whose district included Little Rock, was defeated in his bid for reelection in the 1958 general election by segregationist school board member Dale Alford. Alford won as a write-in candidate who announced his campaign just one week before the election. Hays had worked unsuccessfully to reach a compromise between Eisenhower and Faubus and was therefore branded as an integrationist.[88]

The crisis gave Orval Faubus exactly what he wanted—in 1958 he won a third term as governor, an achievement last accomplished by Jeff Davis, who served as governor from 1901 until 1907. Faubus remained governor until 1966, when he decided not to run for a seventh term.

Rockefeller's unique position as Arkansas's most famous citizen allowed him to criticize Faubus's actions in the Little Rock crisis while remaining a member of the governor's administration, although relations between Faubus and Rockefeller began to deteriorate noticeably in 1960. While Rockefeller's public disapproval of Faubus's handling of the Central High crisis certainly must have been a factor, it was Rockefeller's decision to work on building the Arkansas Republican party that incurred Faubus's public wrath. Rockefeller was a Faubus appointee in a state that rarely recognized the two-party system as an acceptable form of political expression. With the exception of the Ozark region in the northwest corner of the state, the Democratic primary was almost always the deciding election. Faubus could tolerate a great many annoyances from Rockefeller because of his name and the status it brought to Arkansas, but upsetting the political status quo was not one of them.

On January 14, 1960, several weeks after Rockefeller first let it be known that he was considering a fall run for the governor's office, his term on the AIDC expired. Faubus's response to questions on whether or not he planned to reappoint Rockefeller were vague enough to indicate that the governor was no longer as "enthusiastic about Rockefeller as he once was." Faubus told reporters that any decision regarding Rockefeller's reappointment would require "due consideration," and that there were "many good people in the state" who could head the AIDC.[89] Over a month after expiration of the term, Faubus told Rockefeller that he would be happy to reappoint him if Rockefeller still wanted the job, and on March 9 Faubus did just that.[90]

In the 1960 and 1962 general elections, Rockefeller publicly stated his support for the Republican gubernatorial candidates. In November 1962 a campaign began among state legislators to oust Rockefeller from his chairmanship of the AIDC. This campaign was denounced on the editorial pages of both major newspapers, but apparently encouraged by the governor who wrote to a prominent Little Rock businessman in reference to Rockefeller that "many people feel . . . that his role as an Arkansas businessman and member of a Democratic administration as chairman of the AIDC is not compatible with his role of active political leadership."[91] In his memoirs, however, Faubus denied any affiliation with the oust-Rockefeller movement, stating, "I had nothing to do with it, and did not want the issue to arise." As explanation, Faubus pointed out that, if Rockefeller had been kicked off the AIDC, "he would have 'hit the ground running'—for governor in the next election."[92] But Rockefeller's Republican activities must have infuriated the governor. Political activism and public appointments had always been intimately connected in Arkansas; before this, however, they had rarely been connected in a Republican.

Because of Rockefeller's stature in the state, ousting him appeared too controversial. Attention was turned first to William Rock, the AIDC executive director whom Rockefeller had lured away from Baltimore. Rumors in November 1962 that Rock was being fired were allegedly initiated by Faubus. The governor had distrusted Rock since the Central High crisis when the latter was suspected "of keeping Rockefeller advised of the goings on inside the Faubus camp."[93] In early 1963, amid rumors that some legislators were planning to disband the AIDC, Rock resigned to become a private development consultant.[94]

Less than two weeks after Rock's resignation, a bill was introduced in the Arkansas house that was designed to legislate Rockefeller out of a job by reorganizing the AIDC. This would allow Faubus to appoint a new commission. Rockefeller's work as chairman of the AIDC was never criticized or offered as a reason for the bill. Rather, his activities on behalf of the Republican party were given in explanation by the legislators involved. Faubus gave steam to the bill by publicly stating his doubts as to the wisdom of retaining "a powerful Republican as AIDC chairman."[95]

It became apparent in the days following announcement of the attempt to oust Rockefeller that public opinion in the state was overwhelmingly on the side of the beleaguered Republican. The bottom line was that the additional jobs the AIDC had brought were more important to a majority of the citizens of Arkansas than Rockefeller's political activities. Because of this support, legislators decided that a roll-call vote of the anti-Rockefeller bill would not be in their best interests, and on February 27 state Rep. Paul Van Dalsem withdrew the bill from consideration.[96]

Partisan attacks on Rockefeller and the AIDC did not end here. A week later, Van Dalsem introduced amendments to the AIDC appropriation bill that would in effect turn day-to-day control of the agency over to the governor. Faubus, always cognizant of public opinion, asked the Joint Budget Committee to rescind the amendments, which it did.[97]

Winthrop Rockefeller continued as chairman of the AIDC until April 1, 1964, when he resigned to run for governor. His letter of resignation summarized the AIDC's achievements: a net increase in jobs of about fifty thousand, approximately $270 million in annual payroll, an increase in per capita income of close to six hundred dollars yearly, and the move of over six hundred new plants to the state.[98] During his tenure, manufacturing wages climbed by 88 percent compared to a national rise of 36 percent,[99] further indication that the AIDC had helped move Arkansas into twentieth-century industrial America. The population drain reversed itself during the 1960s, in part due to increased employment opportunities. The 1960s saw a gain in Arkansas's population of 7.7 percent, well below the national average, but a big improvement from the past.[100] Fifteen years after Rockefeller's death, Faubus assessed Rockefeller's performance as head of the AIDC as "excellent. He attended almost all the meetings, he presided, he was a man of very firm opinions and viewpoints, and most of the time he had his own way."[101]

On April 4, 1964, Winthrop Rockefeller announced his candidacy for governor of Arkansas on the Republican ticket.[102] He faced stiff opposition, not only from the Democrats but from within the Republican party, which was by no means unanimous in its support of him.

TWO

Taking Control of Arkansas's Republican Party

V. O. Key, Jr., has laid the groundwork for all postwar studies of Southern politics in his 1949 work, *Southern Politics in State and Nation.* In Arkansas, Key found a state solidly welded to the Democratic party. "Perhaps in Arkansas we have the one-party system in its most undefiled and undiluted form."[1] This one-party system produced factionalized politics based on personalities rather than issues. "It would seem that in Arkansas, more than in almost any other southern state, social and economic issues of significance to the people have lain ignored in the confusion and paralysis of disorganized factional politics."[2] Part of the explanation Key gave for this lack of concern with issues was an "extraordinary consensus" among the electorate concerning them. Conservatives controlled Arkansas politics "without serious challenge," and the only issue that seemed important at election time was to find the "best qualified" candidate. Coming out a winner in a state like Arkansas necessitated winning the support of local political leaders who could deliver votes. This, in turn, created a situation in which "electoral irregularities creep in from time to time," particularly with the poll tax. In Arkansas, an agent could pay this tax for a voter. This resulted in block payments by political leaders and, allegedly, issuance of poll-tax receipts to fictitious and deceased persons. Key concluded that this one-party system was more open to corruption than a two-party system, because in the latter the two parties watched each other, and this tended to keep them more honest.[3]

Key found four different types of Republicans in the South. First were presidential Republicans, those who voted Democratic locally and Republican nationally. Second were mountain Republicans, the people of the Ozarks in the northwest corner of the state, descendents of the pro-Union areas of the South. They controlled local governments only, and in Arkansas they regularly controlled only two counties, Searcy and Newton. The third group of Southern Republicans was blacks, although by 1949 most either had been effectively disfranchised or had converted to the Democratic party under Franklin Roosevelt in the 1930s. The final group of Southern Republicans was the party leadership. The leadership's major concern was not with obtaining votes, but rather with controlling the state party machinery. The leadership controlled patronage, and a weak Republican party ensured that there were fewer to reward when patronage became available.[4]

The Republican party that Rockefeller found upon his arrival in Arkansas was small and practically moribund. Led by a small group of "Post Office Republicans," businessmen and lawyers concerned primarily with dispensing federal patronage, they had not elected even one governor, senator, representative, or state senator in the whole of the twentieth century. Frequently, the Republicans failed even to field a complete slate of candidates for state offices.[5] In the 1952 election, Republican candidates ran for governor, lieutenant governor, and attorney general, and only two of Arkansas's six congressional positions. The gubernatorial candidate, Jefferson Speck, received 12.6 percent of the vote. The only Republicans elected to state office in 1952 were two state representatives, and this in spite of the fact that Eisenhower obtained a then-record Republican popular vote in Arkansas of 43.9 percent.[6] This enormous disparity between the national and local voting percentages shows the total ineffectiveness of the Arkansas Republican party and the inability of presidential Republicanism to influence local elections.

In addition to a dismal showing at the polls, the Republicans experienced growing rifts within the party over leadership since, with President Eisenhower in office, there was now party patronage to dispense for the first time in twenty years. The titular heads of the party, State Chairman Osro Cobb and National Committeeman Wallace Townsend, were longtime supporters of Robert Taft of Ohio. Jefferson Speck, the 1950 and 1952 gubernatorial candidate, headed the Arkansas faction that supported Eisenhower. As such, Speck expected to control patronage after Eisenhower's victory. Townsend and Cobb, who had dominated the Arkansas GOP since the 1930s, were not about to abandon their positions. Townsend won this power struggle and continued to control patronage for the Republicans, while Speck, in retaliation, publicly backed Democrat Orval Faubus for governor in 1954.[7] The rift between "Old Guard" Republicans, as the more conservative members of the party were called, and Eisenhower Republicans widened even further during the 1957 Central High School crisis, with the Old Guard favoring states' rights and the others supporting President Eisenhower's decision to send in federal troops to enforce the Federal court order.[8] Given this background, it is easy to comprehend why Winthrop Rockefeller's attempts to build a strong, active, and unified Republican party in Arkansas met so much opposition and achieved only limited success.

Rockefeller's first efforts to build the state GOP took the guise of a nonpartisan drive to create a two-party system in the state. On October 10, 1960, Rockefeller gave a speech, broadcast on both television and radio, arguing that a two-party system would create a "healthier condition in Arkansas politics by building parties which are stronger than individuals; parties which have reasonable philosophies, continuity of purposes; parties which are strengthened by strong candidates, but not ruled by them." He sought to convince the people of Arkansas that a two-party system created better government by providing organized opposition to the party in power. He decried the lack of a secret ballot in a state with neither voting booths nor machines, arguing that a two-party system would bring better election practices. He urged voters to support a two-party system by voting for Nixon, Lodge, and Henry M. Britt, the Republican candidates for president, vice-president, and governor.[9]

On October 17, 1960, a "Party for Two Parties" was held at Winrock Farms. For fifty dollars each, participants received dinner and entertainment by Tex Ritter, Edgar Bergen, and Kathryn Grayson, among others. The event's purpose was two-fold—fund raising and publicity for the newly formed Committee for the Two-Party System. The chairman of the committee was William Berry, a nominal Democrat who was also chairman of Volunteers for Nixon-Lodge. According to the Committee for the Two-Party System's literature, the organization was remaining independent of the state GOP so that it could build up a two-party system without having to work within the rules established by the national Republican party. In other words, the committee wanted to be free to endorse Democratic candidates whenever it was advantageous.[10]

The underlying reason Rockefeller chose to cloak his drive to build up the Republican party in Arkansas with this two-party drive was not hard to fathom. As he explained in a letter to his brother:

> The concept of drumming for a two-party system—as against talking straight Republicanism—has been most effective, for in many parts of Arkansas the word Republican is still a dirty word. Under the guise of a new name we have been able to bring out Independents and many Democrats who are disgruntled with the present situation.[11]

It appears that Rockefeller had another reason for forming his Committee for the Two-Party System—lack of enthusiasm within the Arkansas Republican party for his involvement. From the beginning of his plunge into Arkansas politics, Rockefeller refused to limit himself to the resources and expertise available from in-state Republicans, often relying instead on financial help and political experience from outside. For instance, Winthrop's siblings and mother contributed a total of six thousand dollars to the Committee for the Two-Party System.[12]

In September 1960, prior to public announcement of the existence of the Committee for the Two-Party System, Rockefeller hired David Hunter, a professional campaign public relations man from San Francisco.[13] Hunter acted as an advisor to both Rockefeller and the Arkansas GOP, as well as a middleman between the two when friction developed. In an early memo, Hunter outlined what he saw as the three major shortcomings of the party: lack of a serious status, factionalism, and amateurism. Five days later, he wrote to Rockefeller: "Ben Henley [the state chairman of the Republican party] has reached the point of being downright un-cooperative. . . . I sense a certain feeling that his rights to the GOP in the state are being challenged by the mere presence of WR."[14]

But Henley's attitude changed rapidly. In a September 28 memo, Hunter reported to Rockefeller that Henley had become "completely friendly, and even communicative." The relatively enormous amount of money and publicity that Rockefeller was affording the Republican party less than six weeks before the election was very likely responsible for the change of heart. In the same memo, Hunter advised Rockefeller that he had "informed both Henley and Britt that WR's contribution to the campaign is already large" and that he (Hunter) was being "courted" by various Republican factions, presumably to "win the favor of WR."[15] The *Arkansas Gazette* confirmed that Rockefeller had done a great deal for the 1960 Republican effort. An October 12 editorial stated, "New weight has been given to the Republican campaign of 1960 by the active part that Winthrop Rockefeller is taking in it."[16]

Henry Britt, an attorney from Hot Springs who later won election as a circuit judge, was the only Republican candidate for a statewide office in 1960, and Rockefeller publicly endorsed and financially supported him. But it was apparent to Rockefeller that after the election changes would have to be made if the party were to grow along the lines he had in mind. David Hunter wrote to Rockefeller that "it is more and more apparent that our candidate is far from the ideal choice as a standard bearer." Hunter went on to suggest that after the election, a coup be undertaken in which the "younger elements" of the party take over leadership and "hail the commencement of a new Republicanism" in Arkansas.[17] This sentiment was echoed by another friend of Rockefeller's: "It is obvious that the Republican machinery in the state needs complete overhauling. . . . it would seem that the best method to proceed is to develop an organization of young intelligent workers on the precinct level up, who will be able to move into positions of authority whenever vacancies occur."[18]

The 1960 Arkansas Republican party platform is a good indicator of the philosophical slant of the party at that time, before Rockefeller's moves to revitalize it. The first major plank in the platform was "states' rights," the standard Southern byword for an anti-integration stance. The platform explained that the state government's failure to take responsibility for domestic affairs had permitted the federal government to intrude. Specifically referring to *Brown* v. *Board of Education*, the Republican platform asserted:

> The dual citizenship status of our people [meaning both federal and state] requires the assumption of leadership and responsibility by the Republican party in this area of disagreement because of the principles of government in which we believe and pursue. We propose that this matter be resolved in the communities by the people involved. . . . We reject federal subsidization of our public schools because that would permit federal domination of our schools within the forseeable future if accepted.[19]

The second plank in the party's platform was entitled "Government and Economic Opportunity." It called for a re-assertion of the free enterprise system by reducing the number and functions of the state regulatory boards and commissions. The platform also endorsed Arkansas's Right-to-Work law, the bane of the state's labor unions, on the basis that it produced more jobs and assured "equal work for equal pay." The last major plank concerned education. Reiterating the theme of local control of schools, the Republicans called for both the commissioner of education and the state universities' boards of trustees to be replaced by elected bodies. By removing public schools and colleges "from the domination of the chief executive," the quality of education might be improved and tighter budgetary supervision realized. The platform also called for higher salaries and state-supported continuing education for teachers.[20]

Results of the 1960 gubernatorial election showed that while the increased Republican party activity had made some inroads into Democratic strength, it was only a start. Faubus received 292,064 votes, or 69.2 percent, while Britt received 129,921, or 30.8 percent. On the positive side, this was the first time since 1954 that Faubus's margin had fallen below 70 percent.[21]

For the four years following this 1960 election defeat, Arkansas's Republican party was in constant turmoil. This condition could be directly attributed to Rockefeller's attempts to transform the party into an active contender for political office. A long memo to Rockefeller, written shortly after the election, outlined the steps necessary to make the Republican party a viable alternative in Arkansas. It showed that his goals were in direct conflict with maintenance of the status quo within the party. The memo, from Don Hall and David Hunter, indicated that the perception of the Arkansas Republican party, "with some reason," was of "a weak party, hopelessly divided into numerous factions at the State and County level." The state GOP was also hurt by the almost continual lack of a positive platform. Improving this image and reality would be difficult because of the contention by "the old guard GOP in Arkansas" that Rockefeller was trying to take over the party. These leaders, according to Hall, were jealous and "suspicious of new leadership from any source, especially new leadership commanding considerable general respect and economic authority."[22]

On May 24, 1961, Winthrop Rockefeller was unanimously elected the Arkansas GOP national committeeman by the Republican State Committee. Rockefeller's election was made possible by the retirement of seventy-nine-year-old Wallace Townsend after thirty-three years in that post, and on Townsend's recommendation.[23] Those Republicans who were suspicious of Rockefeller were willing to overlook their fears because he "gave instant respectability, instant resources that the party had never had."[24] In the fall of that year, Rockefeller toured the state to publicize the Republican party and recruit grass-roots support. He acknowledged to the press that part of his goal was to determine just how conservative the state's Republicans were—the state GOP, like the national party, was split in the early 1960s between right-wing Goldwater conservatives and more left-wing liberals, many of whom supported, on the national level, Nelson Rockefeller.[25]

From the beginning of Winthrop Rockefeller's involvement in the Arkansas Republican party, personality differences and struggles for control of the party caused ever-widening and more public divisions. Through 1961 and 1962, Rockefeller worked to gain control of the state party organization by easing "Old Guard" Republicans such as Ben Henley out of positions of power. Henley's term as state chairman ended in 1962. In August, at the Republican State Committee meeting, Rockefeller publicly backed William L. Spicer of Fort Smith for the position against Henry Britt, the 1960 gubernatorial nominee. After Spicer's election, in a move toward reconciliation, Spicer appointed Britt the party's general counsel. Rockefeller made the necessary motion to have the appointment confirmed. The *Arkansas Gazette* identified both Spicer and Britt as Eisenhower Republicans, stating that "if any member of the Old Guard was in the running for the chairmanship this year his name never reached the floor."[26] However, in two respects Spicer and Britt were both very much "Old Guard." First, they were both ideologically conservative. They may have been Eisenhower Republicans, and in the 1950s that was new, but this was 1962, and both men were strong Goldwater supporters. At the committee meeting, Spicer stated: "I'm a conservative Republican. I am opposed to socialism and these liberal pinkos in every form and fashion."[27] Second, both Spicer and Britt were Old Guard in that they fully expected that the state committee would control the Republican party, and any patronage that might fall its way. Neither was willing to surrender any authority to the national committeeman. After the 1960 elections, Henry Britt discovered that Rockefeller had held a meeting at Winrock with his political advisors to which Britt had not been invited. Britt wrote to David Hunter, "If I am not included, then it is possible that I might take a direction not palatable to those whom I consider my friends."[28] Spicer, within a year after his Rockefeller-supported election as state chairman, was engaged in bitter attacks on the character, power, and politics of Winthrop Rockefeller.

In the 1962 election, more Republicans ran for office in Arkansas than at any time since Reconstruction. In addition to the gubernatorial candidate, Willis Ricketts, Republicans challenged two of Arkansas's four congressional seats, and Dr. Kenneth Jones ran against Sen. J. William Fulbright.[29] As evidence that this far-from-complete slate of candidates was in reality a remarkable show of Republican strength, the Democrats established a state-wide campaign organization, something that had not happened "within memory." Furthermore, at their state convention, the Democrats lambasted the Republicans "with a venom generally reserved for the Federal Government" and wrote a party platform that promised to "pulverize" the Republicans.[30]

Fielding candidates and pushing the Democrats into increased activity was one thing; getting voters to seriously consider a Republican candidate was quite another. A September 1962 public opinion poll showed that none of the Republican candidates for office were known by even half of the voters interviewed. The interviewing firm concluded: "There is obviously little hope for the GOP this November in the minds of the electorate. And there is little wishing that the GOP *could* win. . . . given Republican candidates 'with a chance,' the picture could be much different."[31] The prediction was accurate—Jones received 31.3 percent of the votes to Fulbright's 68.7 percent, and Ricketts received only 26.7 percent to Faubus's 73.3 percent.[32] The election, and Rockefeller's activities on behalf of the Republican party, resulted in the campaign in the state legislature to have him ousted from the chairmanship of the AIDC.

Between the 1962 and 1964 elections, the problems between factions of the Republican party broke out into a full-blown feud. The major players in this drama were Winthrop Rockefeller on the one side, with his supporters Everett Ham and Marion Burton, and William Spicer, Henry Britt, and Walter Stouffer of Fort Smith, chairman of the Sebastian County Republican Committee, on the other. The fundamental causes of the feud were both an Old Guard fear of losing control of patronage, and a genuine difference of political opinion within the party. Winthrop Rockefeller was determined to build the state's Republican party into a strong vote-getting competitor to the Democratic party, with a moderate platform and widespread grass-roots support. His opponents were willing to allow the party to remain small, as long as it retained its conservatism and strongly supported Barry Goldwater. They also wanted Rockefeller to abandon all efforts to build the party unless his activities were conducted through the "State Organization," that is, through William Spicer's office. This way, tight control could be maintained over the national committeeman's activities.[33]

In 1963, as chairman of the AIDC, Winthrop Rockefeller was one of Arkansas's most popular citizens. His opponents within the GOP, therefore, directed their attacks at Rockefeller's assistants, especially Everett Ham. Ham's official title was assistant to the national committeeman. Rockefeller hired Ham shortly after his election to that post because he wanted someone familiar with Arkansas's Republicans. Ham was employed by Rockefeller personally, not the Republican party. He went into the counties for Rockefeller, drumming up new recruits for the Republican party and fresh leadership for the county organizations. This was enough in itself to make him unpopular with the state chairman. In addition, Ham was an activist, and not always diplomatic. According to John Ward, Rockefeller's public relations director from 1964 to 1971, getting along with those he disagreed with was not Everett Ham's strongest quality. Ward wrote that Ham "could be—and frequently was—quite heavy handed, excusing it in the name of building a two-party system. Ham knew how to roll heads, and he did it. You could go with Rockefeller or get out of the way. The old mossback Republicans did neither."[34] This led to constant feuding. Everett Ham acknowledges that he "was the focal point for anything that [the Post Office

Republicans] didn't like," but attributes this primarily to the Republicans' fear of Rockefeller and his popular support.[35]

As early as May 1963, Spicer was asking Rockefeller to give Ham a "more behind the scenes status" in the Republican party, arguing that Ham was damaging party "unity and harmony." Spicer wrote a letter to Ham, a copy of which was sent to Rockefeller, telling him:

> There is strong resentment towards you from all sections of the State....
>
> ... What our Party in Arkansas needs ... more than anything else ... is harmony ... and it is high time the State Operation start moving the way I wish it to move, considering the thinking of friends from all over the State.[36]

The letter clearly showed that Spicer wanted harmony, but on his own terms. Spicer and Ham seemed to be guiding the Republican party in opposite directions, with no room for compromise. Since Ham was employed by Rockefeller, presumably Rockefeller felt his way. Certainly, Rockefeller resisted all attempts to oust Ham from his position in spite of the fact that Ham was personally causing an uproar within the Republican party. Such a public uproar could have been beneficial to Rockefeller's attempts to build a two-party system. It certainly kept the party in the news and kept Rockefeller's goals before the people in a way that did not appear to be self-aggrandizing. On the other hand, the public bickering could prevent some from seeing the Republican party as an attractive alternative to the Democrats.

By June 1963 Spicer was asking Rockefeller to transfer Ham from his Republican party work "to some other capacity in your enterprises in Arkansas."[37] Throughout the summer, the feud intensified and expanded. Marion Burton was a North Little Rock attorney, hired by Ham and paid by Rockefeller, who was on loan to the Republican party to serve as executive assistant to Spicer.[38] In a letter that was sent to the entire state executive committee, the chairman attacked Burton for "cooperating with the other state officers in the performance of their duties" without first obtaining permission from Spicer.[39]

The executive committee met in Little Rock on August 31. The meeting had been called by Spicer, Britt, and ten other members who had six proposals to present, all of which were designed to limit Rockefeller's influence in the party. One of these proposals even recommended removal of the state party office from the Tower Building, Little Rock's first skyscraper, built by Rockefeller and also housing Rockefeller's personal business offices. This proposal was passed, and on September 25 the office and its one employee were moved.[40] Another proposal concerned eliminating Marion Burton's job. This proposal was defeated, but on September 19 Burton submitted his letter of resignation to Spicer. The resignation was retroactively effective to September 1, "in view of the resolution presented to abolish my job." The letter, which was made public, attacked Spicer for refusing the help and cooperation given him by Rockefeller and Ham, for concentrating on national affairs rather than on building a state party organization, and for violating party rules by passing resolutions at the August 31 meeting without first holding hearings.[41]

Rockefeller consistently argued that he was trying to build the party at the grass-roots level because no one else was doing it. Spicer did appear to be more concerned with national politics and with trying to establish complete control over the party. He admitted in a January 1964 letter that "there is considerable truth in the charge of my not having done anything as State Chairman."[42] Spicer and other Post Office Republicans did not want the state GOP to grow because they would then lose control over patronage. According to Marion Burton, they also "had a working relationship with a lot of the politicians and office holders in the state and also at the national level."[43] This meant that Republicans agreed not to challenge Democrats in most races, and, in exchange, a certain amount of political favors would be passed on to the GOP. Everett Ham went even further, stating that the Post Office Republicans were afraid of being replaced at the county level because some of these county Republican leaders were Democrats masquerading as GOP members so that they could control county election commissions.[44]

But it also appears true that once Rockefeller began building the party, he would not be satisfied until he had accomplished a philosophical takeover. According to Rockefeller, Spicer's followers were "politically antagonistic to my basic philosophy. They were the right-wingers up to and including sometimes Birchers, and they were power-crazy."[45] When Spicer refused to hire field men to recruit precinct workers at the county level, as recommended by the national party, Rockefeller hired the men, paying them himself. Despite Spicer's objections, the party's state executive committee approved this action, an indication that sentiment was shifting toward Rockefeller.[46]

By May 1964, after Rockefeller had announced his candidacy for the governorship, Spicer seemed desperate. He wrote two letters that were photocopied and sent to his supporters. The first reported "confirmed" and "not confirmed" information about the "Rockefeller Forces," and their "continued kicking in the teeth of the OLD GUARD . . . BONAFIDE . . . TRUE BLUE Arkansas Republicans" [capitalization and ellipses in original]. Most of the information concerned the 1964 Republican national convention and Spicer's fear that Winthrop was trying to assemble an Arkansas delegation that would vote for Nelson Rockefeller rather than Goldwater. The second letter contained excerpts from a 1952 anti–Rockefeller family and Standard Oil book that Spicer said "gives the lowdown on the Rockefeller people."[47]

But by June Spicer appeared to acknowledge defeat. Discussing a proposed executive committee meeting, he told Rockefeller: "Win, I seriously doubt that any other than those known as the people on the 'Rockefeller' side of the argument would be there. You would have the majority. That's been demonstrated before. In fact, I don't know that I would bother to go." Later in the conversation, Spicer reiterated that Rockefeller had "taken control of the Party," but Spicer felt that "40 percent of the Party is still very dissatisfied with the way things are going." Rockefeller suggested that Spicer might want to resign after Spicer said that he was "rapidly reaching the point where I am going to wash my hands of the whole thing." But Spicer's response was that "the control of the vote can change."[48]

William Spicer did not attend the meeting he discussed on

the phone. At that meeting on June 14, the executive committee voted to move the Republican party offices back into the Tower Building because of "the need for facilities that are housed in National Committeeman Win Rockefeller's office—such things as printing and mailing equipment and volunteer workers."[49] Rockefeller had successfully taken control of the Republican party. He had by no means, however, silenced the opposition. This conflict would continue at full steam throughout the 1964 election. Rockefeller's inability to reconcile some Arkansas Republicans to his view of the goals of the party seriously hindered his attempt to build a valid second party in the state.

While fighting entrenched, stagnant power within the Republican party, Rockefeller also immersed himself in the political situation in Conway County, where Winrock was located. He joined forces with a newspaper editor named Gene Wirges against the county's Democratic machine headed by Sheriff Marlin Hawkins.

Wirges, an Arkansas native, bought the *Morrilton Democrat* in September 1957. He began using the paper to fight alleged corruption in county government in 1960. By July 1961 the county machine was fighting back, using financial pressure as their primary means of assault. Wirges made it easy for his enemies by overextending himself and, on more than one occasion, sale of the paper was forestalled only by the intervention of those who supported Wirges's fight and were willing to put up the money necessary for him to continue it. Rockefeller became a direct participant in Wirges's struggle to stay in business in late 1962. The Internal Revenue Service threatened foreclosure of the newspaper if Wirges could not come up with seventy-five hundred dollars in personal income taxes. Rockefeller posted a surety bond to guarantee Wirges's tax payments. Several years later, Rockefeller justified his intervention, explaining: "I didn't consistently agree with the way that Gene was running that newspaper. . . . But I felt it was a matter of principle. The machine was obviously out to get him. He was fighting not only for personal survival but also for freedom of the press."[50]

The Republican party also became involved in Wirges's crusade in 1962, sending Marion Burton to Conway County to help investigate alleged voting frauds. This assistance did not deter the machine in its fight against Wirges, but merely intensified the struggle. In October 1963 Burton was jailed for the first time by Circuit Judge Wiley Bean on a contempt of court charge for refusing to answer questions in the judge's chambers after the jury was already in deliberations. The charge was later dismissed by the state supreme court. And in February 1965 Burton and three other men, including Everett Ham, were indicted by a Conway County grand jury for conspiring to have Hawkins falsely arrested. That charge was dismissed in September 1966, on the basis that the state had failed to prosecute the case for three terms of court.[51]

Wirges himself, meanwhile, lost two libel suits against him in Conway County's circuit court. The judgments totaled $275,000.00, and to prevent seizure of the *Morrilton Democrat* to satisfy the claims, ownership of the paper was transferred to Transportation Properties, Inc., a Little Rock firm owned mainly by Rockefeller. To prevent further suits against the paper, Wirges's wife became the editor. Both libel suits were later dismissed on appeal.[52]

Wirges's legal problems continued through June 1967, when the state supreme court dismissed the last charge pending against him, a perjury conviction that would have meant a three-year prison term.[53] But the struggle against Hawkins and the county machine continued. A taxpayers' suit initiated by the Republican party alleged Hawkins had misappropriated more than $200,000.00 in county funds between 1954 and 1967. The judge found Hawkins liable for $10,082.20 and stated his conviction that the missing funds were only the result of "faulty bookkeeping."[54]

There were other charges, countercharges, and court dates too numerous to detail here.[55] The whole episode is significant because of Rockefeller's involvement and the impact this had on politics. In an October 1964 statement to the Conway County grand jury, Judge Wiley Bean claimed that the crusade against Hawkins was initiated "in order to build an effective two party system . . ." but that "as long as the tactics are used that I have just outlined there will never be a two party system in Arkansas. . . God forbid another millionaire from migrating to Arkansas."[56] Marlin Hawkins also claimed that the "strife, turmoil and publicity in our county has been created, nourished and constantly kept aflame by the ambitions and finances of Winthrop Rockefeller."[57] But G. Thomas Eisele saw Rockefeller's involvement in Wirges's struggle as "one of the greatest examples of the man's [Rockefeller's] stand on principles."[58] In a 1965 memo, Eisele had called to Rockefeller's attention that "from the political viewpoint, it is my judgement that the 'Conway County–Morrilton Democrat–Wirges' problem, to date, has been harmful to your overall cause."[59] Hawkins was a very popular man. Both his constituents and politicians owed him favors, were indebted to him, and saw him as their friend. Wirges, on the other hand, had many enemies, including some within the ranks of Conway County Republicans.[60] Yet Rockefeller helped fight Wirges's battles. With so little to gain politically, Rockefeller had to be fighting on principle, and, being stubborn, he was determined to continue battling what he saw as an abuse of the public trust, even after the battle appeared futile and the end result not worth the cost. This trait would surface again in Rockefeller's crusade against the Game and Fish Commission.

When Rockefeller announced his candidacy for governor in April 1964, it ended speculation about his political ambitions that began even before he was first eligible in 1960, the year he completed Arkansas's seven-year residency requirement. As early as late 1959, in response to queries from the press, Rockefeller had kept his options open regarding future races. Stating that he had been urged to run, he responded at that time that if he did, it would be as an independent, not as a Democrat. "Unfortunately, the Republican label is still fatal in Arkansas."[61] In the 1960 Democratic primary, Faubus was renominated in a landslide, receiving almost four times as many votes as his closest competition. This may have influenced Rockefeller's decision not to run as an independent that year, as was speculated by the *New York Times*.[62]

After the 1960 general election, David Hunter prepared a memo for Rockefeller outlining a "plan of action" for electing a Republican governor in 1962. The memo was written under two assumptions: that the Republican candidate would be Rockefeller, and that Faubus would not seek reelection in 1962. Hunter addressed the problem of organizing grass-roots support for a Rockefeller campaign. This would be difficult, he asserted, because Rockefeller's nomination by the GOP "is already taken for granted." In order to combat the lack of a primary battle, three things would be needed: vigorous Republican primaries for other positions in the state; cooperation with the state's "professional Republicans"; and a petition campaign urging Rockefeller to consider running, to be conducted prior to his public entrance into the race.[63]

Public opinion polls were commissioned by Rockefeller's staff in October 1960 and February 1961. The first dealt with many topics including national political issues, since the presidential election was only a month away. But the poll also looked to the future, asking people to rate the effectiveness of four well-known Arkansans (and presumably potential gubernatorial candidates), including Faubus and Rockefeller. Rockefeller came in second to Faubus in every category except the revitalization of industry, where Rockefeller led. The second poll was aimed specifically at assessing Rockefeller's popularity within the state in relation to other possible gubernatorial candidates and at evaluating potential election issues. The study concluded that Rockefeller was "indeed a *potentially strong* candidate for governor." However, if Faubus decided to run again in 1962, "he would be difficult to defeat."[64]

In April 1962 Rockefeller announced that he would not be a candidate in the 1962 gubernatorial race. His explanation for not running was that "I can do more for the Republican party in Arkansas by making it clear that I am not seeking something for myself." In a televised speech, Rockefeller stated that, despite denials, Faubus would probably run for a fifth term. And at a later press conference, Rockefeller would not rule out the possibility of being a candidate in 1964.[65]

The chain of events described above would seem to indicate that Winthrop Rockefeller wanted to be governor and was waiting for the election in which he would have the greatest chance of winning. But, according to his former advisors, this was not the case. Everett Ham said that Rockefeller decided to run "after I pounded away at him for years."[66] And, according to John Ward, "Rockefeller 'tried every way in the world' to get others to run for governor in 1964, until finally everyone turned to him and asked, 'What about you?'"[67] This agrees with Alvin Moscow's assessment. In *The Rockefeller Inheritance* he asserted: "Personally, he did not want to campaign for or to hold public office . . . it ran counter to his fundamental shyness. He preferred to be the power behind the throne, a guiding and helping hand in political reform."[68] Rockefeller ran not because he wanted to or because he was personally ambitious but because he was ambitious for Arkansas. He wanted to help build the state economically, socially, and culturally. Putting someone who felt the same way in the governor's office seemed the best way to achieve these goals. When it became apparent that only Rockefeller had a chance of defeating the Faubus machine, he agreed to run.

The tone of the campaign that Winthrop Rockefeller would conduct in 1964 was indicated shortly after he announced his candidacy. On May 3, 1964, he was the guest on NBC-TV's *Meet the Press*. He spoke of possible corruption within the Faubus administration because, as a result of Faubus's long tenure in office, the governor had appointed every member of the state's 187 regulatory boards and commissions. Responding to a query whether he would run as an integrationist, he stated, "I have always been a moderate." He called for better educational opportunities for blacks but came out against the 1964 Civil Rights Act then under debate in the Senate on the grounds that it was too vague and granted "certain police powers to the administrative, Executive branch of the government." Regarding the slow pace of integration in Arkansas (of 117,000 black students, 300 were in integrated schools), he said that the problem should be solved on a local basis "with encouragement." Rockefeller also came out against proposed legalized gambling in Hot Springs.[69]

Faubus stressed his experience as compared to an "untried, inexperienced former New York playboy." The governor listed his administration's accomplishments. When he discussed his plans for the next two years, they were in general agreement with Rockefeller's own promises. Faubus pledged to work for more paved roads and teacher salary increases, and he opposed legalized gambling. He avoided, whenever possible, any mention of racial issues. But Faubus's campaign speeches spent little time on his record and goals. Instead, they focused primarily on personal attacks against Rockefeller. Faubus criticized Rockefeller's admission that he served liquor to guests at Winrock, that he got his hair cut in New York, and that he was divorced. The governor accused Rockefeller employees of desecrating a cemetery in Lonoke County. He attacked the Rockefeller family, especially John D. Rockefeller, Sr. Faubus talked of the hardships his family endured purchasing coal oil when he was a boy because the price was set by Standard Oil.[70] These attacks showed that Faubus took his opponent seriously. He later recalled, "I had evaluated the Rockefeller threat as genuine and real with a good possibility of success."[71] After Faubus won, Rockefeller commissioned a postelection poll, which showed that Faubus's personal attacks were a contributing factor in the loss.[72]

Rockefeller's 1964 campaign was tremendously complicated by the divisions within the state Republican party caused by the opposing campaigns of Barry Goldwater and Nelson Rockefeller for the Republican presidential nomination. The debate had begun in early 1963, six months before Nelson officially entered the race, when Winthrop came out publicly in support of his brother. In May 1964 Winthrop acknowledged to the *New York Times* that Nelson's campaign was hurting his race for the governorship in Arkansas because "Nelson is branded throughout much of the South as a liberal."[73]

As Arkansas's Republican national committeeman, Winthrop was the head of Arkansas's delegation to the national convention. Two months before the convention, the party's executive committee instructed the Arkansas delegation to nominate Winthrop as the state's favorite-son candidate. Winthrop could then withdraw his nomination as soon as the voting began, and the twelve delegates would be free to vote for the nominee of their choice. This decision was a clear indication that Rockefeller now controlled the state organization, and it enraged Spicer and other Goldwater supporters.[74] Winthrop's favorite-son nomination strategy never materialized. One month before the convention, Nelson withdrew as a candidate. On the convention's first ballot, the Arkansas delegation split: nine for Goldwater, two for Pennsylvania Gov. William Scranton, and one, Winthrop, for Nelson Rockefeller. After Goldwater's nomination on the first ballot was assured, all twelve Arkansas delegates switched their votes to the nominee.[75]

After the Goldwater nomination, a split developed within Rockefeller's own campaign staff over how closely he should be identified with the national ticket. Rockefeller's campaign manager, G. Thomas Eisele, a young attorney, believed that Rockefeller should avoid close association with Goldwater. For one thing, Rockefeller had no chance of winning without a large proportion of crossover votes—Democrats who saw Rockefeller as a more moderate alternative to Faubus's conservatism. Such voters would be supporting Lyndon Johnson for president and might be offended or misled if Rockefeller and Goldwater were closely connected. In an August memo to Rockefeller, Eisele wrote, "I am convinced that further efforts at identification will destroy our ability to obtain a large number of the Lyndon Johnson votes which will clearly be needed for victory."[76] Rockefeller's assistant Everett Ham, on the other hand, believed that the two campaigns should be closely linked, and that Rockefeller's campaign would help Goldwater. Ham had hired Eisele, believing that his law practice would prevent Eisele from working full time on the campaign, thus allowing Ham to run the show. Eisele, however, "shut down his law practice and joined the campaign full time," according to John Ward. "Ham was dismayed." The disagreement over Goldwater became so intense that Eisele threatened to resign if Rockefeller sided with Ham.[77] He did not; on the top of the August 11 memo, Rockefeller wrote, "For record, I agree with GTE [Eisele] . . . my instructions were ignored."[78]

On the Democratic side, Orval Faubus encountered the same problem, only in reverse. Since much of his support came from conservative, rural Arkansas, he did not want to risk alienating those Democrats who supported Goldwater because of Johnson's civil-rights agenda. Thus, Faubus allegedly considered publicly endorsing Goldwater. It was not until mid-September that Faubus announced his support for the Johnson-Humphrey ticket.[79]

All of this confusion did not help Rockefeller's chance of winning, a chance that had always been slim. Faubus received enough votes in the Democratic primary to assure victory in the general election, and Rockefeller's own polls leading up to the election consistently showed him trailing Faubus. Thus it was no surprise that Faubus received 337,489 votes, or 57 percent, to Rockefeller's 254,561 votes, or 43 percent. In the presidential race, Johnson carried Arkansas with 56.4 percent to Goldwater's 43.6 percent. Despite the similarity in the percentage of votes received by Rockefeller and Goldwater, Rockefeller did best in the more urban counties, counties that Johnson also carried. Rockefeller's 43 percent was the largest number of votes received in Arkansas by a Republican gubernatorial candidate since Reconstruction. When speaking to reporters after conceding the election, Rockefeller announced that he would run again in 1966.[80]

While Rockefeller's 1964 campaign had begun in April, only seven months prior to the election, his 1966 campaign began on November 4, 1964. A poll was conducted a month after the election to determine the effectiveness of various aspects of the campaign.[81] Issues that were seen as either important or controversial were discussed and studied. Two subjects given a great deal of attention were voter registration and possible voting irregularities. Arkansas voters had approved an amendment to the state constitution in the 1964 election that abolished the poll tax as required by Amendment 24 of the United States Constitution, ratified in January 1964. A permanent voter registration system was established, but complications arose after the election. First, the state election commission drew up a registration form that asked for race and party affiliation. After the courts struck down these provisions, registration was held up by a lawsuit between two printing companies for the right to print the form. Rockefeller was advised to lead the drive for voter registration, which he did in a public statement on May 11, 1965, although Governor Faubus continued to hesitate.[82]

Voting irregularities were almost a way of life in Arkansas. In the summer of 1964, several lawyers and the president of the League of Women Voters established the Election Research Council, Inc., to investigate vote fraud. They concluded that at least 50 percent of the absentee ballots cast in the 1964 election were invalid. Marion Burton was one of Pulaski County's three election commissioners. He recalled that it took "three to four days just to count the absentee ballots."[83] Everett Ham told the story of one rural voting place in a church where paper ballots were used. According to Ham, a man hid up in the loft with duplicate ballots. The number of each ballot and the voter's name were called out loud enough for the man in the loft to hear. Then the ballot boxes were switched on the way out of the church. Ham concluded that "anytime you get 43 percent of the vote as a Republican, you'd probably have won had every-body been able to vote as they wanted to."[84] Rockefeller's staff tried to verify voting records in Faubus's home county of Madison. After repeated attempts to see and copy the records were refused, all the county voting records were "stolen" and duplicate copies were burned, despite an injunction prohibiting their destruction. This overzealous behavior helped shake up voter apathy regarding fraud and gave Rockefeller an issue for the 1966 election.[85]

In an effort to have federal legislation enacted aimed at protecting votes once cast and at assuring honest elections, Rockefeller sent letters to senators and congressmen involved in drafting the Voting Rights Act of 1965. The act allowed the "chief legal officer or other appropriate official" of any state to petition the attorney general for federal poll examiners, or watchers. The attorney general would then present the evidence to a court of three judges who would decide where to place these officials. Rockefeller was informed by Sen. Jacob Javits that certain counties in Arkansas would be entitled to federal poll watchers.[86]

One issue that Rockefeller and his staff had trouble dealing with was race. His activities with the Urban League and other interracial groups were well known and hurt him in racially conservative Arkansas. A pre-election poll showed that 49 percent of the voters statewide felt that Faubus could do the best job of keeping racial peace in Arkansas, as opposed to 28 percent who thought Rockefeller most likely to do so. This was in spite of the fact that Rockefeller had been very careful not to come out for integration, insisting that it was a local issue.[87]

In early 1965 John Ward outlined in a memo to Rockefeller and his assistants the steps that Ward felt were necessary in order to deal effectively with the question of race relations. He wrote:

> WR, because of his background, his liberal identification, his birthplace and for other reasons, will see his opinions and feelings about the race issue misinterpreted. . . . He has to state what he believes as precisely and consistently as possible. . . .
> . . . He should never become completely identified with either extreme. He should maintain an attitude that takes into account the feelings of those on both sides of the issue, offering guidelines for both leading to a solution both can accept.[88]

All of the preparations made in 1965 for the 1966 campaign were based on the assumption that Rockefeller would once again run against Faubus.[89] Certain steps were taken to counter the Faubus charges that public opinion polls showed had been effective. One such charge was that Rockefeller preferred to spend money out of state, even going to New York to get his hair cut. Therefore, when John Ward ordered publicity photographs from a California firm, he asked that the firm's label not be embossed on the backs because "many Arkansas folks don't like the idea of WR getting his hair cut, his picture made or his pants pressed anywhere else."[90]

Rockefeller formally entered the race for governor on January 11, 1966, still expecting to oppose Faubus. On March 21, Faubus announced that he would not seek a seventh term. His explanation was that he was tired and wanted to retire. In his memoirs, Faubus claimed that he made the decision not to seek a seventh term even before winning the 1964 election.

> One thing that was said in criticism of my administration was true. It had grown "old" . . .
> I tried to maintain the same interest, diligence and zest for the duties of the office in the last years of my service as in the first. For many key people in my administration I observed this was not the case.[91]

In response to those who claimed he feared losing to Rockefeller, the governor asserted that "the poll [of February 1966] showed that I was the only Democrat who could defeat Rockefeller in 1966."[92]

With Faubus stepping out of the picture, eight Democrats ran in the primary, and after an August runoff, Rockefeller finally had a Democratic opponent. He was James D. Johnson, or "Justice Jim," the hard-core segregationist who had made a name for himself fighting integration in Hoxie, Arkansas, and was later elected to the state supreme court. Johnson had campaigned for Goldwater in 1964, and was a close friend of George Wallace's. While his victory in the primary was due in part to racist backlash, it also appeared to be a reaction to the increased government spending and bureaucracy of the Lyndon Johnson administration. Jim Johnson's main theme was a return to what he called "old values."[93]

Rockefeller also faced a primary in 1966, but his opponent was hardly a serious challenger. He was Gus McMillan, a Democrat and Faubus supporter who switched parties on the same day that he entered the race. Republicans speculated that McMillan had entered merely to force the party into the expense of a primary. And in July the Republican State Committee announced in the party's newspaper that McMillan had offered to pull out of the race for eighty-two thousand dollars. In the primary later that month, Rockefeller won by a vote of 19,646 to 310.[94]

The 1966 campaign was a bitter one, because Johnson concentrated on name calling rather than issues. To him, Rockefeller was "prissy sissy" and "Madison Avenue cowboy." Johnson had used the same tactics in the Democratic primary and had thus made enemies of many moderate Democrats. He also alienated Faubus supporters by attacking what he called "machine politics." Johnson had never had the support of blacks or liberals, and he did not back away from his reputation as a segregationist. He walked past blacks as if they did not exist, but claimed he was not a racist, explaining: "I've said many times that if anyone can point out to me where mixing of the races has ever benefited either race, then I would take a new look at the situation. But I've never had it pointed out to me yet."[95] All of this helped swing many Democratic votes to Rockefeller. While an August survey showed Johnson leading 45 percent to 42 percent, by October Rockefeller was leading 51 percent to 43 percent. This lead remained relatively constant up to the election.[96]

For his part, Rockefeller did not like name calling. He tried to avoid personalities and concentrate on his agenda for the state. He called for improved education, increased industrialization, and better roads. His staff used computers for direct mailings, one of the first campaigns to do so. Whenever possible, he avoided mentioning civil rights, but he had representatives lobbying on his behalf in black neighborhoods. Rockefeller's moderate, positive program stood in sharp contrast to Jim Johnson's arch-segregationist past, and this helped.[97] Rockefeller's campaign was also aided by experience gained in the 1964 race, and two years of preparatory work including the work his staff did toward building the Republican party. While the percentage of the population considering themselves Republicans did not grow, the party was better organized. At the 1966 state party convention, all seventy-five counties were represented for the first time.[98]

Rockefeller's running mate, the Republican candidate for lieutenant governor, was Maurice "Footsie" Britt. A native Arkansan, Britt was also a former Razorback football star and a World War II Medal of Honor winner. Raised as a Democrat, Britt converted to the Republican party after voting for

Eisenhower in 1952 and after being convinced by his father-in-law of the need for a two-party system. Britt ran for lieutenant governor at the urging of Everett Ham, and only after his "good personal friend," eleven-term Lt. Gov. Nathan Gordon, decided not to run.[99] On election day, Rockefeller received 306,324 votes, or 54.4 percent, to Johnson's 257,203 votes, or 45.6 percent. Britt also won, although by a slimmer margin, 50.3 percent to his Democratic opponent's 49.7 percent. A Republican, John Paul Hammerschmidt, the state party chairman since July 1964, captured one of Arkansas's four congressional seats.[100]

Rockefeller's victory was due in large part to the black vote. It was estimated that he received more than 95 percent of the approximately seventy-five thousand black votes cast, and this would have been the difference between victory and defeat.[101]

Despite modest Republican gains, Rockefeller's victory in 1966 was personal rather than an indication that the two-party system had arrived in Arkansas. His opponent's extremism was certainly a major factor, for the 1966 Republican and Democratic party platforms were virtually identical, calling for reform in the state constitution, better education, and more industry.[102] In analyzing the 1966 election, Rockefeller later said:

> In '66 the people were not necessarily voting for me. Certainly they weren't voting for a Republican. They were voting against a system they had wearied of. . . . So I have the feeling that the original election [against Johnson] wasn't quite as surprising when you realize that I was running against the type of person I was.[103]

John Ward agreed that Rockefeller's victory was personality based rather than an indication of a shift toward a two-party system. Ward said that the people voted for Rockefeller because "they didn't think he would steal from them, and they liked his positive attitude, he was someone they could be proud of and they could feel good about his going off and representing the state."[104]

Regardless of the reasons for the victory, Rockefeller's election was part of a national trend in 1966. The number of GOP governors grew from seventeen to twenty-five. Republicans also added forty-seven seats in the House of Representatives and nearly tripled the number of state legislatures they controlled.[105] Unfortunately for Rockefeller, this growing Republican strength was a phenomenon that would not hit Arkansas, especially in the very Democratic, and often recalcitrant, General Assembly.

THREE

A Legislative History of Rockefeller's First Term

O n Tuesday, January 10, 1967, Winthrop Rockefeller was inaugurated as Arkansas's first Republican governor since 1874. To accomplish his objectives, he would have to deal with a state legislature composed of thirty-five Democrats in the senate, and ninety-seven Democrats and three Republicans in the house. In his inaugural address, he stated:

> Now is not the time for party politics. . . .
> . . . Any administration must be measured by its goals and by its objectives. Let us spell them out like men. We come here committed not to discord, but to doing . . . not to destroying, but to discovering . . . not to dividing, but by dissolving old problems with new solutions.[1]

Over the next two years, Rockefeller would experience much discord in his relationship with the legislature. But he would also achieve passage of much of his reform agenda. The governor's effectiveness in guiding legislation through the General Assembly diminished as the 1968 election approached.

The obstacles Rockefeller encountered were not exclusively the result of his minority-party status. The organization and procedures of the General Assembly almost assured that problems would surface between the governor and the legislature.

The Arkansas General Assembly was, and is, an amateur legislature. The state constitution permits only one regular session every two years, and this session must be limited to sixty days unless extended by a two-thirds vote of both houses. The governor can, however, call the legislature into special session at any time, stating in his call the items to be discussed. Other matters can be considered only if two-thirds of both houses vote to do so. Salaries for legislators are set in the constitution and can be increased only by amendment. In 1966 legislators were paid twelve hundred dollars a year with a per diem expense allotment of twenty dollars during the regular session. The per diem allotment during special sessions was only six dollars. Arkansas legislators were therefore part-time employees who relied on another occupation as their chief means of support. The low per diem and the additional time spent away from work made special sessions very unpopular with the legislators. Of the six special sessions held in the decade prior to Rockefeller's inauguration, the average length was six days.[2]

Aside from the president of the senate, who was the lieutenant governor, leadership in both houses of the General Assembly was determined by the pledge system; this meant that the speaker's position in the house and the position of president *pro tempore* in the senate went to the individuals who obtained enough pledges in the current session to be elected in the next session. Thus, leadership was based not solely on seniority but also on "fellowship," on placating as many other legislators as possible. Such an atmosphere hardly invited conflict or controversy.

There was, during Rockefeller's two terms, no law restricting lobbying. The most influential lobbyists were former legislators who were allowed unrestricted access to the floors of both houses. There was also no code of ethics for state employees, and the amateur nature of the legislature meant that there were frequent conflicts of interest.

Between sessions, legislative business was conducted by the legislative council, a committee comprised of both senators and representatives. Its duties consisted primarily of recommending legislative programs, preparing research reports, and reviewing and holding public hearings on the governor's proposed budget.[3]

The Sixty-sixth General Assembly convened on January 9, a day prior to Rockefeller's inauguration. On that day, the Arkansas senate voted to confirm ninety-three appointments to various state boards and commissions over the objections of the governor-elect. The appointments had been made by then-Governor Faubus in the almost two years since the adjournment of the Sixty-fifth General Assembly. All ninety-three appointments were confirmed unanimously in spite of, and perhaps because of, an unsigned memo Rockefeller had delivered to the senators' desks asking that the appointments go unconfirmed until he had a chance to review them and make his own recommendations. The senators' vote made headlines, and the senators themselves disagreed as to whether the vote was customary or a slap in the face of the Republican governor. Older senators recalled that lists sent to the senate by previous departing governors had been ignored.[4] Other senators were quick to blame Rockefeller, stating that the unsigned note appeared as a challenge to the senate. The *Democrat* reported that several senators admitted they would have waited if Rockefeller had spoken to them personally. Others challenged the authenticity of the note, since it was unsigned. One senator went so far as to say that Rockefeller was "deliberately trying to alienate this legislature."[5] The *Gazette* editorialized that the vote was indeed intended as a slap at Rockefeller and that "there was no reason—if the matter is to be judged by standards of fairness and good will—for the Senate to have felt compelled to act on the appointees so hastily, without so much as a debate."[6] Reviewing the problem in a letter to Rockefeller, one twenty-year veteran of the General Assembly, Morrell Gathright, noted as one possible reason that not confirming the appointments would have given the Republican party additional patronage appointments.[7] The governor-elect, meanwhile, defended the note he sent on the basis that there was no time to do anything else, having found out about the vote at the last minute.

Rockefeller had expected the "customary privilege" of reviewing the appointments first.[8]

Was this confrontation, and the many others that would follow, inevitable? Many of the legislators themselves thought so. Following Rockefeller's election, there was constant speculation on whether or not a working relationship was even possible between the Republican governor and the overwhelmingly Democratic legislature. It became apparent that cooperation was conceivable only if Rockefeller went out of his way to avoid actions that would in any way enhance the stature of the Republican party. In a state that, for all intents and purposes, had not seen the two-party system at work for one hundred years, this narrow partisanship seemed perfectly natural and was accepted as a fact of life. Shortly after the election, a Democrat who had supported Rockefeller sent the governor-elect a long letter of advice on how to deal with the legislature and pass "a program that will carry Arkansas forward through the next two years." The letter recommended several Democrats who could help Rockefeller in dealing with the legislators and then concluded:

> I know how strongly you feel about your two party system in Arkansas, but I caution you that this drive should be deferred until after the Legislature adjourns. I know that if I were a Democratic Legislator and you were threatening to get me sizable opposition two years from now from a Republican, I would be inclined to fight your program or to throw chunks in your way than to be enthusiastic in helping you.[9]

Many legislators resented what Rockefeller had already done for the Republican party. For the first time in their careers, they had faced opposition in the general election, and they blamed Rockefeller for forcing them into the expense of two campaigns, one in the Democratic primary, and the other in the general election. In the weeks following the election, the press focused on what to expect in the upcoming legislative session. One twenty-year veteran of the senate, J. Lee Bearden, stated that, while he wanted to help make Arkansas a better place to live, he drew the line at "helping Rockefeller build a two-party state."[10]

In the twentieth century, one of the lieutenant governor's

traditional powers, as president of the senate, has been to appoint members and chairmen to the senate's more than twenty committees. In September 1966 thirty-two senators held a meeting and formed a new Committee on Committees, comprised of the senate's five senior members. This new committee would now assume the power of committee assignments. After the Republican candidate, Maurice "Footsie" Britt, was elected lieutenant governor in November, the Committee on Committees met to carry out this duty. At a meeting later the same day, Britt told the committee that he considered the change in rules as "a slap in the face" and invalid since the senate was not in session when the committee was formed. J. Lee Bearden reminded Britt that he was not a senator and that the senate "was in sole control of its internal affairs."[11] As the senators pointed out, the change was planned prior to Britt's election, which had not been expected by many in the state. But the fact that the change was carried out after the Republican was elected served as a source of tension and suspicion between Britt and the senate.

The building tension led four Democratic state representatives to issue a manifesto in December pledging to cooperate "actively and wholeheartedly" with Rockefeller in proposals that were for the good of Arkansas. They stressed that it was "self-defeating" to oppose administration measures solely on the basis that they had originated with a Republican governor.[12] Over the next four years, nonpartisan cooperation was not an easy goal to attain. There was fault, in varying degrees, on both sides. There was also a genuine and deep split between Rockefeller and many legislators over what Arkansas's needs were and how the state government should best go about satisfying those needs.

The regular session of the Sixty-sixth General Assembly ran from January 9 to March 10, 1967, with an extension of the regular session held from March 27 to March 31. During the session, forty-four administration-sponsored bills were introduced in the senate. Twenty-six were enacted into law. Thirty administration bills were introduced in the house and thirteen became law. The majority of these new laws concerned social and political reform. Rockefeller achieved success with much of his program for improving education. Other administration legislative triumphs streamlined state government, established study commissions to examine long-term problems, and improved highway safety.[13]

A substantial portion of the administration's legislative program in this session dealt with improving education, one of Rockefeller's long-term interests. Bills that became law without much controversy were Senate Bill 13, which provided for free textbooks, and Senate Bill 45, which allowed driver education in public schools.[14] A constitutional amendment was approved, to be voted on in the next general election, that would allow state-supported kindergartens for the first time in Arkansas. The state constitution confined free public education to persons between the ages of six and twenty-one. The amendment did not require kindergartens but merely allowed them. Despite this, it met with considerable opposition. One *Arkansas Democrat* columnist complained that the amendment, which abolished the age restriction on both ends, would turn the schools into nursing homes and baby sitter facilities.[15]

One controversial administration measure introduced in the 1967 General Assembly granted teachers salary increases averaging $500 for each of the next two years. Although a pay increase for public school teachers was a goal everyone could agree on, what type of increase they would receive was another matter. The furor over teachers' salaries began with a nonadministration measure, which was the first bill of the legislative session Rockefeller vetoed. This bill would have taken a $2,790,000 surplus in the education budget and distributed it to classroom teachers in the form of two $500 a year bonuses. The surplus was a state tax windfall resulting from the start of state income-tax withholding in 1966. Taxes for both 1965 and 1966 were collected in 1966. This one-time surplus would pay the bonuses but could not provide permanent pay raises. Rockefeller's argument in vetoing the bonus bill was that the state could not afford to give the teachers these bonuses in addition to a permanent raise without seriously damaging other state agency budgets. He wrote, "It is my judgement that the teachers benefit more in the long run by having their basic salary increased than by the receipt of 'bonuses' which necessarily will not be available in future years."[16] Opposition to Rockefeller's veto was strong, especially from the teachers' Arkansas Education Association. Forrest Rozzell, executive secretary of the AEA, asserted that there were sufficient funds to cover both the bonuses and the pay raises. The governor did receive support for his stand from the *Arkansas Gazette*. The paper praised Rockefeller's "considerable courage" in standing up to the AEA and vetoing what was a "questionable method of state financing."[17]

The administration then concentrated on its own answer to the teachers' raise controversy, a bill that would have granted *average* raises of five hundred dollars per teacher for the next two years. The raise due each teacher would be calculated on a formula, taking into consideration current salary as well as training and experience. One of the advantages of the formula method would be to help equalize the salaries of black teachers with that of whites in those districts where two separate pay scales were used. It would also help poorer, rural districts retain teachers. While Rockefeller's bill was supported by the AEA, the Arkansas Teachers Association, and the state Department of Education, teachers in the more affluent districts of the state were vehement in their opposition to a formula bill.[18] It died in the house of representatives, in part because the house had already passed its own salary bill. The house bill passed the senate and was signed by the governor in early March. This bill provided all Arkansas classroom teachers with a flat five hundred dollar salary increase for each of the next two years. Rockefeller signed it "reluctantly" while his own bill was still in the house, hoping that his bill would clear the house, in which case he would "happily sign it," thus superseding the earlier one. A letter and memo asking for support was sent by the governor to Arkansas's teachers, but, not surprisingly, to no avail.[19] The teachers received their flat five hundred dollar raises amounting over the two years to an average salary increase of 20 percent.[20]

One portion of Rockefeller's education program that met total defeat in the legislature was a bill granting tenure to public school teachers. The proposal would have set up a tenure system beginning with the 1970–71 school year. Supported by the Arkansas Education Association, the bill faced opposition from rural legislators who argued that it was a "big city measure . . . tying the hands of local school boards."[21] The bill provided three years teaching in a district before tenure could be granted and gave a broad range of reasons for firing a tenured teacher. Despite this, the attitude of legislators opposing the bill was exemplified by Sen. Robert Harvey, who said that "in instances where teachers were not wanted by the community it was best that they leave."[22] The tenure bill was initially passed by both houses, but was later recalled by the senate for reconsideration. The voting record for the bill was expunged, and it was not voted on again.[23]

A major triumph for Rockefeller was the passage of two bills, creating a new administration department and a personnel division within the department. The new department combined the Purchasing Department and the Comptroller's Office in an attempt to streamline state government. The personnel division would work toward establishing a uniform salary classification for state employees. The idea of an administration department was not new—one had been established during Francis Cherry's term as governor (1953–55) but was dismantled by Faubus. It had the support of many senior members in both the house and the senate. There was one difference between the administration bill and the final version passed by the assembly. An amendment was added to the personnel division bill permitting state agencies to decide whether cooperation with the personnel division study of state employment would interfere with the normal functioning of the agency.[24]

Three administration-sponsored study commissions were established during the legislative session. The first, the Penitentiary Study Commission, was signed into law on January 31. This commission was given broad subpoena and investigative power. The second commission was the Constitutional Revision Study Commission, signed into law on February 21. The state's 1874 constitution, a reactionary document written at the end of Reconstruction, was in desperate need of reform. Earlier in the session, several house members had introduced a bill calling for a constitutional convention to convene in 1968. The new constitution would then be submitted to the voters in the 1968 general election. This bill was defeated, forty-three to forty-four, because many representatives were fearful of what a new constitution might contain and instead favored fixing problems with the present constitution by amending it. The sponsors of the constitutional convention bill then threw their support behind Rockefeller's more conservative idea of convening a study commission.[25] The third commission established in 1967 was the Arkansas Governmental Efficiency Study Commission, nicknamed the Little Hoover Commission.[26]

Rockefeller achieved success with a series of highway safety bills in the 1967 legislature. There was little opposition to most of the program because the bills were necessary to avoid a 10 percent cut in federal highway funds under the federal Highway Safety Act of 1966. There were eleven bills in all, providing for vehicle safety inspection, driver's education, two-year issuance of driver's licenses, central recording of all driver's licenses, additional safety requirements for motorcycles, suspension of driver's licenses of all persons receiving aid on the basis of legal blindness, permanent vehicle registration, the banning of roadside billboards, and the raising of minimum age requirements for drivers of school buses and commercial trucks. All eleven bills passed except for the last one, which was controversial because many school bus drivers were under eighteen, the minimum age under the new law.[27]

While preparing the administration's program in the months prior to his inauguration, Rockefeller announced on television that he would support a minimum wage bill for Arkansas. The bill, which was drafted in December 1966, provided for an immediate minimum wage of $1.00 an hour with increases over the next two years to bring it to $1.20 an hour.[28] At the time, Arkansas had no minimum wage, while the federal minimum wage was $1.20 an hour, rising automatically in February 1967 to $1.40. Though a minimum wage bill was supported in both platforms, opposition from businessmen was fierce and began as soon as Rockefeller made his intentions public. Frank W. Cantrell, executive vice president of the Arkansas State Chamber of Commerce, told reporters: "The state chamber has never thought that minimum wage bills were advantageous. I think the reasons are obvious. . . . They benefit chiefly people at the top of the scale rather than those at the bottom."[29]

The minimum wage bill, introduced by Senators Max Howell and Ben Allen, was strongly supported by the Arkansas AFL-CIO. The union's president, J. Bill Becker, stated in hearings held by the Senate Labor Committee that a state minimum wage law would be the "greatest single step in the war on poverty."[30] But opposition from and lobbying by the business community were too strong to overcome. The bill was defeated amid claims that it would run many enterprises out of business.[31]

Other administration measures that did not make it through the Sixty-sixth General Assembly included Rockefeller's "Little Hatch" Act, restricting the political activities of state employees, and a jury wheel bill, providing for random selection of jurors. The jury wheel bill was opposed by many circuit judges who currently controlled jury selection by appointing three commissioners who had complete control in choosing jurors. The bill was also opposed by representatives who feared that a result would be "more Negroes on juries."[32]

Rockefeller backed a bill permitting municipalities to increase the statewide 3 percent sales tax by 1 percent, subject to local option. The sales tax bill was one administration measure condemned by the usually supportive *Gazette*. The paper, noting the regressive nature of the sales tax, which included groceries, called for more realistic property tax assessments instead.[33] But given Arkansas's agricultural economy, calling for increased property taxes was tantamount to political suicide. The sales tax bill was introduced in the senate by Max Howell at Rockefeller's request. It passed the senate twenty-one to eleven, but died in the house.[34]

One bill that was not administration sponsored but that had Rockefeller's approval would have permitted the sale of alcoholic beverages only in those municipalities and counties where it was approved by the voters. The idea of a mixed drink bill was not new, but it was an extremely emotional issue with tremendous opposition. One senator noted that the last time one was submitted, "the gallery was full of Baptist preachers and no one showed up to speak for the bill."[35] In 1967 the sale of liquor was allowed only by the bottle at liquor stores, and then only by local option. One supporter of the new bill, Rep. Ode Maddox, argued that it was better to have "liquor by the gulp rather than by the gallon." The bill died in the senate by a vote of eight to twenty-six, and an identical measure was defeated in the house by a closer vote, forty-four to forty-seven.[36]

In the two months the Sixty-sixth General Assembly was in session, tension between Rockefeller and the legislature often erupted into public arguments. When the governor sent over his first list of appointments in late January, the senate confirmed fourteen of the fifteen, but only after a heated discussion behind closed doors. Opposition to the appointments was led by Sen. Guy "Mutt" Jones, angry over Rockefeller's public disapproval of the senate's January 9 vote on Faubus's appointees. During Rockefeller's two terms in office, Jones, a twenty-year veteran of the senate and a campaign official for Jim Johnson in 1966, would prove to be one of the governor's most consistent and strident critics. The one appointment not confirmed was that of a woman who had been an unsuccessful Republican candidate for state representative in the 1966 election. Afterwards, Jones announced to the press that the senate, in confirming all but one, had shown Rockefeller "more courtesy" than he had shown them.[37]

On Monday, February 13, Rockefeller spoke before a joint session of the General Assembly. The purpose of the speech was to deliver a budget message, but Rockefeller used the first few minutes to discuss the relationship between his office and the legislature. Regarding the senate, Rockefeller stated:

> A few men have attempted to choke off the development of better government in Arkansas, . . . to embarrass the new state administration in every way possible. . . . they have attempted to

show, at any cost, that a Republican governor cannot possibly accomplish anything with a legislature made up almost entirely of Democrats. . . .

. . . I must tell you now—in the most emphatic terms—that I will not sit by quietly in the governor's office while a few legislators do their best to dismantle the executive branch of government.[38]

Later that month, Lt. Gov. Britt and Sen. William Ingram argued on the floor of the senate when Ingram accused Britt of "making a deal" on behalf of a bill to shorten the workweek of firemen. Despite a public handshaking later that day, bitter feelings remained over Ingram's diversion into charges of voting fraud in the 1966 election and his producing police records regarding a 1964 public drunkenness charge against Rockefeller's new insurance commissioner, J. Norman Harkey.[39] Relations between the governor and the senate were further damaged by Britt's admission that he had agreed to recognize a supporter of the firemen's bill if the bill was in danger of being killed, not in a "deal" but simply because he agreed with the bill. As one senator told Britt: "You're getting a little off base if you did that. You're supposed to be impartial."[40]

Relations between Rockefeller and the Arkansas house were peaceful in comparison to the governor's stormy relationship with the senate. This was due in part to the system of checks and balances. The house did not have to confirm the governor's appointees, nor was it presided over by the lieutenant governor. The size of the house, with one hundred members in contrast to the Senate's thirty-five, worked against the possibility of the house's acting as a single unit, as the senate often did. With the senate feuding with Rockefeller even before his inauguration, the house was particularly sensitive to charges of partisanship. This may also have served to keep relations calm.

The first indication that the house was not as eager as the senate to wage war on Rockefeller came on February 14. The house defeated, by a vote of sixty-five to twenty-four, a senate bill introduced by Guy Jones that would have granted job security retroactive to January 1 to all state employees whose jobs were granted on the basis of patronage. The consensus among house Democrats voting against the bill was that the bill was not a positive program for the good of Arkansas but was merely for the purpose of "sniping at the heels" of the governor.[41] Tension existed between the house and Rockefeller, but it did not usually get to the point where it made headlines. One representative wrote the governor near the end of the session: "I have found that many feel that the Welcome Mat has been removed from the Governor's office. Just how to restore that is the problem, maybe it is the lack of communication or perhaps it is just political stubbornness."[42]

On March 7 the house, along with the senate, voted to override Rockefeller's veto of a bill sponsored by Guy Jones that required senate confirmation of all appointees to boards and commissions. This was the first time since 1953 that the legislature had even attempted to override a veto.[43] Three other bills were passed over the governor's veto in 1967. One required voters to designate their party affiliation before voting in party primaries, another granted increases to nursing homes for the care of welfare recipients, and the third restricted the right of voters to vote for write-in candidates.[44]

The bill introduced in the Sixty-sixth General Assembly that provoked the most controversy, and even national media attention, was a nonadministration measure that would have permitted gambling in Hot Springs, a tourist-oriented town that had seen better days. Gambling had flourished illegally in Hot Springs through much of the twentieth century, and the legislators from Garland County, where the town is located, were anxious to make it legal. A constitutional amendment legalizing gambling had been overwhelmingly defeated by the voters in 1964. This session's bill was passed by both the house and the senate in a total of five days, but by close votes, and placed on Rockefeller's desk. Gambling was in itself a controversial issue, but the controversy was compounded by a disagreement between Rockefeller and the legislature. Rockefeller had announced prior to passage of the bill by the house that he was morally opposed to gambling and would not sign it. This was in keeping with statements made during both the 1964 and 1966 campaigns that he would fight the presence of gambling in Hot Springs. Many representatives, however, were told by the bill's backers that the governor favored it and would allow it to become law without his signature. This, they said, was why they voted for the bill. Sen. Richard Griffin declared that the senate had been "made a fool of" by Rockefeller.[45] Rockefeller aggravated the situation when, after being presented with the bill, he refused to say whether or not he would allow it to become law. Instead, he urged the public to make their sentiments concerning the bill known and expressed hope that the senate would recall it. Aides reported that public response to the governor's office was running eight to one against legalized gambling.[46] One of the sponsors of the bill, Oscar Alagood, wrote Rockefeller urging him to allow the bill to become law on the grounds that gambling would always exist and, if legal, could be controlled.[47] The following day the governor vetoed the bill. Its backers announced that they would not attempt to override it, but they were adamant in their assertions that Rockefeller had promised them he would not veto. Sen. Q. Byrum Hurst told the senate that the governor had "perpetuated a fraud upon me . . . Now I feel that I have been misled, that the people of my county have been crucified."[48]

Despite the many unpleasant incidents that arose during the 1967 General Assembly, the session was a success for Rockefeller. In part this was due to the fact that much of his program had widespread popularity statewide. Most people wanted to see education reform. The highway safety program was necessary to continue federal funding. Because of the income tax windfall, the session was not marred by the threat of statewide tax increases. (The sales tax bill would not have raised taxes, but would merely have permitted municipalities to vote on raising them.)

Another major reason for the relative success of the administration program in 1967 was the spirit of cooperation that prevailed in the house of representatives. The speaker of the house, Sterling Cockrill, Jr., was anxious that the house members not engage in "petty partisanship."[49] Cockrill was one of the four representatives who had issued the December manifesto pledging cooperation with the Republican administration. His leadership helped steer the house away from blatant antagonism toward Rockefeller. Cockrill later recalled that during Rockefeller's first term "there was a willingness [in the house] to wait for him to come forward and let's see what he was going to offer."[50] Of the house's one hundred members, forty-four were serving their first terms, and they were not trying to prove their independence after the executive dominance of the Faubus administration. A much smaller proportion of the senate were newcomers—nine out of thirty-five—and two of the nine had previously served in the house.

The fact that Rockefeller's governorship was preceded by Faubus's twelve years in office accounted for some of the problems between Rockefeller, Britt, and the senate. Faubus had ruled the legislature—his patronage power was increased by his longevity in office. By the time he retired, Faubus had appointed every member of every board and commission in the state. Some of the rule changes that Rockefeller and Britt resented resulted more from a legislative desire to strengthen their branch of government than from narrow partisanship. For example, one of the reasons that Faubus did not have a single veto overridden was that he frequently refused delivery of a bill until the closing days of a session. The bill could then be vetoed after the legislature had gone home. In the 1965 regular session, Faubus vetoed three bills while the legislature was still in session and seventeen after it adjourned. As a result, the legislature enacted a law establishing procedure for the delivery of bills to the governor. Another example of legislative independence that caused problems was the new senate rule that required consideration of the governor's appointments by executive session of the committee of the whole rather than by the senate. This meant that consideration excluded not only the press but also the lieutenant governor.[51]

Rockefeller's first encounter with the legislature was influenced to a degree by the lingering ghost of his predecessor. But as his term in office progressed, legislative politics would be affected even more by upcoming elections. The effectiveness and constructive productivity of the legislative sessions would diminish over the course of the next four years.

At the conclusion of the regular session in March 1967, Rockefeller announced that he would probably call a special session. By the summer, the governor had decided that a special session in 1968 was absolutely necessary. One of the main purposes of the session, which was originally planned for January, would be to implement the recommendations of the Prison Study Commission, the Governmental Efficiency Study Commission, and the Constitutional Revision Study Commission.[52] In addition, a special session would give the governor another opportunity to enact, before his fight for reelection, those parts of his program that did not make it through the 1967 General Assembly. There were several inherent advantages to a special session—the agenda was set by the governor and, while legislators could introduce their own bills, those bills had to be part of the governor's proclamation. Thus, attention was focused on Rockefeller's goals. The distraction of other matters was removed. The lack of sufficient remuneration to the legislators for special sessions worked to the advantage of the governor as it put pressure on the assembly to decide the issues being considered. Debate would be held to a minimum. On the other hand, the meager per diem could cause resentment among the legislators, making them less favorably disposed toward the governor's program. Another disadvantage was that a special session put the governor's prestige on the line. If the session proved to be fruitless, it was Rockefeller's reputation as an effective leader that would suffer the most. Despite these disadvantages, special sessions were not rare. Regular sessions were short and were held only once every two years, leaving relatively little time for lawmaking. At least one special session had been held between every regular session in the previous ten years.

Once the special session was a certainty, legislators began voicing their opinions on the session's scope and chance for success. Rockefeller held regional meetings with the legislators as a forum for these opinions.[53] Despite this, it appeared that the governor's relationship with the General Assembly was no better in the months preceding the special session than it had been when the regular session ended in March. There was little incentive for the legislators to react favorably to any items considered in an election-year special session. While Rockefeller would get the blame for failure, he would also get the credit for success. As the session neared, it became more apparent that Rockefeller would have to request tax increases to pay for the reform programs he proposed. This created even more resentment. Those legislators who did favor Rockefeller's programs felt that the money should be made available without his asking supporters to put their political careers in jeopardy by voting for a tax increase.[54]

In December Rockefeller's executive secretary, Marion Burton, sent a letter to the legislators outlining items under consideration for inclusion in the special session slated to begin on February 5. On January 9 Rockefeller sent a memo modifying the list, eliminating approximately eighty items that had been considered and rejected. The memo broke the topics down into three categories: those items that would definitely be included, those that were "probable," and those that were "still under consideration."[55] The legislative council was presented on January 22, by the state Administration Department's Budget and Accounting Division, with a three volume, two-hundred-plus page synopsis of the items to be considered.[56] All of this paperwork appears to have been aimed at eliminating those proposals with the least chance of success, thus producing as much cooperation as possible between governor and legislature. Because of the tremendous number of items under consideration, Rockefeller decided to call two separate special sessions. The February 5 session would deal only with nonfiscal matters and a second special session later in the year would tackle revenue problems. This decision, made several days before the session was to begin, incensed many legislators who claimed that Rockefeller was wasting state money because he was not prepared to deal with fiscal problems but called the early session anyway in order to "save face."[57] The *Gazette* editorialized that Rockefeller was correct in calling two sessions as "an orderly and sensible way of handling this year's special legislative agenda."[58]

There were too many items to be considered in one special session, a session that was not expected to last more than two weeks. But this illustrates a fundamental problem that plagued Rockefeller in his attempts to get his agenda passed by the legislature. Rockefeller's plans always appeared too ambitious. He never reconciled himself to the realities of an amateur and hostile legislature, and therefore failed to limit his call to what he considered to be the most important issues.

The executive proclamation calling the first extraordinary session of the Sixty-sixth General Assembly to convene consisted of eighty-three items for consideration. In his opening address to the legislature, Rockefeller spent a good deal of time pleading for nonpartisan consideration of his programs and defending the necessity of two sessions.

> The problems that confront us today . . . are not partisan problems; they are Arkansas problems. . . . They are problems to be dealt with honestly, courageously, and promptly. I feel that you will want to join me in doing just this. . . .
> . . . In 1965, the prior administration and the General Assembly, knowing of many urgent needs in our state, created new programs and expanded existing programs in anticipation of the tax bonanza. . . .
> . . . Programs were activated, and possibly too rapidly, without properly calculating the cost of future operations. . . .
> . . . In the past we've had no adequate independent means of evaluating such [financial] demands. Now we can [through the new Department of Administration], and so I'm asking that we postpone, for two or three months, legislation which might be needed to help solve our financial problems.[59]

He went on to emphasize those portions of the call that he felt were most significant: prison reform, tighter regulation of the insurance industry, a minimum wage law, and a proposal to remove the ten-year residency requirement for the director of the Arkansas State Police. The general mood of the legislature at the beginning of the special session was described as "surly" but nonetheless fearful of election-year charges of obstructionism.[60] Nowhere was this more evident than in the fight over the state police director residency requirement proposal or, as it was better known, the Davis bill. When Rockefeller was inaugurated, the director of the state police was Colonel Herman Lindsey. Lindsey retired on July 31, 1967. The Arkansas State Police Commission wanted the new director to be a current member of the department, Major Kenneth McKee. Over their objections, Rockefeller appointed Lynn Davis as director. Davis was an Arkansas native who had, since 1961, been living in California, where he was a special agent for the FBI. A 1945 Arkansas law stipulated that the director must have been a resident of Arkansas for at least ten years preceding his appointment. Rockefeller appointed Davis despite a written opinion by the state attorney general that Davis was ineligible under this law. Davis served as director from the end of July until December 18, 1967, when the state supreme court ruled him ineligible. During those four and a half months, Davis developed tremendous popularity statewide, largely because of his fight to end illegal gambling in Hot Springs.[61] Upon the court's ruling of ineligibility, Rockefeller announced that a bill lifting the residency requirement would be included in the special session.

Davis's popularity did not assure passage of the bill that would permit him to retain his job. Legislators in both the house and the senate opposed it. Though much of the opposition came from Hot Springs legislators, there was also some opposition that was purely partisan. Guy Jones of Conway prepared three amendments to the bill, any one of which would have made Davis ineligible. For example, one amendment stipulated that the director never have spent any time in jail. Davis spent a night in jail in December 1967 on a contempt charge for refusing to reveal the name of an informant in a gambling case. The contempt charge was removed two weeks later by the state supreme court, and Jones's amendments were not passed. But meanwhile another amendment was added to the bill in the house requiring that the director be a qualified voter. In 1968 this meant being an Arkansas resident for one year. Davis would not qualify until late July. This was the final form in which the bill passed, and Davis withdrew his name from consideration for the position rather than leave the state police in limbo for another four months. The legislature received widespread condemnation for acting out of partisan spite in the case of Lynn Davis.[62]

The inclusion of a minimum wage bill was a surprise to many in the state because of both its controversial nature and its defeat in the regular session. Bills with slim chances for passage were usually not considered during special sessions. In his opening address to the legislature, Rockefeller acknowledged this, but urged passage of the bill "because of my concern for the working man and woman." [63] It was quite a political gamble on the governor's part, but it paid off. The minimum wage bill passed both houses by overwhelming margins and was signed by Rockefeller on February 19. It established a minimum wage of $1.00 an hour in 1969, rising to $1.20 in 1971. It was, though, watered down so that only about one-fourth of the workers not already covered by the much higher federal minimum wage would be covered by the new law. This meant that the law applied to approximately twenty-five thousand workers. Agricultural workers were excluded completely.[64]

The fate of bills based on the recommendations of the three study commissions, a primary reason for holding the special session, was mixed. The Governmental Efficiency Study Commission report resulted in eleven items on the governor's call. One of these, the merging of the four juvenile training schools into one Juvenile Training School Department, was passed and signed into law. The merger was the first step toward integration of the four schools that at the time were segregated, two girls' schools and two boys' schools.[65] The remainder of the items were relatively minor, involving internal shuffling in several departments. Five of the nine became law.[66]

According to Rockefeller, the most important issue facing the special session was constitutional reform.[67] The Constitutional Revision Study Commission recommended two measures toward that goal. The first would permit the people of Arkansas to vote on whether or not they wanted a constitutional convention. The second would provide for the election of delegates to this proposed convention. Both measures would be voted on in the 1968 general election. While the need for constitutional reform was recognized, disagreement arose over the timetable for elections and the basis for apportionment of delegate positions. One major difference between the administration-sponsored bills and the others was that the former would hold a special election in 1969 for voting on a new constitution (provided the people voted to hold a convention) while the latter would have the vote on a new constitution incorporated into the 1970 general election. The other major difference was that the administration would base delegate positions on present house membership while other bills based them on the apportionment in effect in 1965. The 1965 apportionment had been ruled illegal by the state supreme court on the basis that it gave a disproportionate share of representation to rural areas. The administration forces carried the day on the delegate position issue, but in order to obtain a vote on a constitutional convention in this session, Rockefeller was forced to compromise and accept 1970 as the year for a vote on a new constitution. The governor vowed, however, to attempt to change this last point through legislation in the 1969 General Assembly.[68]

Prison reform, based on the recommendations of the Prison Study Commission, received the most publicity in this special session. Arkansas's prisons had been the subject of national media attention since late 1966. Rockefeller's reputation as a reformer tended to rise and fall in conjunction with events at the state prisons. Most legislators were aware that it was not just Rockefeller's reputation resting on the fate of prison reform legislation, but also that of the whole state. In drafting penitentiary bills for this session, the administration consulted with the legislative council in an attempt to head off disagreement.[69]

Rockefeller's prison reform package consisted of four major items. The first was the establishment of a Department of Corrections to oversee all activity at the prisons, and a separate Board of Pardons and Paroles. These two agencies would assume the duties of the Penitentiary Board. The second was to modify sentencing procedures. The third was to triple the "free world" staff, those personnel who were not convicts. The fourth involved the appropriation of funds produced by proposed prison industries to give a small incentive pay to inmates. Opposition in the assembly centered around two basic philosophical disagreements—whether prisons were meant to rehabilitate or to punish, and whether prisons should be self-supporting, even at the expense of reform, or use tax money to improve prison conditions and provide educational facilities.[70]

In obtaining passage of his prison reform package, Rockefeller was forced to compromise on several key points. First, he had to agree to include on the call for the next special session any proposals that were requested by either the legislative council or a joint resolution of both houses of the General Assembly, to amend the reforms. Another aspect that suffered concerned corporal punishment of prisoners. Rockefeller's original bill specifically prohibited corporal punishment, in response to charges of brutality at the prisons. All mention of this matter was deleted from the final version of the bill so that use of the strap could be maintained. Finally, the fourth point in the governor's original package, the establishment of a fund for prison industry income, was deleted entirely.[71] Despite these compromises, the prison reform measures that were passed were a big step in the beginning of the long struggle to bring Arkansas's prisons into the twentieth century. It would probably not have passed had it not been for the national public outrage directed at Arkansas's prisons in the months prior to the special session.[72]

In the first week of this special session, the *Gazette* editorialized: "Early indications have suggested that the tone of the Arkansas State Senate's current deliberations may measure up to the standards of the memorable regular session of a year ago."[73] But by the time the session adjourned on February 21, Rockefeller had achieved a substantial portion of his stated objectives—prison reform, the constitutional convention vote, and the minimum wage bill being the most important. Criticism of Rockefeller was still widespread in the legislature, this time charging that the session was not necessary and could have waited until May and that many bills were poorly drafted. Some of this criticism even came from George Nowotny, the house Republican leader.[74] In retrospect, however, Rockefeller appears to have been correct in holding two special sessions. The expected strong opposition to his revenue-raising measures would have provided an even tenser atmosphere in the legislature than normal, affecting the passage of his reform bills.

Rockefeller spoke before the legislative council on April 30, to outline his rationale for calling a second special session in 1968, scheduled for May. He explained that, if Arkansas was to provide the programs and services needed to move the state forward, "then it will be absolutely essential that we convince ourselves and our fellow citizens of the need to substantially increase our tax revenues." The additional revenues were needed in part because of an increase in state employees, over 75 percent of whom were in education, and also to meet prior commitments, particularly in prison reform, grants to welfare recipients, and the teachers' raises.[75]

The second special session convened on May 20, 1968. The governor's call included thirty-one items. Two of those were aimed at amending legislation passed in the first session. Rockefeller included an attempt to have any new constitution voted on in a special election, while the legislative council had an item included to permit changes in the prison reform acts. Rockefeller's proposed tax increases were spelled out in the call. They included a tax on the transfer of real property, increased taxes on cigarettes, a tax on other tobacco products and snuff, and a tightening of allowable state income tax deductions. There were several surprises in the call—a mixed drink bill was included, as were two controversial measures, a riot control bill and a bill reimbursing local school districts for their legal expenses in fighting desegregation lawsuits.[76]

The school desegregation lawsuit bill was strongly criticized by one group that had voted overwhelmingly for Rockefeller in 1966—Arkansas's blacks. The public outcry regarding this bill prompted Rockefeller to issue a statement explaining his actions. He defended the bill on the basis that allowing a local school board its day in court was the "best means of obtaining community cooperation." Rockefeller claimed that the bill was not an administration bill but was placed in the call at the request of "several small school districts."[77] According to Rockefeller's public relations director, John Ward, seemingly out of character actions such as the desegregation lawsuit bill were not an indication of growing conservatism in the governor's goals, but rather were a compromise with the more conservative elements in the Republican party in an attempt to strengthen the party and consequently Rockefeller's goal of a two-party system.[78] This lack of support for the measure by Rockefeller is substantiated by the fact that the bill was not mentioned in the governor's opening remarks to the legislature, and was listed in an internal memo as a nonadministration measure.[79] The bill died in the house by a vote of thirty-six to thirty-five.

The riot control bill, condemned by both the right and the left, was something that Rockefeller himself endorsed. It gave the governor the power to declare a state of emergency when necessary and during it impose curfews, prohibit the sale of alcoholic beverages, and prohibit the possession of deadly weapons. The bill was defeated by a wide margin on the basis that it would infringe on individuals' rights, particularly the right to bear arms.[80]

Rockefeller, the legislature, and the press all agreed that the mixed drink bill was the most controversial bill on the session's agenda.[81] This explains why Rockefeller changed his mind twice about whether or not to include it in the call. Rep. Ray Smith had attempted to have the bill included in the February special session. Smith asked for its inclusion on the basis that a mixed drink bill, and the accompanying liquor tax, was the best way for the state to raise additional revenues. As soon as news of this became public, reaction against the idea was fierce. Rockefeller's staff reported that public opinion dictated that the mixed drink bill not be placed on the call. And Rep. John E. Miller wrote the governor: "The proposed mixed drink bill should *NOT* be included in the forthcoming special session of the legislature. . . . The question is asked in the Bible: 'What shall it profit a man to gain the whole world and lose his own soul?'"[82] While the governor supported a mixed drink bill, he was reluctant to include it in the special session unless he had "firm and unequivocable assurances that a majority of the members of each house of the General Assembly would support and vote for the proposal."[83] He never received this, and finally, several days before the special session was to begin, Rockefeller announced that he would wait until the 1969 General Assembly to introduce the bill.[84]

Several things prompted the governor to change his mind and include the mixed drink bill in the second special session. One was a public opinion survey that concluded "there is a real possibility that most voters would okay a state tax-and-control bill with local option."[85] Another reason was a ruling by the state attorney general that the Alcohol Beverage Control Board regulation allowing private clubs to serve mixed drinks was illegal. The confusion surrounding private clubs was the extra impetus needed to convince Rockefeller to include the bill in the special session, and to label it administration sponsored.[86]

The second special session was, in John Ward's words, a "disaster."[87] The mixed drink bill, along with every other proposed tax increase, was defeated. Only sixteen bills became law before the May 30 adjournment, and these were primarily noncontroversial appropriations bills, six of which were initiated by the administration.[88] The primary reason for failure was politics. The timing of the session made this inevitable—the primaries were only a month away. Q. Byrum Hurst, president *pro tem* of the senate, summed up the feeling of some legislators and pleaded for more constructive attitudes in a television interview.

> This special session is more political than any we have ever had in the twenty years I have been there; but of course this is the first time there has been a real organized effort to get Republican candidates to run against all members of the legislature. . . .
> . . . we need to think a little less about the fact that he's Republican and we are Democrats and try to do something with the bills he has sent upstairs for us to work on.[89]

The warnings of men like Hurst and Sterling Cockrill went unheeded. Most legislators deeply resented Rockefeller's publicly expressed hope that the Republican party would field candidates for all available legislative seats. As one reporter later observed, "One does not court a political enemy by promising him an opponent."[90] Rockefeller further aggravated the situation by going public, attacking the partisanship of the legislature on television, and appealing to voters to go to their representatives and express displeasure with their actions.[91] Legislators did not disagree with the need for additional taxes, evidence that the major cause for the session's failure was partisanship. Those who opposed Rockefeller did so on the grounds that the tax increases could wait until the 1969 General Assembly when they could be combined with a more comprehensive program and when the legislators would no longer have the threat of imminent reelection campaigns hanging over their heads.[92]

Some of the blame for the session's failure must lie with Rockefeller. The timing of the session was terrible. While the call was better organized and streamlined in comparison to the call for the first special session, the mixed drink bill probably should have been left off. The traditional purpose of a special session had been to enact legislation that the governor felt could not wait for the next regular session. The other tax revenue proposals may have had a better chance without the mixed drink bill acting as a thorn in the legislators' sides. The mixed drink bill certainly did not lessen the adversarial relationship between the governor and the assembly. But it is the legislators who must shoulder the primary responsibility for their inaction. Not only did they destroy the governor's program, but, despite recognizing the need for additional revenues, they offered no alternatives. There may have been more than spite involved in this course of action. With an election approaching, they may have been trying to convince the state's voters that only a Democratic governor could work with the legislature.

The Rockefeller administration made great strides in the Sixty-sixth General Assembly toward social and governmental reform. The governor scored his greatest successes in the regular session and in the first special session. Education received considerable attention, resulting in free textbooks, teachers' raises, and a constitutional amendment to be voted on in the next election permitting kindergartens and adult education. Arkansas obtained its first minimum wage law. The legislature addressed severe problems in the state's prisons and passed reform legislation. The creation of a new administration department streamlined state government. And a bill was passed permitting a vote on whether or not to hold a constitutional convention.

But as Rockefeller's first term progressed, it became more difficult to get administration measures through the legislature. The second special session was a disaster. The novelty of having a New York–born millionaire in the governor's chair wore thin, and legislators grew increasingly resentful over the fact that Rockefeller's private resources would help provide many legislators with new Republican competition at the polls.

The Rockefellers, circa 1916. Left to right: Abby, Laurance, David, John D. Rockefeller, John D. Rockefeller, Jr., Winthrop, Abby Aldrich Rockefeller, John D. III, and Nelson.

The Rockefeller brothers, 1958. Left to right: David, Laurance, John D. III, Nelson, and Winthrop.

Aerial view of Winrock Farm, August 1960.

Ten Years in Arkansas appreciation dinner held in Winthrop's honor in Little Rock on August 7, 1963. Winthrop and Jeannette cut the cake at left while Gov. and Mrs. Nelson Rockefeller look on at right.

The beginning of the 1964 gubernatorial campaign, May 23, 1964, in Winthrop, Arkansas.

Campaigning in 1964.

Rockefeller's inauguration as governor, January 10, 1967. Front: Arkansas state Supreme Court Justice Carleton Harris and Rockefeller. Back: Speaker of the House Sterling Cockrill and Lt. Gov. Maurice "Footsie" Britt.

After the inauguration, January 10, 1967. Left to right: Sal Pappa, Blanchette Rockefeller, Anne Bartley Pappa, John D. Rockefeller III, Winthrop Rockefeller, Winthrop Paul Rockefeller, Sherry Bartley, Jeannette Rockefeller, and Bruce Bartley.

Singing "We Shall Overcome." The memorial service for Dr. Martin Luther King, Jr., on the steps of the state capitol, April 7, 1968.

Portrait taken during the 1970 campaign.

Winthrop Paul and Winthrop Rockefeller with Vice Pres. Spiro Agnew in 1972.

Winthrop Rockefeller at Petit Jean Mountain, undated.

FOUR

A Reform Agenda and the Fight for Reelection

As chief executive, the governor of any state must deal with more than just achieving passage of his legislative program. For Rockefeller, this meant developing a working relationship with state agencies, boards, and commissions and occasionally involved conflict between the governor and his Democratic subordinates. Rockefeller worked for reform of the Welfare Commission and Insurance Department, achieving moderate success. His crusade against members of the Game and Fish Commission proved more frustrating. The governor also dealt with human rights issues that governors all across the nation were forced to face during these years, particularly prison reform and civil rights. Finally, all of this had to be accomplished while facing an upcoming fight for reelection in 1968.

When Rockefeller became governor, state government had become stagnant after twelve years without a change in administration. In addition, regulatory agencies and commissions were frequently controlled by the industries they were supposedly watching. The new governor found that the quickest way to clean up some state agencies was to put his own people in charge of them. But this was not always done without opposition.

Rockefeller met success with the state Insurance Department, in part because reform had widespread bipartisan support. Throughout 1966, the legislature had been asking Faubus and the Insurance Department to rid the state of unscrupulous insurance companies. According to one observer, lax regulation "had enabled a number of gubernatorial cronies to become millionaires during the latter years of Faubus' tenure."[1] Legislative disapproval intensified in June, when the department approved rate hikes for automobile liability insurance averaging 25 percent, on top of a 17.5 percent hike approved the previous year. Public outrage caused the rescinding of the increase in July, but nothing more was done before Rockefeller took office.[2]

On February 1, 1967, he appointed John Norman Harkey, an attorney, as insurance commissioner. At the time, there were over a thousand insurance companies authorized to do business in Arkansas. By comparison, New York, with thirty times the population, had approximately five hundred licensed companies. Harkey stayed in office until February 1, 1968, when he resigned to return to his law practice. In his letter of resignation, he reported that "the cancerous situations which existed . . . have been largely torn out. . . . I have set up the necessary machinery to complete the work with respect to refinement of regulation in the insurance industry."[3] Thirty-nine companies were no longer selling insurance in Arkansas, and legislation sponsored by the department had been passed, tightening regulation of the remaining companies. Harkey was succeeded by his assistant commissioner, Allan Horne. Horne continued to tighten up the insurance industry, prohibiting mail-order solicitation by companies not licensed in the state.[4]

Political pressure proved to be a source of trouble in the Welfare Department. When he first took office, Rockefeller asked the present welfare commissioner, A. J. Moss, to continue in his job. But in April 1967 the governor appointed Len Blaylock welfare commissioner, apparently due to allegations of Moss's heavy drinking. From the moment Blaylock took over, the Faubus-appointed Welfare Board grew insistent that it have a direct role in personnel matters in an obvious effort to maintain Democratic control over county welfare jobs. Blaylock refused to give up his authority. Both he and his predecessor dismissed several employees for engaging in political activities.[5]

Rockefeller's attempts to control the Game and Fish Commission were much less successful. Amendment 35 to the state constitution, approved by the voters in November 1944, created a Game and Fish Commission independent of the governor's office, in order to remove "politics" from the commission. While the governor appointed seven commissioners to serve staggered seven-year terms, the commissioners could not be removed during their terms except for "the same causes as apply to other constitutional officers, after a hearing that may be reviewed by the First District Chancery Court with the right of appeal to the state Supreme Court."[6] Trouble between Rockefeller and the commission began on April 7, 1967. On that date Bob Scott, from the governor's office, and Joe Gaspard, a Republican party official, were denied access to commission records by Hugh Hackler, executive director of the Game and Fish Commission. Hackler was a paid employee, not one of the commissioners. This was a violation of the Freedom of Information Act passed earlier that year. Rockefeller wrote Stanley McNulty, chairman of the commission, to protest. The governor reminded McNulty that he had tried unsuccessfully to convince the legislature to audit the commission. "I request that I be advised immediately as to the attitude of the Board with respect to this incident and as to what action, if any, your Board intends to take." McNulty's response, which was very defensive, did not address the governor's inquiry but stated, "We do not desire to be harassed, but have instructed Mr. Hackler to make available to your office any matters of public record over which we have jurisdiction."[7]

Rockefeller had been "hearing reports for months about wrongdoing in the Game and Fish Commission."[8] This was why Scott and Gaspard had gone to view commission records. On May 26 Rockefeller took action, asking all seven appointed members of the commission to resign, concluding that "the public interest can best be served, and public confidence regained" by the resignations. Rockefeller warned that if the members did not resign, "it will be necessary for me to consider other alternatives which may be available to me as Governor."[9] On May 31 the commission voted unanimously not to resign, explaining, "Under Amendment 35, we have an obligation to the sportsmen of Arkansas to serve out our legally appointed time." The commission members alleged that the move was political, that the Republican party was trying to obtain half of the jobs in the commission.[10]

Legal complications held up any further action until September, when Rockefeller named the three-member hearing board, all Democrats and past presidents of the Arkansas Bar Association. H. W. McMillan was appointed evidence officer.[11] In October five commissioners filed a lawsuit challenging the legality of the hearing. The Arkansas Supreme Court ruled in July 1968 that the governor had the authority to hold the hearing. It was then that Rockefeller made public what charges would be leveled. At this time, charges were filed against only one commissioner—Raymond Farris. The charges centered around Farris's alleged use of state equipment and employees for his own business. Two other commissioners, Newt Hailey and Ernest Hogue, were charged in August. On October 8 a new injunction was issued to prevent the hearings, scheduled to begin the next day, from taking place. The legal question this time was whether or not Rockefeller could delegate responsibility for conducting the hearing. This held things up until July 1969, well into the governor's second term in office. In the end only one commissioner, Raymond Farris, was actually removed from office.[12]

It was impossible to remove politics from Rockefeller's relationship with state agencies, boards, and commissions. Since he was the first Republican Arkansas governor in the twentieth century, the party was anxious to place as many Republicans in state positions as possible. This was what was supposed to happen as far as they were concerned. As John Ward related: "There was a strong patronage group that simply said, 'Fire every state employee, fill every job with a Republican or supporter.' They'll still argue that one of his greatest mistakes was that he didn't do so."[13] Rockefeller told Ward in a 1972 interview that his first objective was to fill state jobs with "competent" persons.[14] But there were not many Republicans in Arkansas, and once the incompetent or ideologically unacceptable ones were weeded out, that left an even smaller number. In addition, Rockefeller had to face the reality of a Democratic legislature. He could not afford to go out of his way to alienate it. Finally, the governor had not been elected exclusively by Republicans, and there were Democrats who also deserved rewards for their support.

The difficulties surrounding Rockefeller's decisions concerning appointments became readily apparent in August 1967, when he attempted to appoint a Republican, Roy Orr, to the Real Estate Commission. Orr was unpopular with several members of the commission and the Arkansas Real Estate Association, a voluntary professional organization, which had publicly supported Jim Johnson in the 1966 campaign. This problem was compounded by the association's contention that the governor was required, by law, to appoint commission members only if they had been recommended by the association. Their contention was based on the ambiguous 1929 statute creating the commission, and reinforced by Faubus, who had accepted all of the association's recommendations in his twelve years in office. In essence, Faubus had abdicated his appointment power to the association. Eventually, Rockefeller succumbed and appointed the person nominated by the association. Another opening occurred in 1968, and again Rockefeller wanted Roy Orr. This time the governor ignored the Real Estate Association and appointed Orr. The man Orr was to replace, B. B. McCarley, then sued, claiming Orr's appointment was invalid. The state supreme court finally ruled, in September 1969, that Orr's appointment was valid and that recommendation by the association was not a prerequisite for appointment. This decision made it possible for Orr to serve his term and for the governor to make another appointment in 1970 of Bert Sigsby, who also was not approved by the association.[15]

Attracting the best men to state government, whether Republican or Democrat, was difficult for another reason—the salaries of state employees in Arkansas were among the lowest in the nation. As governor, Rockefeller continued a practice he had begun as head of the AIDC, supplementing official salaries with increments from his own funds. He announced publicly in April 1967 that he planned to supplement the salary of the director of the new Department of Administration. In the bill creating the department, the legislature had fixed the salary at eighteen thousand dollars, although Rockefeller's original bill called for a twenty-six-thousand-dollar salary. Joe Purcell, the state attorney general, issued an opinion that the supplements were illegal because only the General Assembly could set state employee salaries. Despite this, Rockefeller announced in May that he planned to supplement "some" salaries. He pointed out that many state employees received income from other sources without criticism, including members of the attorney general's staff who were permitted to have outside law practices. In a December 1968 letter to the chairman of the legislative council, Marion Burton defended the practice, pointing out that there were many opportunities for state employees to take advantage of "questionable fringe benefits." He continued: "I feel very strongly that both private employers and public employers get no more than what they pay for. Inadequate salaries and substandard compensation only breeds dishonesty and corruption. . . ."[16]

The idea of using money from outside sources to run the state was not new, though using it specifically to raise salaries appears to have been. The Arkansas legislature had a tradition of stinginess when it came to paying for necessary services. In Neal Peirce's *The Deep South States of America*, W. R. "Witt" Stephens, head of the Arkansas-Louisiana Gas Company (Arkla), explained where Faubus got the money to run the state.

> The governor's office pays $10,000, so what happens when a man without a quarter comes in? It must have cost Winthrop Rockefeller a quarter to a half million a year to be governor. How in hell can one of our Democratic boys be governor when it costs that much? . . . Faubus got his support from people like me and a lot of other people who would chip in and pay the expense.[17]

Stephens's admission helps illustrate the negative side of running the government with private funds—corruption. In the 1950s, while Faubus was governor, the Public Service Commission approved three yearly rate increases for Arkla, totaling $3.2 million.[18] They may have been legitimate rate increases, but the conflict of interest that existed certainly calls them into question. No one doubted that Rockefeller's motives were altruistic and meant to serve the public interest. However, as much of the press pointed out, it was a bad precedent to set. Salary supplementation by less honorable people could easily lead to divided loyalties.[19]

The condition of Arkansas's prisons—and Rockefeller's efforts toward prison reform—was the most widely publicized crisis of his four years in office. The state's prisons were in the 1960s what Central High was in the 1950s: the magnet attracting public attention to Arkansas. And once more that attention proved an enormous embarrassment to the state.

The Arkansas State Penitentiary consisted of two prison farms, Tucker and Cummins. In August 1966 then-Governor Orval Faubus ordered the Criminal Investigation Division (CID) of the Arkansas State Police to investigate conditions at Tucker, the smaller of the two. Faubus did not release the sixty-seven-page report to the press before leaving office. On January 14 Rockefeller, who had received the report ten days before his inauguration, told reporters that when he released the report's findings and his prison reform recommendations, the facts would "shock you beyond anything you can imagine."[20] The following day, one of Faubus's investigators, Eugene Hale, released his own account of prison conditions that was essentially a condensation of the CID report. Hale did so in order to "minimize whatever political gain he thought Governor Rockefeller might seek when the official report was released."[21] No longer having any reason to delay, Rockefeller released the report on January 16.

The CID report lived up to all the advance publicity. It included interviews with inmates and staff, as well as observations of the investigators. The investigators described the bug-infested kitchen, the inmates' ragged clothes, and the filth of the barracks. In the kitchen, "flies were very thick and there was no screen on the door. . . . The food and meat were piled on the cook tables completely exposed to the flies." The meal being prepared consisted of "one large spoonful" of "very thin, watered down" rice and one slice of "tasteless cornbread." Kitchen personnel told the investigator that meat was served once a month, eggs once a year, and milk never. The inmates themselves "appeared to be forty to sixty pounds under their normal weight." Their clothes were "filthy, torn up, and in bad states of repair." In the barracks the investigator found mattresses that were "filthy and rotten and appeared to be badly discolored. The cotton was spilling out of the majority of the mattresses." He also noted: "The urinals were stopped up and in general disrepair. The entire barracks smelled from filth."[22]

The most shocking part of the report was the descriptions of various torture devices found on the premises, such as brass knuckles and rubber hoses and whips, and the explanations by the inmates of how the inhuman tools were used. One particularly vicious instrument was the "Tucker Telephone," which

> consisted of an electric generator taken from a ring type telephone, placed in sequence with two dry cell batteries, and attached to an undressed inmate strapped to the treatment table at the Tucker hospital, by means of one electrode to a big toe and the second electrode to the penis, at which time, a crank was turned sending an electric charge into the body of the inmate.[23]

The CID report detailed what criminologists already knew—the Arkansas prison system was, as one expert wrote, "unquestionably the worst in the country."[24] Unfortunately for those interested in reform, not everyone in Arkansas was upset by the revelations. John Ward wrote that "an alarming number of Arkansans" felt that "criminals should be confined and forgotten, that whatever happened to them, no matter how brutal, was what they deserved."[25] The state Penitentiary Board had refused to accept the CID report. One state representative, a former chairman of the Penitentiary Board, called "95 percent of the complaints . . . [in the report] lies."[26] Given this atmosphere, reform would have to proceed slowly. A Penitentiary Study Commission was established by the legislature at Rockefeller's request. The legislature also appointed a joint house-senate committee to make its own investigation into prison conditions.[27]

Rockefeller's best chance for instituting prison reform appeared to be in appointing his own people to key positions in the prison system. The first opening on the state's five-member Penitentiary Board came in January 1967. Rockefeller named John Haley, a Little Rock attorney, to the position. The governor also had the authority to appoint superintendents for the prisons. Between August 1966 and February 1967, Tucker prison farm was run by three different superintendents, all Faubus appointees. In between superintendents, the state police were called in to take over security. In February Rockefeller named his own man to head Tucker. The new assistant superintendent of the Arkansas State Penitentiary was a criminology professor from Southern Illinois University, Thomas O. Murton.[28]

In retrospect, Tom Murton was Winthrop Rockefeller's most famous, and most controversial, appointee. Murton's account of his year in Arkansas, *Accomplices to the Crime*, was a best seller. The movie *Brubaker*, with Robert Redford in the title role, was loosely based on the book. It is probably too early to evaluate all the charges, countercharges, and refutations surrounding his administration, but what is certain is that during Murton's tenure strides were made toward reform. They were not enough, however, to end the problems in Arkansas's prisons.

Murton was hired to run Tucker. The man in charge of Cummins, and the titular head of the penitentiary system, was O. E. Bishop, a Faubus appointee. Murton and Bishop clashed, both personally and philosophically, from the first Penitentiary Board meeting after Murton's appointment in April 1967. The meeting turned into a contest between the old and the new, with Haley, Murton, and Bob Scott, Rockefeller's advisor on prison affairs, on one side, and Bishop and the remainder of the board on the other.[29] In June Murton prepared a status report on Tucker and sent it to the Penitentiary Board. The last five pages of the report listed what Murton called "obstacles which have been placed in our path to prevent any success." All of the obstacles were attributed to Bishop and his staff at Cummins. These obstacles included refusal of access to necessary records kept at Cummins, discrepancies between goods delivered to Tucker from Cummins and records of those goods, and a deliberate refusal to supply additional inmates and requisitions necessary to run the farm. Murton concluded, "This institution will never progress under continued harrassment and interference by Cummins officials."[30] Bishop responded to Murton's charges at the July Penitentiary Board meeting, denying any harassment and claiming it was Murton who was the harasser. He asserted that "any failure at Tucker belongs to Mr. Murton and cannot be passed on to me, the penitentiary board or anyone else."[31]

In August Bishop and Murton issued requested reports to Rockefeller and the board on the status of their respective institutions. In releasing the reports to the press, the governor showed his preference for Murton's ideas.

> The recommendations made by these two men differ greatly, but each deserves careful study and review by the citizens of Arkansas.
>
> I must state, very frankly, that I am greatly impressed with the recommendations of Mr. Murton, looking toward complete reform of our state correctional program.[32]

Bishop's 6-page report endorsed the trusty system, the use of convicts in various prison jobs, although he did condemn the current practice of arming trusties. Bishop also defended corporal punishment and recommended the continued maintenance of both prison farms. Murton's 103-page report harshly condemned both the extensive trusty system and corporal punishment, a practice that he had already stopped at Tucker. At this time neither prison farm had an education or vocational training program of any kind. While both Bishop and Murton endorsed the idea of vocational training, Murton suggested that such programs, along with the establishment of prison industries, might eventually replace the farms. Furthermore, Murton had often condemned the practice of training men to pick cotton when, outside of the prison, all cotton was picked by machine.[33]

Murton's recommendations for prison reform were extensive and enlightened. But the tone of his report highlighted the reason he was in Arkansas only one year—his abrasive personality. He leveled public criticisms at anyone he felt deserved it, with no consideration for the backlash from public opinion. For example, in listing the reasons penal reform had not yet come to Arkansas, Murton included a "reluctance of officials to forego profiteering, and magical thinking" relegating convicts to "the category of a sub-human species."[34] While the charges may have been true, including them in a formal report could not but alienate many public officials whose support he might need for success.

John Ward quotes Rockefeller: "Murton's ego equals only his ability as a penologist." And Ward himself wrote,

> Murton's continuing stream of highly quotable criticism was not all well aimed; and his almost psychopathic disregard for channels of authority and the need to get along with those with whom he must work soon had Murton and the administration in hot water with nearly everyone but members of the press, who loved the whole thing.[35]

Murton's zeal and single-minded passion inspired loyalty and admiration among his subordinates, most inmates, and the out-of-state public. But in dealing with other state agencies, Bishop, and the Penitentiary Board, he could appear less reasonable. In a letter to G. Thomas Eisele, Murton complained that promised funds for construction were being held up: "I do not understand the problem. All I know is a need exists and I could care less how it is resolved as long as the obstacles are removed from my path. This job is difficult enough without being ambushed."[36] The following day Murton wrote Sidney Kegeles, the director of the state Purchasing Department, that there appeared to be a "breakdown somewhere in your agency," holding up funds meant for Tucker. He went on to list four pages of specific examples. Murton criticized the Purchasing Department for second-guessing his requests and concluded, "I would not presume to suggest to you how your office should be operated and ask that you extend the same courtesy to me."[37]

Murton's frequent outbursts prompted Bob Scott to write him in August 1967, referring to a letter Murton sent the governor. "I detect a note of sarcasm in the last paragraph of your letter to the Governor which to me is uncalled for. . . . I have, however, several times tried to express my concern over your apparent overly defensiveness of criticism of you and the operation of the Tucker Unit."[38]

In *Accomplices to the Crime*, Murton did not deny difficulties in dealing with his superiors. Regarding the board, Murton wrote: "They may have had a point about my personality. . . . It took abrasion to rub through their shell of ignorance. . . . There is no way to tiptoe through the quicksand of social and bureaucratic inertia."[39] He justified his attitude by stating, "True reform is an intolerable irritant to the Establishment."[40]

While Murton was cleaning up Tucker and alienating state officials, O. E. Bishop was running into problems at Cummins. In October 1967 the penitentiary system's new medical director, Dr. Edwin Barron, reported to the board on his discovery of drug peddling and filthy conditions at Cummins. That same month, the board ordered a "shakedown" of the trusty barracks at Cummins, amid reports of smuggled-in weapons. The shakedown was canceled at the urging of state police director Lynn Davis. The trusties had weapons anyway, and Davis warned that a search would only provoke unrest. Murton added to Bishop's problems when, in a speech to the Hot Springs YWCA, he stated that Bishop's reforms at Cummins had been "more superficial than real" and that "the prisoners still run the place."[41] Finally, on November 1, Bishop submitted his resignation effective December 31. The reason given was that "many circumstances and a number of people have rendered it impossible for me to do my job in the manner in which I think it should be done."[42]

Upon Bishop's resignation, Rockefeller and the Penitentiary Board reached a standoff on his successor. Rockefeller wanted Murton named superintendent and put in charge of both farms. The board had to either agree with the governor's choice or name its own appointee, which the governor then had to approve. Neither side would give in. The board's four Faubus appointees resigned in protest, giving Rockefeller complete control of the board. On January 15, 1968, the new board, including the first black ever appointed, unanimously named Murton superintendent.[43]

Murton's promotion was the beginning of the end of his career in Arkansas. Shortly after assuming his duties at Cummins, Murton disclosed to Walter Rugaber of the *New York Times* that he believed inmates had been murdered and buried on the prison's grounds and then written off the records as escapees. Rugaber's January 28 article brought the press flocking to Cummins, and there were television crews present when Murton began digging in a spot pointed out by prisoners as the graveyard. The following day, three coffins were found. After the discovery, Murton notified Rockefeller's office, and the state police were called in to investigate. Newspapers all over the country picked up the story.[44]

The actual identities of the three skeletons were never determined. Murton never wavered from his claim that they were the bodies of three murdered prisoners, basing his belief on allegations of several long-time prisoners at Cummins.[45] The state police investigation reported that prison records were inadequate to identify the skeletons but noted that the area where the bodies were found was an old prison cemetery used until the 1940s. The cemetery, known as Bodiesburg, "was a matter of common knowledge to inmates, prison officials and local citizens." The report also stated that "evidence points to prior existence of a 'Free World' cemetery in same general area."[46] The medical examiner determined that none of the three bodies showed evidence of a violent death. The official conclusion, based on the length of interment of the skeletons, was that two of the bodies were paupers and the third an unclaimed prisoner.[47] In 1972 the ages of the skeletons and the length of their interment were determined by Dr. Clyde Snow, an Oklahoma physical anthropologist. The skeletons had been given to Snow a year earlier by Arkansas's state medical examiner. Snow concluded that the skeletons were prison inmates buried fifty to seventy years earlier in what was probably a formal cemetery. He found no conclusive evidence of violent death. This finding refuted both the state police report and Murton's accusations.[48]

Rockefeller called the 1968 state police report a "mishmash of information." It primarily consisted of the investigators' transcripts of interviews with prisoners who alleged witnessing the murders of other prisoners. In an internal memo, John Ward called the report "unspoken hearsay" containing "major discrepancies and inconsistencies . . . indicating that much of the material, if not all of it, has little value."[49] The report made no recommendations. Rockefeller pursued the matter by sending a copy to U.S. Attorney General Ramsey Clark. Clark informed Rockefeller that federal statutes applying to the allegations in the report were governed by a five-year statute of limitations. Only one of the deaths had allegedly taken place in the previous five years, and the information concerning it was turned over to the FBI. However, Clark added:

> Under Arkansas law, prosecution for these offenses, being capital crimes, would not be barred by a statute of limitations. I understand, however, that the local prosecuting attorney, Mr. Joe Holmes, has announced he does not intend to follow up the report of the prison investigation. If further State action is contemplated, and our assistance is desired, please let me know and I will be glad to arrange to have members of my staff confer with the appropriate Arkansas officials.[50]

No action was taken within the state to further investigate the allegations of murder. The prisons came under the jurisdiction of the Lincoln County prosecuting attorney, Joe Holmes, who, as Clark stated in his letter, declined to conduct any follow-up on the state police report.[51]

Murton's opinion of the state police report was that

> The public statements made by Major Streubing [of the state police] and Dr. Carlton [of the medical examiner's office], the quality of the investigators assigned, the method of conducting the investigation, and the final preparation on Colonel Scott's report, lead ultimately and inevitably to only one conclusion: the investigation was a deliberate fraud, perpetrated upon the people of Arkansas and the inmates of the Arkansas State Penitentiary in order to suppress the truth about atrocities within the prison.[52]

While Murton's conclusion seems extreme, it is apparent that there existed in Arkansas an obsession with avoiding uncovering past crimes within the prison system. For example, while the Penitentiary Study Commission recommended, in

November 1967, that an annual audit of the prison system be conducted, it declined to request an audit for 1966, despite reports of misuse of prison goods in the August 1966 CID report.[53] Part of the problem was politics. Any investigation of past abuses would mean that a Republican administration would be exposing possible sins of the Democrats. The Democrats were adamant in their opposition to this, and Rockefeller could not afford to further antagonize the Democratic legislature. A second problem was public opinion. Arkansans as a group seemed extremely sensitive to criticism of the prisons while remaining unwilling to correct the system's abuses. The fact that most prisoners were black only served to increase public apathy concerning their treatment. According to John Ward, after Rockefeller was elected he was warned by some close friends to avoid prison reform because the people of Arkansas "didn't want to hear about brutality" in the prisons.[54] For example, a grand jury in Lincoln County was empaneled to investigate whether the law was violated when Murton dug up three bodies without a court order. The grand jury's findings indicated tremendous hostility to both Murton and prison reform. Their report called the digging "a publicity stunt" and declared that Murton "has displayed a more sincere desire for publicity for personal gain than for operating the Arkansas State Penitentiary for the protection of her citizens from the criminal element." It went on to recommend that use of the strap for discipline be reintroduced.[55]

The atmosphere of Arkansas's prison system certainly makes the murder of inmates a plausible idea, regardless of whether or not the three bodies found were those of murder victims. But Murton had been digging for bodies at Tucker for a year, and with no results. This, plus the negative publicity and lack of overwhelming evidence, militated against further inquiry. On February 8 Rockefeller ordered the digging stopped until its legality was determined. The state attorney general ruled that a court order would be needed for further excavations, and no more digging was done.[56]

Murton, meanwhile, had dug his own grave. Simultaneous with the grave-digging uproar, the state legislature passed the bill creating a Department of Corrections. Murton wanted the job of commissioner, but the publicity surrounding the grave digging, and the fact that the press seemed to know what Murton was doing before the governor did, angered Rockefeller. At a press conference, the governor stated that "as to the department of corrections, I am not sure Murton would be the man I would like to see in that particular job." As justification, Rockefeller cited Murton's penchant for informing the press before informing the administration and his unwillingness to "work with other people outside the penitentiary administration."[57] Murton alleged that, when he was first hired in February 1967, he was promised the commissioner position. In a rather sarcastic letter to Rockefeller, sent on February 28, Murton claimed that "as one of the terms and conditions of my employment . . . Tom Eisele, John Haley and yourself agreed to appoint me as Commissioner of Corrections at such time as the department would be created."[58] According to Rockefeller and his staff, no such deal was ever made. In response to Murton's letter, Eisele wrote Rockefeller a lengthy memo, outlining his recollection of the commitments made to Murton, as well as Murton's shortcomings as superintendent.

> In the attached letter, Murton refers to a "commitment" by us as part of the "terms and conditions" of his employment. The suggestion that there was any formal contractual negotiations is about as far from the truth as one can imagine. . . .
> . . . He has not demonstrated the capacity to deal with his own board, other agencies. . . he has not shown the interest or capacity to deal with the fiscal problems or the legal red tape to warrant his appointment to this most sensitive position.[59]

On March 1 the Penitentiary Board became the new Board of Corrections. With this change, the power to hire and fire the commissioner and prison superintendents transferred from the governor to the board. On March 4 Rockefeller sent a letter to Murton and the board stating that he had made no commitment to Murton regarding the commissioner position. The governor went further by telling the board, "not only are you under no commitment to appoint Mr. Murton to this position, but you are under no commitment to retain him in any position whatsoever in the Arkansas prison system."[60] The Board of Corrections fired Murton on March 7, replacing him as superintendent with Victor Urban, the director of pardons and paroles, who had originally been hired by Murton. The board produced a list of complaints to justify its action, all of which centered around Murton's insubordination and unwillingness to work within the system.[61] No one in the administration at any time questioned Murton's ability as a penologist. During his year in Arkansas, Murton had made tremendous strides in improving the living and dietary conditions of the prisoners and in seeing that all prisoners were treated fairly. But his ego and overwhelming sense of righteousness made him ineffective in achieving further reform.

Upon his hiring, Urban told the press, "We will carry on the reforms in the old Murton tradition."[62] But in *Accomplices to the Crime*, Murton claimed: "Rockefeller lacked the courage to be great. And, as a result, the prison system reverted, in essence, to the low established during the Faubus era."[63] An incident in the fall of 1968 at least partially confirmed his allegation. In October approximately eighty prisoners presented a list of complaints and staged a demonstration, refusing to work until the complaints had been addressed. Under the order of the associate superintendent for security, guards fired birdshot into the penned-up prisoners, wounding twenty-four. Urban called the shooting "reasonable," while John Haley, who was now chairman of the Board of Corrections, said that some of the complaints had "considerable merit" and that firearms were supposed to be used only to prevent property damage or injury.[64] Corporal punishment had supposedly been abolished by the board in February. On the other hand, the incident wound up in the courts in 1969, something that probably would not have happened before Rockefeller's tenure.

In fact, in December 1968 the Eighth Circuit Court of the U.S. Court of Appeals ordered Arkansas to abolish use of the strap. The court determined it a violation of the Eighth Amendment's protection against cruel and unusual punishment. As noted, the Penitentiary Board had abolished use of the strap in February. However, until this ruling, it was still legal and could have been reinstated. In the 1960s the only other state still whipping prisoners was Mississippi.[65]

A commissioner of corrections was not named until after Rockefeller's reelection, when, on November 8, the Board of Corrections named Charles Robert Sarver Arkansas's first commissioner. Sarver was a Charleston, West Virginia, lawyer, and an outspoken advocate of rehabilitation in the prisons. Sarver thus became the chief administrative officer of the prison system, furthering Rockefeller's own commitment to prison reform.[66]

Throughout 1967 and 1968, while the Arkansas prison system was making headlines, studies of the prisons continued. The first report made after the release of the 1966 CID report was the February 1967 report of the joint legislative committee formed in the previous month. The committee dealt with present rather than past problems, and suggested three major improvements: first, that more paid personnel be hired; second, that control over hiring and firing be transferred from the governor to the Penitentiary Board; and third, that the prisons no longer be required to pay their own way. All three suggestions became part of the administration's February 1968 prison legislation package. The major portion of Rockefeller's prison bills was based on the findings of the Penitentiary Study Commission, which had submitted its two-volume report on January 1, 1968. They included the establishment of a Department of Corrections, which would also encompass the then-separate Board of Pardons and Paroles, the establishment of an integrated youthful offenders facility at Tucker, the instituting of educational and vocational training programs, the construction of a maximum security facility, an increase in the number and quality of civilian employees and the elimination of armed trusty guards. The commission also recommended that corporal punishment be replaced at Cummins with methods approved by the American Correctional Association, such as solitary confinement and the loss of "good time."[67]

Next to prison reform, it was probably civil rights that brought Rockefeller the most national attention during his first term as governor. His philosophy was one that he had learned as a child, believing, basically, in giving blacks the education and opportunity to succeed and then letting them triumph or fail based on their own merit. No special favors—just rectify the inequalities. This was a very moderate approach, and, as the civil rights movement grew more militant in the late 1960s, Rockefeller looked more and more conservative to many blacks. But for his first term, at least, the governor was able to work with the black community.

Rockefeller's primary achievement was in giving blacks a voice in government by hiring or appointing them whenever possible. A September 1967 progress report by the Republican party reported that in the first eight months of his governorship, Rockefeller had appointed 10 blacks to boards and commissions and 23 to various advisory councils and employed 123 in state jobs outside of custodial and menial labor.[68] By far, the greatest advances could be seen on Arkansas's draft boards. When Rockefeller was inaugurated, no black had ever served on a local draft board in the state. Though the Selective Service was a federal agency, the state director was appointed by the governor. Rockefeller appointed Colonel Willard A. Hawkins in January 1967. By the end of that year, thirty-five blacks were appointed, two of whom were on the state appeal boards. Eighty percent of Arkansas's black population were under the influence of integrated boards, and there were more blacks on draft boards in Arkansas than any other Selective Service division in the nation.[69] This dedication to increasing minority representation on the local draft boards continued throughout Rockefeller's two terms in office, in spite of pressure from other groups, particularly the Republican party, to obtain draft board appointments as political rewards.[70]

Other attempts by Rockefeller to improve race relations were less successful. In June 1967 he issued an executive order forming the Governor's Human Resources Council. The purpose of the council was to strive for better opportunities for blacks and improved relations between the races. But, as John Ward concluded, "the organization, for all its high purposes, never did much."[71] Approximately half of the council's forty-eight members were black, including its director as of June 1968, Ozell Sutton. Its achievement seems to have been the encouragement it offered to the community to improve race relations in various areas.[72]

Dr. Martin Luther King, Jr., was assassinated in Memphis, Tennessee, on April 4, 1968. Riots flared up in 110 cities across the United States, including a minor one in Pine Bluff. Violence was avoided in Little Rock, thanks in large part to Rockefeller's actions. When the city police informed the governor that black leaders had requested a marching permit, he, at his wife's suggestion, proposed a prayer service on the steps of the state capitol instead. On Sunday, April 7, approximately three thousand people, two-thirds of whom were black, gathered to hear the governor and the state's black leaders eulogize King. Rockefeller was the only Southern governor to publicly do so. The governor stood hand-in-hand with black leaders and sang "We Shall Overcome." He cautioned the crowd: "Let us not forget the importance of equal education. . . . Let us not forget the importance of elimination of the ghettos. Let us not forget that we are all creatures of God."[73] As expected by Rockefeller's aides, the political repercussions were not all favorable. One disgruntled Republican county committeeman wrote, "your actions in regard to that criminal [King] who got just what he deserved . . . is [sic] the last straw and we are withdrawing our support of you and the state party."[74]

King's murder appears to have been the turning point in relations between Rockefeller and the black community. Black leaders were no longer willing to wait for the results of Rockefeller's more moderate approach. They demanded more jobs, in proportion to the percentage of blacks in the population, in state agencies, public utilities, and new industries brought to the state by the AIDC.[75] Rockefeller, on the other hand, still believed that training and communication would bring equality, and that jobs could not be filled by blacks until they had training equal to that of white job seekers. But William L. "Sonny" Walker of the Economic Opportunity Agency warned that poverty-stricken young blacks were getting restless and wanted action, not more studies. There were plenty of facts to substantiate claims by black leaders that not enough was being done. In 1968, while blacks made up 21.9 percent of Arkansas's population, only 3 percent of state agency jobs were held by blacks. And Arkansas's entire congressional delegation voted against the 1968 Civil Rights Act, passed a week after King's death.[76]

Urban riots had been erupting throughout the United States for several years—Watts in 1965, New York and Chicago in 1966, Newark and Detroit in 1967. They grew out of frustration and despair, and occurred in black neighborhoods and ghettos. In August 1968 violence broke out in Little Rock following the death of an eighteen-year-old black youth at the county prison farm. Rockefeller called out the National Guard and imposed a curfew. The city quieted down after several days, but racial disturbances would become more frequent during Rockefeller's second term.[77]

There were other matters that, as governor, Rockefeller had to address. He did so with varying degrees of success. One of his biggest triumphs was the state police crackdown on illegal gambling. The only legal gambling in Arkansas took place at the horse track in Hot Springs and at the greyhound track in West Memphis. Illegal gambling—slot machines, blackjack, and the like—had flourished in Hot Springs and to a lesser extent in Little Rock for decades, on the thin legal basis that private clubs enjoyed the same privileges as a private residence. In 1965 the Arkansas house of representatives passed a resolution calling on local officials to enforce gambling laws, and, according to then-Governor Faubus, "illegal gambling in Hot Springs ceased completely."[78] But Faubus obviously did not consider the gambling clubs illegal. Once in office, Rockefeller tried to convince local officials to enforce the law in private clubs. When the county sheriffs refused to act, Rockefeller sent in the state police. Between February and October 1967, raids resulted in the confiscation of nearly five hundred slot machines. While raids were periodically necessary after October 1967, the state police raids effectively ended open illegal gambling.[79]

When Rockefeller was elected governor in 1966, there was never any doubt that he would be a candidate for reelection in 1968. He knew it would take more than two years to accomplish all that he had intended. But 1968 was also a presidential election year, and Rockefeller's governorship and reelection campaign were complicated by the candidacy of Nelson Rockefeller for the presidency.

In the spring of 1968, Richard Nixon was the front-runner for the Republican presidential nomination. Nelson Rockefeller stayed out of the race officially until late April, when he formally announced his candidacy. When the announcement was made, Winthrop was already a member of the Rockefeller for President Committee.[80] Despite adverse pressure from both within and outside Arkansas, Winthrop supported Nelson in the months leading up to the Republican convention. He was able to do so because the Arkansas Republican party had voted in January to nominate their governor on the first ballot as a favorite-son candidate. The delegates would be free to vote for their own choice on the second ballot.[81] The schism among Arkansas Republicans between conservatives and liberals still existed, making it impossible for the state committee to endorse one candidate outside of the ceremonial endorsement of the governor. It helped Rockefeller by not forcing him to choose between loyalty to his brother and loyalty to the state party.

The Republican National Convention was held in Miami in early August. Rockefeller supporters believed that if Nixon could be prevented from a first-ballot nomination, their candidate would have a better chance. However, when Winthrop tried to hold the Arkansas delegation to his favorite-son candidacy through the second ballot, a minor revolt forced him to back down. On August 8 Nixon was nominated on the first ballot, ending Nelson Rockefeller's final bid for the presidency.[82]

While Rockefeller campaigned for his brother, he also had

to prepare for his own reelection fight. Arkansas Democrats viewed Rockefeller's 1966 election as a fluke, owed largely to the extremism of his opponent, Jim Johnson. The disastrous May special session of the legislature made Rockefeller look vulnerable, and there was no shortage of Democrats willing to try to unseat him. The leading contenders for the Democratic nomination were Bruce Bennett, the former state attorney general who had been defeated for reelection in 1966; Virginia Johnson, the wife of "Justice Jim" (Johnson was running in the primaries against Sen. J. William Fulbright); Marion Crank, an eighteen-year veteran of the Arkansas house of representatives; and Ted Boswell, an attorney and member of the Constitutional Revision Study Commission. Rockefeller also encountered opposition from within the Republican party—Sidney C. Roberts, an unemployed heating equipment salesman.[83]

The primaries were held on July 30. Rockefeller easily defeated Roberts, 26,541 votes to 1,195. On the Democratic side, the number of candidates almost assured a runoff between the top two vote-getters. Marion Crank and Virginia Johnson faced each other in an August 13 runoff, with Crank winning the opportunity to oppose Rockefeller in November.[84]

Senator Fulbright's fight for reelection complicated Rockefeller's campaign. Fulbright was seen as a vulnerable candidate. His stand against the Vietnam War made him unpopular among conservatives, while his civil rights voting record hurt him among black voters. He faced three opponents in the Democratic primary, but the only real threat came from Jim Johnson. Understandably, this gave the black vote back to Fulbright, who defeated Johnson almost two to one. Fulbright's Republican opponent in the general election was Charles Bernard, a businessman and treasurer of the state party. Rockefeller's staff saw Bernard's candidacy as damaging to Rockefeller's since many Rockefeller supporters also supported Fulbright. Rockefeller faced a dilemma. If he ignored Bernard, he angered Republicans, but if he supported Bernard, he lost Democratic votes. Bernard ran "against the governor's advice."[85] His loss angered him and his followers and became one more source of bitterness within the Republican party.

The state Republican party platform was an endorsement of Rockefeller's achievements and goals. It included constitutional revision, administrative reorganization, election reform, a "little Hatch Act" limiting the political activities of state employees, teacher tenure, establishment of free kindergartens and adult education, continuance of prison reform, and industrial expansion. The Democratic platform endorsed many of the same items, but with several glaring differences. Concerning the prisons, the Democrats said that inmates should not be "coddled" and made no mention of rehabilitation or vocational training. In an obvious attack at Rockefeller's hiring of talented out-of-state residents, the Democrats pledged to give employment priority to "qualified residents." The platform also criticized the governor for what it called "one-man rule" and pledged to represent Arkansas's four hundred thousand Democrats.[86]

The campaign was a difficult one for Rockefeller. Polls showed that his popularity had been declining throughout his term. An early September poll suggested that if the election were held then, Rockefeller would have lost to Crank, 60 percent to 40 percent.[87] Much of the dissatisfaction with the governor centered around public perceptions of Rockefeller's personal flaws rather than his accomplishments, or lack of them, as governor. A great deal was made of the amount of time Rockefeller spent, or rather did not spend, in his office and in the state. Another major source of criticism was his drinking. Unlike his predecessors, Rockefeller made no secret of the fact that he enjoyed alcohol. Rumors about the degree of the governor's alcoholic consumption ran rampant, much to the Democrats' delight. The governor was also hurt by his lack of administrative skills. In conducting day-to-day business, Rockefeller necessarily depended on his staff to handle most of the details of daily operations. Unfortunately, according to John Ward, Rockefeller was a "terrible" administrator. For instance, getting mail answered, and making sure that staff members were accountable for the mail, was a constant problem.[88] This naturally cut down on the governor's effectiveness and image, as did his habitual tardiness, which raised questions about his interest in serving.[89] His reputation was further damaged by the disastrous May special session of the legislature. Many felt a Democratic governor would be more successful, and Crank used all of these avenues of attack repeatedly.

Rockefeller's campaign managers, Ward and Robert Faulkner, had ammunition of their own against Crank. They had uncovered evidence that, while he was in the legislature, Crank's entire family was on the state payroll, including his eight-year-old daughter. In an attempt to defuse the issue, on October 8 Crank made the information public himself. But he held back and did not tell the whole story. This allowed Rockefeller's people to release their documentation to the press. The "family plan," as it was called, was extremely damaging to Crank's campaign. Prior to this, Rockefeller's most effective charge had been that Crank was a Faubus crony, a member of the Old Guard. The family plan suggested that there were also serious questions about his personal and public honesty.[90]

Arkansas's two major newspapers, the *Democrat* and the *Gazette*, endorsed Rockefeller over Crank. Rockefeller's polls on the eve of the election agreed, predicting a victory over Crank, 51 to 49 percent. The polls were amazingly accurate— Rockefeller received 322,782 votes to Crank's 292,813. The closeness of the race suggests that a more progressive candidate not associated with the Old Guard might have defeated the governor. In other races, Fulbright easily defeated Bernard, and George Wallace won Arkansas's six electoral votes. Arkansas's one Republican congressman, John Paul Hammerschmidt, also won reelection. The voters likewise approved Amendment 53, permitting state-supported kindergartens, and voted for the calling of a state constitutional convention, both of which received strong support from the governor.[91]

That the Arkansas electorate voted for Rockefeller, Fulbright, and Wallace appears at first glance contradictory. But an examination beneath the popular labels of "conservative" and "liberal" reveals more of a pattern. Arkansas voters were extremely dissatisfied with Lyndon Johnson's Great Society of welfare programs and civil rights acts, and this was naturally transferred to Humphrey. George Wallace was a Southerner, and many

Arkansans agreed with his views. Arkansas's dislike of Johnson also helped Fulbright, whose domestic record was quite conservative, opposing every civil rights bill. Fulbright's opposition to the Vietnam war did not hurt him among white voters as much as his anti–civil rights stand helped him. At the same time, his anti-war stance helped him with liberals and blacks. And Bernard had run a nasty campaign, alienating many voters by accusing Fulbright of being soft on communism. The *New York Times* observed that "white conservatives evidently still fear Negroes more than communism, and the Negroes apparently have not found Mr. Bernard's racial stance believable."[92] While Rockefeller once again received approximately 90 percent of the black vote, Bernard received only 30 percent in his race for the Senate.[93]

Rockefeller's victory once again was a personal one rather than an endorsement of a two-party system. The only other Republican state constitutional officer elected was Lt. Gov. Maurice Britt, even though Republicans ran for every statewide office. Most voters were willing to give Rockefeller the traditional two terms in office to prove himself. They were not willing, however, to abandon their Democratic roots. In contrast, the vote for George Wallace did indicate a shift in presidential voting patterns that was not limited to Arkansas. The only Southern state to vote for Humphrey in 1968 was Texas. Georgia, Alabama, Mississippi, and Louisiana, like Arkansas, voted for Wallace. The rest of the South gave their electoral votes to Nixon.

Rockefeller's first term in office was relatively successful. He made strides in prison reform, civil rights, and education. He ended gambling in Hot Springs. Arkansas had its first minimum wage law. He streamlined state government through the new Department of Administration. But if Rockefeller wanted to continue and expand upon these achievements, the state would need additional revenue, and this would prove to be an almost impossible goal. Furthermore, Rockefeller, in the 1968 elections, had once again helped finance the campaigns of Republicans running against many legislators. The resentment existing within the General Assembly grew during his second term, making further success difficult to obtain.

FIVE

Minor Victories and Major Defeats in the Legislature

As Rockefeller began another two years of dealing with the legislature, he faced problems even more difficult than the ones he had encountered in 1966. The legislature's political composition had changed only slightly—it now boasted four Republican representatives and one Republican senator, an increase of two legislators. Rockefeller had pledged during the campaign not to seek a third term, and legislators therefore looked upon the governor as a lame duck. All they had to do was maintain the status quo until a Democrat could be elected in 1970. Yet the public expected more from a governor with two years' experience. Rockefeller's difficulties were compounded by the fact that his election margin was slim—he could by no means claim a mandate for his programs. In a pre-election memo to the governor, Eisele discussed the problems Rockefeller would face if he won.

> Frankly, you will have no success on any major legislative program unless you are able to deal effectively with the "enemy." That enemy still controls the legislature, and we will have nothing but two more years of turmoil—and very little program—if we are unable to devise ways and means of bringing them in line.[1]

Rockefeller's dilemma lay both in drawing up a new legislative program and in convincing the legislators to give that program a fair chance. A post-election telegram from six prominent Democratic legislators invested the situation with a sense of urgency. While pledging to work with the governor "for the good of our state," they warned that "if the administration does not come up with a program, the Democratic leaders will plan a program of their own. . . ."[2]

The regular session of the Sixty-seventh General Assembly would begin in early January 1969. Within a month of his re-election, Rockefeller went on television to request public support for the tax proposals that would be the cornerstone of his legislative program. He argued that additional revenues were needed to keep Arkansas "in step with the rest of the nation."[3] On December 10 the governor unveiled the scope of his proposals in a speech to the legislative council. His tax program would produce $90 million in additional revenues the first year, and $105 million in the second. These revenues would come from increases in the sales tax, personal and corporate income taxes, and taxes on tobacco products and alcohol.[4]

In the remaining weeks before the session, Rockefeller tried to sell his tax package to legislators and to the public. Legislative reaction to his December 10 speech demonstrated that his job would not be easy. Most legislators recognized the need for a tax increase—a minimum of $16 million was needed to maintain the current level of spending—but they were almost unanimous in their feeling that Rockefeller's requested $90 million was too ambitious. Rockefeller's staff adopted a campaign slogan, "Arkansas Is Worth Paying For," and spread it across the state on bumper stickers in an effort to convince the public to pressure their legislators. But, as a former aide to the governor noted, legislators quickly turned this around with their own slogan, "Rocky Ought to Know—He's Bought It Twice."[5] The legislators themselves were fed and wooed in groups of twenty at Winrock. The specifics of the program were outlined prior to these meetings, and "constructive criticism" welcomed.[6]

Rockefeller delivered his second inaugural address on January 14, 1969. He spent most of the speech discussing his tax program, explaining why it was needed, how the money would be spent, and how it would be raised. Rockefeller argued that his reelection indicated a desire by the people for progress, since he had made the need for new taxes and consequent service programs known during the campaign. He proposed spending 50 percent of the new revenues on education, 12 percent on health and welfare, 10 percent on local government, and the remainder on improving state services and the salaries of state employees. He ended by stating: "There are no frills in what I am proposing . . . no luxuries . . . no monuments to me as an individual. . . . I implore every member of the General Assembly as I have myself: Listen to the voice of the people . . . not to the selfish interests."[7]

The tone of Rockefeller's closing remarks indicated a continuation of his adversarial relationship with the legislature, particularly the senate. There were only three new senators, including the one Republican, and returning senators had not forgotten the problems of the last two years. In the house, a full twenty-five of the one hundred members were new. While this presented a potential for more independent voting, the house's Democratic leadership worked very hard to gain the loyalty of these new members.[8]

Rockefeller's tax proposals contributed to what was the longest session in the history of the Arkansas General Assembly. The session lasted ninety-three days, finally adjourning on May 8. The last major adjustment in state taxes, including the income tax, had been in 1957. Then-governor Faubus had worked for two years prior to passage building support for a tax increase. In 1955 Faubus had appointed a commission that outlined the need for new taxes and had then organized pro-tax groups in all seventy-five counties to help the governor push the program through the legislature in 1957. In order to win support for the program in eastern Arkansas, where the highest concentration of blacks lived, Faubus had agreed to support school segregation bills, which became the justification for the governor's involvement in the Central High crisis that fall. Despite these deals, and even considering Faubus's political clout over the legislature, a petition drive had referred his proposed sales tax, one part of the tax program, to the voters, absolving legislators from responsibility for the tax. It won approval in the 1958 election.[9]

Legislators were traditionally reluctant to act on tax increases, lest their political careers suffer. Arkansas's tax burden was both relatively low and extremely regressive because most legislators saw that as the will of the people. This attitude was ingrained in Arkansas's political consciousness. State taxes had only been raised four times since Reconstruction. Anti-tax sentiment was so strong during the Depression that then-governor J. Marion Futrell had persuaded the legislature and voters to pass the Futrell Amendment to the state constitution, requiring a three-fourths vote of both houses of the legislature to raise the rate of any tax on the books in 1934. Furthermore, Arkansas was not paying its share of the costs of New Deal programs. In January 1935 President Roosevelt had told the state that he would cut off all federal aid to Arkansas by March unless the state began paying its fair share toward relief programs. The tax legislation passed in response to this threat legalized horse and dog racing, and imposed the first sales tax and the first taxes on beer, wine, and liquor. Following this, taxes were not raised substantially until Faubus's tax package in 1957. Fear of raising taxes permeated the 1969 legislative session, quickly prompting some senators to propose that the legislature again delegate its responsibility on this matter to the people. The president *pro tem* of the senate, Morrell Gathright, proposed that a sales tax increase be voted on in a special referendum. However, as the session progressed, the legislature refused to give the tax proposals even that much of a chance.[10]

While the legislature avoided action on tax increases, Rockefeller's staff conducted public opinion surveys to determine which branch of government was really reflecting the will of the people. A January 23 survey showed a "resignation" toward the need for higher taxes. Sixty-eight percent of the public agreed with an income tax increase, and 49 percent agreed with a sales tax increase. But as Rockefeller and the legislature haggled over the necessity of taxes, public support for the program dropped dramatically. A February 24 survey showed only 33 percent of the public supporting an income tax increase, while sales-tax support had dropped to 28 percent. It appears that the legislature was influencing public opinion rather than the other way around.[11]

In mid-February, and again in March, Rockefeller addressed joint sessions of the legislature. His February 19 speech revealed the frustration he felt. He pleaded with the General Assembly to assume a leadership role and vote for the taxes necessary for Arkansas to progress. The governor denounced the apparent unwillingness of legislators to vote for anything not entirely endorsed by public opinion, warning:

> Public opinion will fault no man for doing what is right. To the contrary, public opinion today will expose the man whose political habit is fashioned from cloakroom expediencies. He will find that such a garment becomes thin and transparent on election day. . . .
>
> . . . I hold it to be significant, too, that coincidental with my election as the first Republican governor in 94 years, virtually 60 percent of the House is made up of first and second year members. I believe this represents a revolt by the people against the ways of the past; a desire on the part of the people to have a greater voice in shaping their future. Do not underestimate the intelligence of the people of Arkansas.[12]

On March 10, shortly before the scheduled end of the regular session, Rockefeller again pleaded for additional revenues. Those bills expected to pass would yield no more than $20 million, and Rockefeller argued that "twenty million dollars would not keep us from going backward in relation to the other states." He went on to caution that "if I must seek a third term to finish my job, then I will." The governor had two proposals: first, that a two-week recess be called, and, second, that a joint legislative committee be appointed to work with him and his staff on the tax proposals during the recess. Rockefeller got the committee, but only a four-day recess.[13]

During the regular session's extension, the house and senate feuded over what types of revenue bills to pass—the house voting down senate bills while the senate opposed the house bills. The house approved tax increases totaling $36 million, but these measures died in the senate. More than a month after the Sixty-seventh General Assembly's scheduled adjournment, the legislature took a three-week recess, having approved measures increasing revenues by approximately $20 million, exactly what had been predicted in March. The bills that cleared the legislature increased taxes on beer and cigarettes, imposed taxes on cigars and other tobacco products, created a realty transfer tax, removed some use tax exemptions for corporations, and raised corporate income taxes. The largest portion of Rockefeller's tax package, the increases in sales and personal income taxes, was never seriously considered after early March.[14]

Was the failure of Rockefeller's tax program inevitable? Was it justified? Did Rockefeller ask for too much? The state had clearly been spending beyond its means for the past four years. State income tax withholding was started during Faubus's administration, and the 1965 General Assembly passed massive spending programs in anticipation of the windfall. No one wanted to curtail state services once they had been increased, but the income tax windfall quickly dissipated. Spending also expanded as a result of federal programs enacted during the mid-1960s requiring state participation—Medicare, Medicaid, and Food Stamps among the most prominent. Arkansas had swallowed a $22 million increase in 1957 for far fewer services. Even without taking the rate of inflation into consideration, the $20 million approved in 1969 was low in comparison. Having fewer taxes was traditionally more important to many Arkansans than improved state services. One historian noted that, during World War II, the state enjoyed unprecedented prosperity. "For the first time in a decade people were able to pay their state taxes which increased the financial resources of state government. However, little of the increased revenues was used to improve basic human services—housing, health care, and education."[15] Even in 1969, Arkansas ranked quite low in state salaries and services when compared with other states, and its tax burden in 1970 was the lowest of any state in the nation, when considered as a percentage of per capita income. Rockefeller's proposed tax increases would not even have brought the tax rates up to the national average.[16]

Still, Rockefeller's program was an ambitious one. He never seemed able to grasp the fact that Arkansans were not interested in competing with other states or the nation. He wanted desperately to lead the state to a position it was not willing to take. Support for his program came from urban business leaders and the Arkansas Education Association. But Arkansas was predominantly rural and blue collar. The AFL-CIO strongly denounced the tax increase proposals. Tax increases were difficult to pass under the best of circumstances, and Rockefeller, as a Republican governor in a Democratic state, had no leverage to use, no way to force legislators to vote his way other than public opinion. But the "Arkansas Is Worth Paying For" campaign was a total failure, as public opinion polls showed. Faubus had passed unpopular legislation through intimidation and bargaining, but Rockefeller did not pose a threat to legislators. His Republican coattails were barely large enough for his lieutenant governor. If the legislature was unyielding in its refusal to increase taxes, Rockefeller was just as stubborn in his insistence on approval of his entire tax package. He seemed to possess neither a knack for gentle persuasion nor a willingness to compromise, flaws fatal in a politician. The failure of Rockefeller's tax program was inevitable but, with one exception, it was not justified. As evidence of this, Dale Bumpers, the Democrat who defeated Rockefeller in 1970, passed an income tax reform bill in 1971 almost identical to Rockefeller's income tax proposal. The one portion of the program for which legislators' arguments appeared valid was the sales tax increase. Arkansas's tax burden was already extremely regressive, and an increase in the sales tax, which applied to food purchases, would only have added much more to the tax burden of the poor in proportion to the rest of the population.[17]

While Rockefeller's tax program dominated his legislative program in the Sixty-seventh General Assembly, he did not abandon other goals. His nonbudget agenda, presented to the legislature several days before the session began, included many goals that were not reached in the first term. One of these was the bill permitting the sale of mixed drinks in those counties where it was approved by the voters. The inclusion of the mixed drink bill in the administration's package was no surprise, but the fact that it passed surprised many.

After the governor's mixed drink bill failed in the May

1968 special session, there was never any doubt that it would be reintroduced in 1969. The bill was evaluated and redrafted for its resubmission. While there were the expected denunciations from church groups, support for the bill was more widespread than before. The Little Rock Jaycees endorsed it, as did several state senators and the state's major newspapers. The primary reasoning behind support for the bill was to bring Arkansas's liquor laws into the twentieth century, to end the hypocrisy in the existing law that allowed liquor to be sold by the gallon but not by the ounce, and to permit the state's citizens to decide for themselves, through local option elections, whether or not to legalize the sale of mixed drinks.[18] The state's sole Republican senator, Jim Caldwell, a Church of Christ minister, pointed out that while, as a minister, he was a "dry," as a legislator, he felt an obligation to allow the people the right to decide the issue themselves.[19] And the student newspaper of Ouachita Baptist University, while being careful to note that it was not condoning "the consumption of liquor," endorsed Rockefeller's proposal, citing the hypocrisy of people "who shout 'dry' through a hangover in church."[20]

Rockefeller's polls showed that a large majority of Arkansas's citizens favored a mixed drink local option law provided that emphasis was placed on a tax to be levied on the drinks. The January 23, 1969, poll showed a 91 percent approval rating, and the February 24 poll an 83 percent approval rating. But the opposition to the bill came from a vocal and aggressive minority. A February 17 mail count by Rockefeller's staff recorded the receipt of 444 letters against the bill with only 13 in favor.[21]

The administration's bill was introduced in the house on January 20. Representatives delayed voting on it until February 20, when it was defeated, fifty-six to forty. However, notice of reconsideration was given, meaning that the bill could be brought up for a second vote. On the second try, after strong lobbying efforts by the governor's staff and Little Rock legislators, the house approved the bill, fifty-two to forty-six. Several days later, the bill passed in the senate, nineteen to sixteen, one vote more than necessary. The governor signed it within hours.[22]

One major difference between the 1968 bill and the new

version helped explain the voting change between May 1968 and January 1969. The 1968 bill allowed local option elections only in communities with a minimum population of twenty thousand. The 1969 bill permitted elections in any incorporated town where the sale of alcoholic beverages was legal, making the bill more amenable to small-town legislators. Passage of the bill was also aided by the confusion over the legality of the sale of mixed drinks by private clubs. Legislators became convinced that they would have to pass a mixed drink law or possibly see mixed drink sales completely eliminated in the state. If that happened, business would suffer, particularly convention and tourism-related industries.[23] So while passage of the mixed drink bill was a triumph for the Rockefeller administration, it did not indicate any improvement in the ability of the governor to obtain the support of recalcitrant legislators for the administration's program.

The remainder of Rockefeller's reform program met with much less success than the mixed drink bill. There were a few exceptions. The governor signed House Bill 16, repealing the law that required blood for transfusions to be labeled by race. Passage of the bill came easily, since the blood labeling requirement had become an embarrassment to the state and its repeal had been requested by the Department of Health, Education and Welfare. The blood-labeling bill had been signed into law by Faubus in 1959. His explanation denied any racial motives. "At that time sickle cell anemia, an ailment which afflicts only black people, was rather wide spread. No physician could assure me that it could not be transmitted by transfusion."[24]

A bill lowering the maximum work week for urban firemen from seventy-two to sixty-four hours won approval. This was a part of the governor's program that met defeat in the Sixty-sixth General Assembly. Prison reform continued on a limited basis. A first-offenders bill passed, converting Tucker prison farm into an intermediate reformatory.[25]

Rockefeller's attempts to streamline and professionalize state government received a boost with the passage of a bill establishing a uniform personnel classification and compensation plan for state employees. Amendments were added to the legislation by the senate to exempt some state agencies from the plan, but it was still a step forward. Though the Rockefeller administration sponsored this bill, the idea had originated during Faubus's governorship.[26]

Administration bills meeting defeat in the Sixty-seventh General Assembly included some bills that had also failed in the Sixty-sixth Assembly. Teacher tenure, a riot control bill, and a jury wheel, or random selection of jurors, bill were all rejected once again. The bill representing an administration goal meeting with the most unusual fate was House Bill 32, establishing a code of ethics for public officials. Rockefeller vetoed the code of ethics bill because of two amendments added to the bill in the senate by Guy Jones that would have made it illegal for a state employee to have his salary supplemented from private sources or from tax-exempt foundations. The amendments were an obvious attack at Rockefeller's admitted supplementation of state salaries, and in his veto message the governor reiterated the necessity of the supplements. Some senators bitterly attacked the veto, including the bill's author, Doug Brandon. An override attempt was not possible, however, because the bill had passed the house on the last day of the session.[27] Earlier in the legislative session, when the bill had shown little chance for passage, Rockefeller issued an executive order establishing a code of ethics for state employees. The executive order covered conflicts of interest and rules of conduct. The legislation was needed to deal with the financial interests of state officials.[28]

The Sixty-seventh General Assembly merged the private Little Rock University with the University of Arkansas into what became the University of Arkansas at Little Rock. This was not an administration bill, but Rockefeller kept his reservations about the matter to himself, giving the bill tacit approval. This was likely due to the fact that the merger proposal's strongest support came from Little Rock's representatives. Much of Rockefeller's own meager support in the legislature came from the Little Rock area, and the governor could not afford to alienate them.

While, at first glance, the merger of Little Rock University and the University of Arkansas appeared a rather routine matter, emotions on the subject ran high. The University of Arkansas is located in Fayetteville, isolated in the Ozark mountains in the northwest corner of the state. Little Rock officials wanted a state university in the capital, while many Fayetteville supporters feared a decline at the main campus if a branch were allowed in Little Rock. The matter was complicated by the presence of the State College of Arkansas in Conway, thirty miles from Little Rock. Guy Jones, Conway's state senator, wanted his constituents' school to become the center of higher education in central Arkansas. In addition to Little Rock's legislative delegation, the merger had the support of David W. Mullins, president of the University of Arkansas, as well as the institution's board of trustees. All three of these groups pressured Rockefeller to include the merger proposal in the February 1968 special session. Rockefeller did so, though he cautioned that the merger would have a greater chance of success if it had the "unqualified backing of the Governor's office," and he personally felt the proposal was premature, that it should wait for "an over-all study of the needs of higher education in Arkansas."[29]

The merger proposal did not get anywhere in 1968 and was introduced again in 1969. Despite delaying tactics employed by Jones in the senate, the bill passed both houses. Rockefeller took the full five days allowed before signing it. He did so only after meeting with the Pulaski County legislative delegation, to elicit their support for his tax measures in exchange for his signature on the merger. Also, mail to the governor's office was running strongly against the merger, and Rockefeller wanted it clear that he was reluctant to sign. In his remarks at the signing ceremony, the governor reassured other parts of the state when he said, "This is not something that is going to take the place of the colleges and universities that we have, but it is going to add to, and it is going to be an institution of quality."[30]

Nonadministration-sponsored measures introduced and passed by the Sixty-seventh General Assembly over the governor's veto reflected a resentment toward Rockefeller. Arkansas was, in 1969, one of six states in the Union requiring only a simple majority to override a gubernatorial veto. Still, until the two-party system came to Arkansas, veto overrides were very rare since there was too much of a political advantage to be gained by legislators who stayed friendly with the governor. But the Sixty-seventh General Assembly broke with tradition, passing six bills over Rockefeller's veto. The first bill passed in this manner diluted part of Rockefeller's prison reform program by tightening parole provisions. The bill overturned an administration-sponsored measure passed in February 1968.[31]

Most of the veto overrides were obvious attempts to dilute the governor's power. Senate Bill 340, passed over Rockefeller's veto, was regarded by the press as the worst bill passed in the session.[32] It transferred responsibility for auditing the books of county officials from the Department of Administration to the Division of Legislative Audit. This meant that the legislature, rather than the governor's office, now controlled the audits. In his veto message, Rockefeller noted:

> I cannot help but be aware that this Legislature has devoted a disproportionate amount of time to diluting or restricting the powers of the Chief Executive of this state. . . .
>
> It [the bill] is obviously an attempt to transfer an auditing responsibility of the state government to a place where those activities may be more sensitive to political pressures.
>
> I must further note that during the process of this particular proposal through the General Assembly, Sheriff Marlin Hawkins of Conway County was prominent in his activities to obtain the passage of this bill.[33]

Winrock Farms was located in Conway County. Rockefeller and the Democratic Hawkins had been publicly feuding for years. The *Arkansas Gazette* also noted Hawkins's lobbying for the bill's passage.[34]

Another bill passed over the governor's veto was the one changing the definition of the "majority party" in the state for purposes of selecting county election commissioners. When Rockefeller was elected, the majority party, which was entitled to select two of each county's three election commissioners, was the party of the governor. When the law was passed in 1948, no one envisioned the election of a Republican governor. The new law made the majority party the party with the most constitutional officers. The legislature had passed a similar bill in 1967, but the governor's veto of that bill stood. This time, Rockefeller was unable to sustain the veto.[35]

In all, Rockefeller vetoed twenty-eight bills in 1969. Of the vetoes that were not overridden, the bill posing the greatest threat to the governor was the one that would have removed control of the Department of Welfare from the governor's office and placed it in an independent welfare commission, its members appointed for nine-year terms.[36]

The adversarial relationship between Rockefeller and the legislature surfaced in the problems the governor encountered regarding agency budgets. In late March the Joint Budget Committee cut the AIDC's budget by forty thousand dollars, claiming the cut was based on the governor's recommendation. But Rockefeller's "recommendation" was part of his December speech to the legislative council, in which he outlined what would happen if additional funds were not raised. In a letter of protest to the committee, Rockefeller wrote: "It is inconceivable to me that anyone would refer to those figures as the Executive recommendations for the next two years. . . . I cannot more strongly express my resentment in this matter."[37]

The controversy over gubernatorial appointments that arose at the beginning of Rockefeller's first term in office continued. The senate was upset over Rockefeller's method of appointing people to boards and commissions. The senators were accustomed to prior consultation before appointments in their districts were made. Rockefeller did not make a general practice of this. While the law permitted approval of appointments by a simple majority in the senate, in reality, if a senator did not approve of an appointment in his district, the rest of the senate deferred to his wishes. Appointments were a continual sore point, for two reasons. First, Rockefeller was a Republican and senators wanted to limit Republican patronage as much as possible. Second, Faubus had always been very careful to follow the will of individual senators when it came to making appointments in their districts. Patronage served as an effective tool for controlling the senate and passing administration-sponsored legislation.

Most appointments to boards and commissions were routine and approved without debate. When the senate rejected one, it was usually because of some slight, real or imagined, against the senate or one of its members. Dr. Richard Springer, appointed to the Racing Commission in late 1967, was rejected by the 1969 senate for declining to meet with Sen. Q. Byrum Hurst concerning his appointment. Three minor, and usually routine, appointments were also rejected at Hurst's request after the appointees failed to consult with the senator. George Fisher, a political cartoonist, was turned down for a position on the Publicity and Parks Commission, reportedly because of a cartoon critical of the senate. Unsuccessful Republican candidates receiving appointments were usually approved, provided, of course, that they had not run for the senate.[38]

There were several explanations for the increasing tension between the executive and legislative branches. Democrats had considered Rockefeller's 1966 election a fluke. When he was re-elected in 1968, they resented the political mileage he gained from the achievements of the Sixty-sixth General Assembly. Once the second term was a reality, legislators resented being told that taxes had to be raised and were further incensed by the governor's pledge to seek a third term if he did not achieve his goals. Arkansas voters had a tradition of giving governors two terms to prove themselves, and Democratic legislators wanted to be sure that Rockefeller was not successful enough to have an opportunity for a third term. Many legislators considered the governor a lame duck and were busy making alliances to support their own agendas after Rockefeller's term.[39]

The regular session of the Sixty-seventh General Assembly ended on May 9, 1969. House Speaker McClerkin declared in closing ceremonies that the session "accomplished more than any other session in modern times," a standard closing statement in the General Assembly, and particularly inaccurate for this session.[40] The *Gazette*, noting the legislature's failure to pass a comprehensive tax program, expressed the hope that legislators would awaken to the necessity of increased taxes before the expected special session, when they would be faced with "a fresh confrontation with responsibility."[41]

The marathon regular session of the Sixty-seventh General Assembly was only half over when Rockefeller announced that he planned to call a special session in the fall to raise taxes. Legislators lost no time in expressing doubts as to the wisdom of this idea. In July 1969 Rep. Grady Arrington wrote Rockefeller concerning input Arrington had received from his constituents: "I am sorry to relate that there is, seemingly, almost unanimous disapproval of more taxes at this particular time. For this reason I trust that you will deem it unnecessary to call a special session later this year."[42] Rockefeller responded that he had no desire "to waste the taxpayers money nor the time of the individuals involved to call a Special Session if that session has no chance to succeed."[43]

The governor did not call a special session in the fall, waiting instead to build support for the idea of tax increases, traveling around the state meeting with county and city officials, as well as legislators. In October Hayes McClerkin, the speaker of the house, wrote the governor, urging him to give adequate notice of when the session would occur and what items would be included. Rockefeller's response admonished McClerkin that he and other legislators were "well aware of the critical areas in which I feel we must make progress. . . . Our greatest difficulty will not be in identifying the needs, or the legislation which should be enacted; rather it will be the determination of how far the General Assembly might be willing to go in meeting these needs."[44]

While Rockefeller was trying to convince the state of the need for new taxes, the press was reporting the dissatisfied rumblings of legislators. The Associated Press polled fourteen of the state's thirty-five senators, and only one, Q. Byrum Hurst of Hot Springs, responded that he thought his constituents would exchange higher taxes for increased state services. The consensus of the remaining senators was that, while more services would be nice, they did not appear necessary. The senators felt they could vote for a tax increase only in case of a "desperate, necessary need."[45] McClerkin predicted in December that no new taxes would result from the upcoming special session, charging that current revenues were not being used efficiently. This sentiment was echoed by Rep. Worth Camp, who wrote Rockefeller that the governor's refusal to work with the Joint Budget Committee in "a realistic appraisal of the state fiscal policies including necessary economies and the recommendations therefor" had caused the "impasse between the governor and the legislature."[46] Even George Nowotny, senior member of the small Republican minority in the house, announced in January that he would oppose any proposed sales tax increase, observing, "At the present time, with the basic tone of the legislature, I believe there would be very little chance of having any increase in taxes."[47]

Rockefeller sent letters to members of the legislature on January 26, 1970, and again on February 3. The first letter outlined items being considered for inclusion in the special session, while the second included specific proposals. Rockefeller was requesting approximately $35 million in additional taxes from three major sources: an increase in personal income taxes, the extension of the sales tax to services, and the removal of some sales tax breaks given to utilities and mass transit. Rockefeller dropped his attempts for a general sales tax increase. The governor asked legislators for their views before making the final decision on the program for the session, slated to begin March 2. Rockefeller received letters of support from some legislators. Rep. John Purtle of Little Rock wrote: "I feel I will be able to support the general program you have outlined. When you eliminated the four percent sales tax you convinced me that you have developed a reasonable course of action."[48] The most prophetic letter, however, came from Rockefeller's nemesis in the senate, Guy Jones, who announced, "It is my settled conviction that a special session for taxation purposes is futile and useless."[49]

Little Rock's newspapers divided on the necessity for the session. The *Democrat* editorialized, "As we have been saying for months, the special session is 90 percent politics on the governor's part." The *Gazette*, meanwhile, defended Rockefeller, stating that he had "made a persuasive case before the legislature yesterday for the $35 million tax program he proposes."[50] The newspapers agreed, however, on the chances for the session's success. The *Gazette* was forced to admit that "whatever he says, Mr. Rockefeller has poor chances of getting any of his three main tax measures through the legislature in this special session."[51]

Rockefeller's official proclamation, issued in two parts on February 13 and 24, included eighty-six items for consideration by the General Assembly. The tremendous number of items indicated that Rockefeller had not learned from his experiences in 1968 to limit and focus the special session on only those needs he felt were most important. It also indicated a conviction, on Rockefeller's part, that having legislative sessions only once every two years was totally inadequate. While addressing the special session, he asked, "What other enterprise involving the expenditure of more than $800 million annually has its Board of Directors meet once every two years to conduct its business?"[52] While Rockefeller was correct in this, he could not ignore the realities of the Arkansas constitution that made special sessions very unpopular. Legislators would not tolerate turning a special session into anything other than a forum to discuss emergency matters. Most of the items on the session's call, aside from the three tax proposals, consisted of appropriations to various state agencies. Among the most important were those intended for the prisons. Federal Judge J. Smith Henley had ordered changes in the state's prisons in order to eliminate cruel and unusual punishment. Rockefeller asked for funds to hire personnel to replace armed trusties and to construct new facilities for both the juvenile training school and the prison. Many other appropriations were aimed at raising salaries in various state agencies. The average salaries of state employees in Arkansas were the lowest of all fifty states, and as a result many vacancies existed. One other item called for the repeal of the "Fair Trade" liquor law and increase of the liquor tax.[53]

On March 2, opening day of the session, Rockefeller spoke before a joint session of the General Assembly. He acknowledged that, while he still believed his original $90 million program was the best avenue, it was unrealistic to expect its passage. However, the $20 million passed in 1969 "would not even allow us to hold our own." Rockefeller asked for the additional $35 million in revenue to "consolidate our gains and keep them from going by the wayside." He explained in detail where the money would go and how it would be spent, and concluded:

> As yet my administration has not been granted enough money to achieve the progress you believe in just as I do. Still, hope springs eternal, and you don't wait until somebody gives you a watch to find out what time it is.
>
> Your executive branch has put together programs that can dramatically affect the future of our state. . . .
>
> . . . The sole issue before us, here and now, is meeting our obligations.[54]

Legislators responded coolly to Rockefeller's speech and program. The consensus seemed to be that the tax bills did not have a chance of passage so close to election time. Many legislators complained that the session was strictly a political move, called by Rockefeller to boost his popularity and put the legislature in an unfavorable, partisan light.[55]

The special session of the Sixty-seventh General Assembly lasted one week, adjourning on Friday, March 6. On Tuesday, both houses of the legislature had voted overwhelmingly to defeat the heart of Rockefeller's tax program, the income tax bill and the bill extending the sales tax to services. The vote on the income tax bill was ten for and eighty-five against in the house, and four for and twenty-nine against in the senate. Debate in both houses on the tax bills was almost nonexistent, indicating that legislators already knew how they were going to vote. The third tax bill, to repeal sales tax exemptions given certain corporations, was defeated the next day.[56]

The General Assembly authorized a total of $9 million in new expenditures. The money was taken from state agencies that had accumulated surpluses and from the remaining balance in the state's general fund, based on a program put together by the legislative council. Rockefeller, in his opening speech, had condemned the legislative council program, saying: "Yes—we have so-called 'balances'—but we also have a severe shortage of state-employed nurses. . . . What good are balances without bodies? What good are balances to the state if the people get inferior services, or no service at all?"[57] And Dr. Max Milam, head of the state's Administration Department, warned of the danger of leaving the state with a balance of "nothing or less."[58] In spite of these warnings, the attraction of satisfying the state's most pressing needs without an increase in taxes was too appealing politically for the legislature to resist.

The prisons received $2.3 million of the $9 million. Rockefeller had requested $4.2 million. Even though this money was recommended by the legislative council, the assembly's leadership, passage was difficult. In both the house and the senate, opponents of the prison reform package concentrated on two themes: that the prisons were being mismanaged and money was being wasted, and that appropriating additional funds amounted to abdicating control of the prison to the federal courts. The prison appropriations did not pass both houses until the last day of the session. The remainder of the $9 million went to construction, most of it at state colleges and universities, and to state salaries. The inadequacy of the $9 million was demonstrated by the fact that teacher salaries were increased an average of only seventy-seven dollars a year.[59]

None of the reform bills on Rockefeller's call came close to passage by the legislature. The repeal of the fair-trade liquor law, the creation of a public defender's office, and the consolidation of the state's tuberculosis program with the Health Department were only a few of the bills meeting defeat. Aside from the legislative council's appropriations measures, the only other bills passed were noncontroversial. A number of bills raising interest rates on municipal bonds were passed, as well as a bill permitting University of Arkansas dental school students to receive out-of-state training.[60]

The only one expressing surprise at the dismal failure of the special session was Winthrop Rockefeller. The *Gazette* pointed out that the governor had failed to sell his tax program to the people before the session. True, Rockefeller had been traveling the state for months, pushing the necessity of additional taxes. But the largest chunk of his tax program, his income tax bill, would have been a major step toward tax reform, redistributing the tax burden from the poor to the wealthy. Under the bill, almost three-fourths of the state's population would have received no increase or a tax cut. It was not until the week prior to the session that the bill's supporters began pushing its reform aspects but, by then, public sentiment was so strong against new taxes that defeat was inevitable.[61] Legislators used the governor's seeming inattention to tax reform as proof that the session was a political move. Failure of the legislature to pass tax reform would provide Rockefeller with great rhetoric in the 1970 election. This seems unlikely, however, because Rockefeller was truly bitter at the results of the special session. He lashed out publicly at not only the legislature but also at the press for purportedly sensationalizing his program's defeat. Furthermore, the governor's staff had to realize that continued friction between Rockefeller and the legislature could only hurt the governor, causing people to believe a Democratic governor could accomplish more. Rockefeller's victory margin in 1968 had been slim enough. If he could not establish a cooperative and productive relationship with the legislative branch, his days in office would be numbered.[62]

An April opinion poll by the governor's staff confirmed that the special session damaged his popularity. The approval level on Rockefeller dropped eleven points to 39 percent between December 1969 and April 1970, and only 36 percent of voters felt he should seek a third term. His approval rating among blacks dropped to 71 percent, with only 50 percent feeling he should run in November. While Rockefeller's own popularity was dropping, his program was gaining approval. A majority of voters were reported as being resigned to some tax increases in the next General Assembly. The discrepancy between Rockefeller's approval rating and the acceptance of his program was attributed to the voters' desire for more stability and less dissension in state government.[63]

The conclusions of the April opinion poll would be validated in the following year. The special session's failure helped convince Rockefeller that he had to go back on his pledge not to seek a third term. The session's failure also helped ensure the governor's defeat in that election. And, as the polls indicated, the session helped convince the public of the need for tax increases and reform. Success for both would come in the 1971 General Assembly.

Rockefeller's program met with little success during his second term. Prison reform continued, and the mixed drink bill became law. Revenues were increased, but not nearly as much as the governor wanted. The greatest indicator of Rockefeller's declining influence in the legislature was the number of bills passed over his veto. In particular, the power to audit county records passed from the executive to the legislative branch, and the definition of the majority party was changed to remove any chance of Rockefeller's controlling county election commissions.

The lack of cooperation between the governor and the General Assembly had many sources. The novelty of having a Rockefeller in Arkansas's capitol had worn thin. In his first term, many legislators feared obstructionist labels. But by the time Rockefeller won reelection, criticizing the governor had become more acceptable. He was viewed as just another politician in the eyes of the legislators. In addition, Democrats considered him a lame duck. His margin of victory in 1968 was small, and Rockefeller's defeat in 1970, should he run again, seemed a real probability.

Rockefeller must share responsibility for failure of his program. He created some of the resentment legislators felt when he appealed directly to the public for support of his tax program. Legislators also never forgot who bankrolled their Republican opponents. The governor failed to learn how to deal successfully one-on-one with legislators. As one former house member noted: "Rockefeller didn't spend time to talk to the legislators. He didn't remember their names."[64] Sterling Cockrill, who was house majority leader during the Sixty-seventh General Assembly, also felt that Rockefeller himself contributed to his problems. "His personality was distant, he appeared to be aloof, he appeared to be superior in attitude."[65] The art of persuasion was a gift no governor, especially one from the opposition, could afford to be without. Rockefeller's inability to work with the legislature would be a major factor in his 1970 defeat.

Fighting for Progress and Keeping the Peace

Rockefeller's stormy and unproductive relationship with the legislature was just one reason why his second term was anything but dull. The renewed controversy over prison conditions could be blamed, in part, on the legislature's failure to enact adequate reform measures. The loss of the head of the state's Administration Department, Mike Frost, was due, according to Frost, to legislative interference in matters that were "really day-to-day operating decisions."[1] Other problems in Rockefeller's second term were holdovers from his first two years in office. School integration and his crusade against the Game and Fish Commission made headlines in both the first and second terms.

Still more issues Rockefeller encountered were symptomatic of the troubled and turbulent late 1960s. Vietnam was the most pervasive. As a governor, Rockefeller had no direct involvement in foreign policy.[2] However, whenever asked, he expressed support for Nixon's attempts to achieve a "just and honorable peace" in Vietnam.[3] The governor's attitude was that "regardless of whether or not American troops should have been committed," once committed, "the winning of that war becomes the first order of business."[4]

Controversy nationwide over the undeclared war in Vietnam culminated in the Vietnam Moratorium on October 15, 1969. On that day, millions of opponents of the war gathered at rallies and prayer vigils. While organized and dominated by college students, the moratorium gained the support of the United Auto Workers and civil rights leaders. New York City's mayor, John Lindsay, had the flag at City Hall flown at half-staff, as did the mayor of Atlanta, Ivan Allen, Jr.[5]

In Arkansas, on the day preceding the moratorium, Rockefeller issued a statement calling for support of the president. The governor noted that while Vietnam was a "dirty, horrible and unpopular war," Americans should refrain from protests conducted "just because we do not have all of the facts and just because we are angered and frustrated." Rockefeller's rationale was that protests would hinder the "cause of peace" by contributing to the "misguided belief on the part of our nation's enemies that we are a divided people who lack the strength to finish what we start or the courage to support our own beliefs."[6] Arkansas Senator John McClellan issued a statement similar to the governor's, while Sen. J. William Fulbright applauded the students' "peaceful petition for an end to the grievous war which is draining away the life blood of this nation."[7] Moratorium activities in the state were lightly attended. The largest rally in the state took place in Fayetteville at the University of Arkansas, where approximately six hundred students and faculty members held a protest march. Rockefeller met with a small group of Little Rock demonstrators on the steps of the state capitol and listened to their proclamation. Though the governor made it clear that he agreed only with the ultimate goal of ending the war, one of the leaders of the group, the Reverend William L. Holshouser, Jr., noted that the governor's willingness to listen indicated a "drastically different attitude toward public dissent and expressions of public concern than President Nixon has shown."[8]

A second national Vietnam Moratorium was held on November 13–15, 1969. Again, anti-war activities in Arkansas were limited. Most of the state's college campuses were sites of small rallies, and a rally in Little Rock drew less than a hundred people. This was reflective of the region. Whether an indication of apathy or acceptance of Nixon's policies, protest against the war in the nation's midsection was limited. In Arkansas, the former seems more likely, since Fulbright's very vocal anti-war stance had little impact on his popularity with Arkansas voters. Rockefeller's personal approach to dealing with what protesters there were, publicly hearing their complaints, surely helped keep anti-war protest peaceful, in the same way that his public display of concern helped maintain peace in Little Rock following Martin Luther King, Jr.'s, assassination.

In May 1970 Rockefeller publicly endorsed Nixon's invasion of Cambodia, a stand contrasting sharply with that of many other elected officials, including New York's governor, Nelson Rockefeller, but one that drew no real opposition from the public in Arkansas.[9]

The civil rights issue also produced controversy and turbulence during the 1960s. And it was a subject of lifelong interest to Rockefeller. While Arkansas was virtually free of strife over Vietnam, the state did not escape the unrest and violence resulting from black impatience for and white resistance to improved civil rights.

Rockefeller continued, in his second term, his practice of filling state jobs with qualified blacks whenever possible. In November 1969 the governor appointed William "Sonny" Walker as head of the state Office of Economic Opportunity. Walker was the first black department head in Arkansas and the first black state OEO director in the South. Walker resigned a year later, after Rockefeller lost his bid for a third term, when the legislative council refused to increase his salary. Walker's salary was paid in federal funds, but the disposition of these funds was determined by the state. His salary was the lowest in the region and $1,680 less than the top salary authorized for his assistant. Despite these factors, the legislative council refused Walker's request, and he left for a position with the federal government.[10]

Rockefeller's staff kept close tabs on both the hiring of

minorities and the types of jobs available. Ozell Sutton, the black executive director of the Governor's Council on Human Resources, kept track of black employment statistics and, at Rockefeller's request, sat in on appointment planning meetings. Sutton also compiled a list of blacks qualified by background and experience for appointments to state boards and commissions. The Arkansas Republican party took advantage of the presence of the Republican administration in Washington to attempt to secure federal patronage positions for blacks. Patronage in fact was a valuable tool in the Republican party's drive to transfer Rockefeller's large black vote to the rest of the party. Qualified, educated people of any color were sometimes hard to interest in government employment in Arkansas. Rockefeller occasionally used his connections with the National Urban League to find jobs for both blacks outside of Arkansas and out-of-state blacks for jobs in Arkansas. Rockefeller also had a special assistant within the governor's office, York W. Williams, Jr., who coordinated input on locating qualified blacks for appointments, acting as both a clearing house and a watchdog for the governor's staff.[11]

On the first anniversary of Martin Luther King, Jr.'s, assassination, a prayer service was again held on the steps of the state capitol, attended by about six hundred people. Rockefeller spoke before the crowd, stating, "We are dedicated to making this a better world where we can call ourselves not just our brother's keeper, but our brother's brother."[12]

These efforts, while admirable, were hardly sufficient to achieve equality of opportunity for Arkansas's blacks. The Thirteenth Amendment was a century old, and blacks were tired of waiting for social, economic, and political equality. The civil rights movement had been relatively quiet in Arkansas in comparison to the rest of the South. Most of the leadership was local. Litigation was the primary means of desegregation, with the assistance of the NAACP and its Legal Defense Fund. But in 1969 several major civil rights demonstrations occurred in Forrest City.[13]

Forrest City, in 1969, had a population of fourteen thousand people, half black and half white. Located in east-central Arkansas, it lay in a traditional farming area approximately forty miles west of Memphis. The town was ripe for confrontation. Mechanization had, for several years, been sending tenant farmers into town where industrial jobs were available. Working in unionized factories made blacks more aware than ever of their lack of social equality. The spark igniting confrontation came in March, when members of the John Birch Society gained a majority on the Forrest City school board. A week later, the board, with no explanation, fired the Reverend J. F. Cooley, a teacher for eleven years at the all-black Lincoln School and a civil rights activist. As a result, the junior high students went on a destructive rampage inside the school. Four of them were sentenced to juvenile training schools. This action, in turn, led to a series of protests and a black boycott of white merchants.[14]

Press reaction to Forrest City's unrest probably precipitated, without meaning to, future confrontations. Forrest City's newspaper expressed surprise at the unrest in a town where "race relations have always been so good."[15] In its report, the *Arkansas Gazette* called Forrest City's schools "desegregated." The *Gazette* went on to explain that the Lincoln School had fifteen hundred students, all black and many of them bused in from other parts of the city, while the other junior and senior high school in town were "predominantly white."[16] Desegregation in Forrest City meant freedom of choice in a student's selection of a school. But whites were unwilling to select an all-black school that was likely to be physically and academically inferior, and very few blacks were willing to brave the isolation attached to being the first to integrate. White intransigence led to black frustration, making further disturbances unavoidable.

Over the next several months, race relations in Forrest City remained tense. In April ten local civil rights leaders, calling themselves the Committee for Peaceful Coexistence, issued a statement listing grievances and requesting intervention by federal and state civil rights agencies. The leaders of the group were Cooley and the Reverend Cato Brooks, Jr. Forrest City's mayor, Robert L. Cope, responded to the statement with the remark: "I see no need to comment since it's the same thing they've been saying for six months. They're just like all these groups. They can't come up with anything."[17] In June the grand jury impaneled to investigate the March riot issued its report, calling the riot a spontaneous disturbance rather than a planned conspiracy. Unfortunately, as the *Gazette* editorialized, the most disappointing aspect of the report "was the failure to conceive any justification for either the riot in March or a student walkout in April." The *Gazette* went on to mention the Reverend Cooley's firing as well as the poor physical condition of the school, noting that, while the newspaper could not condone the violence, "it is not difficult to understand . . . the destructive response of some students."[18] White leaders' refusals to acknowledge that a real problem existed kept racial tension in Forrest City "explosive," as Ozell Sutton called it.[19]

In early July Brooks and other Forrest City activists began planning a "poor people's march" from West Memphis to Little Rock, a distance of 130 miles. The purpose of the march, scheduled for August 20–24, was to "dramatize outdated conditions black people are forced to live in throughout the state of Arkansas," according to Brooks.[20] At this point, Rockefeller became directly involved in Forrest City's racial problems. The situation was no longer a local matter. If the march took place, it would directly affect every town on its route. On August 6 Rockefeller met with both blacks and whites from Forrest City, promising to visit the town in an effort to soothe racial tensions. The governor also met with Brooks, who had not been present at the earlier meeting, on August 11. On August 16 Rockefeller went to Forrest City.[21]

From the outset, the governor was against the march, but as August 20 drew nearer, it seemed even more important that the march not take place. Racial conflict and disturbances were cropping up in several communities along its route, including Little Rock. Ralph Scott, director of the state police, reported that "it is inevitable that the proposed march will adversely effect [*sic*] relations in the Little Rock area."[22] Glen Jermstad, a Republican party leader, put pressure on the governor not to allow the marchers to "walk the first mile."[23] Rockefeller did not believe he could or should prevent a legal march, and doing so would have done tremendous damage to his standing in the black community. Rather, he persistently tried to persuade black leaders to call it off. Rockefeller met again with Brooks and Cooley on August 19. After this meeting, the two ministers announced a thirty-day postponement of the march in order to give the governor time to meet their demands and because racial tension in the state "makes it dangerous at this time." They also praised Rockefeller for his showing of "good faith in responding promptly" to their demands.[24]

Forrest City white leaders had been complaining since March about outside agitators, claiming that there would be no race problem in town if militants had not come in and created hate. These whites felt vindicated when, on the day Brooks and Cooley postponed their march, Lance "Sweet Willie Wine" Watson of Memphis announced that he would conduct his own "walk against fear" along the same route. Watson was the leader of a militant Memphis group called the Invaders. Brooks had invited Watson to Forrest City earlier that summer to assist in the black boycott of white businesses. Ralph Scott urged Rockefeller to "prohibit this march which is bound to result in serious problems if it is permitted to take place."[25] Scott based his warning on an FBI report. In it Watson promised that, if faced with violence, the marchers would "survive and defend ourselves if necessary."[26] This possibility was not remote. City leaders in Hazen, a small town on the route, had barricaded side streets and armed one hundred auxiliary policemen with shotguns. Rockefeller did nothing to prevent the march, but urged all citizens, "black and white, to completely ignore the marchers."[27]

Watson left West Memphis on August 20, accompanied by only five other marchers instead of the two hundred he had predicted. While the number of marchers varied as the march progressed, it remained small. The marchers were escorted by plainclothes state policemen, and Rockefeller declared a state of emergency in Prairie County, where Hazen was located, to ensure the ultimate authority of the state police. Hazen authorities dismantled the barricades. The town's extreme overreaction did more to highlight why the marchers were walking than any of Watson's pronouncements. The march ended without incident in Little Rock on August 24. Watson praised the state police accompanying the marchers. "If police were like them all across the United States, we wouldn't have any police brutality."[28]

The march did nothing to improve race relations in Forrest City. After three black youths were arrested for the rape of a white girl, whites calling themselves the Concerned Citizens Committee began picketing, demanding "law and order." One local businessman told a reporter that what the demonstrators really wanted was "for the police to shoot some Negroes. . . . some show of force."[29] The demonstrations erupted into violence on August 26, when a crowd of approximately five hundred whites attacked three white reporters and two blacks, one of them "Sweet Willie Wine" Watson, who had returned to Forrest City after rumors of lynching the black youths spread. No whites were arrested as a result of the incident, but Watson was charged with disorderly conduct. Rockefeller declared a state of emergency and moved in about fifty state troopers. The *Gazette* noted "how far eastern Arkansas has still to go in the pursuit of racial peace and justice."[30]

In mid-September Brooks and Cooley announced the indefinite postponement of their march. Racial tension was especially high in the schools, resulting in boycotts by white students. On September 17 the school board closed all city schools indefinitely, blaming the problems on communism. Two days later, white crowds attacked three newsmen and slashed their tires, accusing the newsmen of not treating Forrest City whites fairly. Rockefeller publicly criticized city police for allowing the attacks and made arrangements with newsmen and the state police for state protection of reporters covering future events in Forrest City. The schools reopened on September 21. On October 27 Watson was convicted of disorderly conduct by an all-white jury. Unrest simmered in Forrest City for several more years, though not on the scale of the summer of 1969.[31]

Rockefeller, even with the minimal role he played at Forrest City, embroiled himself in a political misunderstanding because of it. On September 9 the governor told the press that four members of the six-man congressional delegation had expressed approval of his handling of racial problems. Two days later, however, Rockefeller issued a statement claiming in part: "For the record, I neither asked the members of the delegation for pledges of support, either direct or implied, nor were they given."[32] There is no evidence to indicate why the governor backed down from his original statement. The obvious conclusion is that Arkansas's congressional representatives wanted to distance themselves from the state's racial problems, in order not to damage their political careers.

School desegregation and busing were the causes of other racial incidents in the state as well as continuing headaches for Rockefeller. Carthage, Arkansas, a small rural town in the southern part of the state, had integrated its school district in 1966. At the beginning of the 1969–70 school year, the black community organized a boycott against the schools because of the firing of several black teachers and a counselor, and the expulsion of some black students. In a district where 180 of the system's 300 students were black, only 4 of the 17 teachers were black. The parents organized volunteer schools in local churches, but these were found by a member of the governor's staff to be "completely inadequate."[33] The state NAACP condemned the boycott on the basis that it hurt the children without solving the district's problems. The boycott went on for six months before the school board made concessions to black demands. The state board of education ruled that the students could not receive credit for time spent in the volunteer schools. When federal funds for a summer school were denied, Rockefeller gave the district fifteen thousand dollars from the governor's emergency fund to operate the summer session. One hundred and fifteen students attended.[34] The school problems at Carthage and Forrest City were representative of small communities across the South, where protests, boycotts and harassment disrupted life but attracted little attention outside the locality. A 1969 report on racial protest in the South, for which Forrest City served as a case study, found that the small-town South would enter the 1970s in "widespread ferment."[35]

Obviously, the 1954 Supreme Court decision voiding "separate but equal" educational facilities did not mean an end to segregation. Southern school districts adopted a policy of gradualism in complying with the Court decision, desegregating slowly, a few children at a time.[36] Aside from the obvious effect of postponing total desegregation as long as possible, gradualism allowed two tragic side effects. The first was white flight to the suburbs, and the second was the inordinate amount of attention focused on those few black students who chose to be the first to integrate. Integrating by sending whites to black schools was never contemplated under gradual plans—an indication of both continuing racism and the inferior conditions in all-black schools.

Little Rock serves as a perfect example of the effects of gradualism. The Central High School crisis came about when nine black students were enrolled in a school with over one thousand white students. Those nine became symbols, easily identifiable, toward whom white reactionaries could direct their wrath. Because desegregation was gradual, those fearful of it were able to move to outlying areas. In Little Rock, as these predominantly white suburbs were assimilated into the city limits, their schools remained independent, separate from the city school district, an obvious attempt to avoid desegregation. When Rockefeller was governor, there were 8,661 black students in the Little Rock schools. According to the *New York Times*, 25 percent of these students were in integrated schools, while the rest went to schools that were all or 75 percent black. The *Times* saw Little Rock as typical of Southern cities in which gradualism had produced resegregation, exchanging "de jure segregation for de facto segregation, with all of the problems of racial isolation and distrust that go with it." Only those schools in lower-income, transition neighborhoods were ever truly desegregated, and housing patterns soon undid even this. Those school board members who tried to increase desegregation were voted off the board in 1968 and 1969.[37]

Under the Civil Rights Act of 1964, dual school systems had to be merged or desegregated by September 1969 or lose federal funds. When it was reported that President Nixon would probably extend this deadline, Rockefeller sent the president a telegram urging him to reconsider "because it breaks faith with the black community and compromises to a disturbing degree the position of those who have courageously gone ahead with objectivity and a sense of justice—if not always with enthusiasm—in the implementation of federal desegregation guidelines."[38] But the Department of Education, with Nixon's support, did relax desegregation guidelines. This move was consistent with the president's Southern strategy. During the 1968 election, Nixon's campaign statements on desegregation were encouraging to white Southerners. Most significantly, he had endorsed freedom of choice desegregation plans as long as they were not used as a "subterfuge to perpetuate segregation."[39] After the new desegregation policy had been in operation for several months, criticism came from the United States Civil Rights Commission. The commission, headed by Rev. Theodore M. Hesburgh, issued a 105-page report in September. The report stated that administration actions since the July announcement appeared to be a "major retreat in the struggle to achieve meaningful school desegregation."[40]

While the Nixon administration dragged its feet in eliminating dual school systems in the South, the Supreme Court was stepping in as federal watchdog. In October, in the case *Beatrice Alexander et al., petrs.* v. *Holmes County (Mississippi) Board of Education et al.*, the Court ruled that school districts must end segregation "at once" and operate integrated school systems "now and hereafter." The decision replaced *Brown* v. *Board of Education*'s ruling that desegregation should proceed with "all deliberate speed" and was a setback for Nixon's Justice Department, which had argued that delays were permissible in some districts to provide continuing education.[41] In December the Court made clear what it meant by "at once" when it ordered six school districts in four Southern states to desegregate by February 1, 1970. In January the Court extended the scope of the February 1 deadline to include the six states of the Deep South—Alabama, Florida, Georgia, Louisiana, Mississippi, and Texas. But February 1 came and went with only six of the forty districts affected by the ruling in compliance.[42]

In Arkansas, Rockefeller was notified in April 1970 that forty-nine school districts in the state operated dual school systems and were therefore not in compliance with the Civil Rights Act of 1964. The governor asked the Justice Department to delay formal action in order to give the districts time to comply voluntarily with the order. The Justice Department, while expressing appreciation for Rockefeller's efforts to establish voluntary compliance, emphasized that "plans should be laid now looking to full desegregation by September 1970."[43] The Justice Department also wrote the state board of education as "the appropriate agency to be called upon to adjust the conditions of unlawful segregation and racial discrimination existing in the public school systems of Arkansas."[44] This was significant, because the Arkansas Board of Education had traditionally made it a policy to not involve itself with desegregation. In September 1968 the board issued a lengthy statement to T. E. Patterson of the Arkansas Teachers Association on discrimination in education. Regarding integration, the board backed away from both its own involvement and the principle of swift compliance. The statement read in part:

> The right to require the interpretation of the court decision as applied to individual school districts cannot be questioned. . . . Thus when a local school board goes to court in order to determine requirements as applied in their local district it is exercising a basic right and criticism of such action is unwarranted. . . .
>   . . . It shall not be our purpose to give unsolicited specific advice to local boards. . . . We believe it sufficient to state that we favor compliance at the earliest practical date as determined by the circumstances in each case.[45]

The board of education's public response to the Justice Department reflected this attitude. Education commissioner A. W. Ford, a Faubus appointee, expressed the hope that federal action would be handed over to Arkansas's three federal judges, instead of the Department of Health, Education and Welfare. This was done in a similar case in Georgia, and Ford said the Georgia decision was more reasonable "than what HEW had demanded of many of our school districts, although the Georgia order does mandate an end to dual school systems."[46] The unwillingness of the state board of education to take an active role in promoting desegregation left blacks virtually on their own against individual school districts. Federal intervention, coming as it did at the eleventh hour, was at times too little, too late. Nixon's Justice Department, having argued before the Supreme Court against forced integration, did only what the courts required.[47]

On July 9 the Justice Department filed desegregation suits against nine Arkansas school districts. The remaining forty districts named in April had all submitted acceptable desegregation plans prior to that date. By the time school began, six of the nine had submitted voluntary plans, with the other three, Watson Chapel, Wabbaseka, and Hazen, under court order to abolish their dual school systems. By the fall of 1970, while truly unitary school districts were far from a reality due to the large number of racially identifiable schools, steps were being taken to eliminate the last vestiges of *de jure* segregation.[48]

Another aspect of school desegregation was the issue of busing students. Rockefeller, in his public statements on busing, alienated both blacks and segregationists because his position changed as the 1970 election approached.

In September 1969 the sixteen-member Southern Governors' Conference, meeting in Williamsburg, Virginia, tackled the emotional issue of busing. Two resolutions were proposed. One condemning busing was rejected, but in the voting, there was one abstention—Rockefeller's. Gov. Mills E. Godwin, Jr., of Virginia, offered a substitute resolution, urging "restraint and good judgement" in the use of busing as a means to end school desegregation and favoring a "quality, nondiscriminatory education for every child." This resolution passed by a vote of nine to three, with Rockefeller voting for the resolution. (Four governors had already left the conference.) The three dissenting votes came from Democratic governors Albert P. Brewer of Alabama, Lester G. Maddox of Georgia, and John Bell Williams of Mississippi. The resolution was significant in that it put the governors' stands on record. The Nixon administration, on the other hand, announced at this same conference that it opposed busing.[49]

Busing became an even more controversial issue in the wake of the Supreme Court decisions of October and December 1969.[50] In January 1970 Rockefeller stated regarding busing, "It should be used and used with discretion, but neither do I think we should blatantly disregard the usefulness of the bus in implementing the court orders, and the law working toward sound integration." The *Gazette* praised Rockefeller for not joining in the "hypocritical" Southern cry against busing "after whole generations of whites and blacks alike were bused all over kingdom come to keep the schools totally segregated."[51] But many Arkansans disagreed with the paper, including some prominent Republicans. Dorothy Webb, president of the Arkansas Federation of Republican Women, and Charles T. Bernard, Senator Fulbright's unsuccessful 1968 Republican opponent, publicly opposed both Rockefeller's statement and the use of busing to achieve racial balance. An internal memo in the governor's office reported that "this misunderstanding seems to be costing a lot of votes."[52] On February 21 the governor issued a new statement to clarify what he called the "distortion" of his position. In a brief statement that was not at all clear, Rockefeller stated:

> I endorse the position wholeheartedly which the Southern governors have taken on the resolution [of September 1969], and I want to make it perfectly clear that I have *not* recommended busing—and am *not* recommending it now.
> . . . The decisions will be made in the local school districts, and the responsibility for carrying out those decisions also rests with each individual school board, working within the limitations of the law and the various court orders.[53]

The next day, at a Little Rock rally led by Freedom, Inc., a conservative organization, Rockefeller stated that he had never endorsed and was not then endorsing busing. The *Pine Bluff Commercial* pointed out that "if the governor's strategy was to antagonize those who have admired his courage and candor in this area, while making a futile bid for a bloc of voters who are the natural prey of candidates like George Wallace, then he succeeded this weekend."[54]

It was obvious that Rockefeller had backed down, rather clumsily, on the busing issue in order to appease the more conservative elements of the voting public. Robert Faulkner, the governor's executive secretary in 1970, later recalled that "there was a lot of discussion" about changing Rockefeller's stand on busing. "I was one of them that suggested, and it was strictly a political [move], that he modify, or 'fuzzy' if you will, his support of busing." Faulkner explained that they were trying to reach people who "weren't sure how they felt about" busing, but he reflected, "That may have been a mistake."[55]

Busing had become a political hot potato. At the National Governor's Conference in February, the busing issue was completely avoided. It appeared, in the spring of 1970, that integration advances had reached a plateau and could easily backslide. But the Supreme Court had never ruled directly on the busing issue, and when it did in April 1971, it unanimously backed busing to combat the South's dual school systems while rejecting the Nixon administration's legal arguments against busing. Busing remained controversial, and total integration remained a dream into the 1980s, but the Supreme Court remained committed to halting segregation.[56]

In higher education, integration started earlier but was no nearer to being complete at the end of Rockefeller's governorship than it was in the lower grades. Blacks were first admitted to the University of Arkansas's law and medical schools in 1948.[57] The decision to desegregate postgraduate programs at that time was simplified by the fact that similar black programs did not exist. At the undergraduate level, Arkansas had one black state-supported college—Arkansas AM&N in Pine Bluff. Blacks were admitted to the University of Arkansas's main campus at Fayetteville and other white campuses in 1955, the year after the Brown decision. But by 1969, integration at the state's white campuses was still minimal and there were virtually no white students at the Pine Bluff facility. In 1969 Leon Panetta, director of the Office for Civil Rights in HEW, notified Rockefeller and Arkansas's colleges and universities that the campuses were racially segregated. He asked for and received a desegregation plan, but he eventually rejected it as too vague. In 1970 the NAACP's Legal Defense Fund sued HEW to take action against Arkansas and nine other states for operating dual higher education systems in violation of the Civil Rights Act of 1964. Arkansas submitted a plan acceptable to HEW in 1974, but this was rejected by the courts in 1977. A second plan was submitted in 1978, which expired in 1985. In 1987 the federal Education Department's Office for Civil Rights and the NAACP's Legal Defense Fund were still in disagreement over the success or failure of Arkansas's plan. The Legal Defense Fund charged the Education Department with failing to explore a possible connection between Arkansas's lack of recruitment efforts and the low number of blacks enrolled in college.[58]

The problems in Arkansas's prisons did not disappear either when Rockefeller was reelected. Both past problems and current conditions made headlines, and Rockefeller was forced to deal with both.

In March 1969 Tom Murton, the controversial superintendent who was fired in March 1968, appeared before the United States Senate Juvenile Delinquency Subcommittee headed by Sen. Thomas J. Dodd, a Democrat from Connecticut. Murton testified on Arkansas's prison conditions before and during his tenure, displaying various instruments of torture. He also alleged that, since his dismissal, the "old head knockers" had resumed control of the prisons, and that exploitation and abuse of the prisoners had continued.[59] Rockefeller reacted angrily to Murton's testimony, and Corrections Commissioner C. Robert Sarver asked the Subcommittee to allow rebuttal.

On March 11, Sarver testified for two hours before the subcommittee. The *Arkansas Gazette* reported that Sarver was consistently frustrated by Dodd while attempting to refute Murton's testimony. Sarver's primary objection to Murton's testimony was that Murton made it appear that the conditions he found when he arrived at Tucker were reinstated after he left. Austin MacCormick, a criminologist from the private Osborne Foundation who served as an occasional consultant to Rockefeller, was present during Sarver's testimony. MacCormick himself testified that the tortures and conditions Murton described "are just not happening today." MacCormick further testified that Murton was undermining prison reform in Arkansas through his allegations.[60] Senator Dodd's public reaction to Sarver's and MacCormick's testimony was that "my position is that Murton was telling the truth."[61] The day following Sarver's testimony, Rockefeller sent Dodd a telegram accusing the senator of "ulterior motives" in arranging Murton's appearance before the subcommittee. The governor condemned the "constant interruptions and harassment to which you, as chairman, subjected" Sarver in "his efforts to refute the misleading and at times wholly untrue statements made by Thomas O. Murton."[62] Rockefeller was not alone in his outrage. The attacks from an "outsider" put the governor and the state legislature on the same side for once. The state senate adopted a resolution condemning the "abusive" treatment Sarver received.[63]

Murton would once more become a thorn in Rockefeller's side in 1970 when his book, *Accomplices to the Crime*, was published. Murton appeared on the "Dick Cavett Show" in September, promoting his book and claiming that the reason he had been unemployed since leaving Arkansas was Rockefeller's "vindictiveness."[64]

In 1969 action was finally taken on the 1966 state police report that first detailed the horrors of the Arkansas prison system. A federal grand jury, meeting at the request of Judge J. Smith Henley, delivered thirty-nine indictments against Jim Bruton, former superintendent at Tucker prison farm, and seven of his subordinates for alleged brutality in the punishment of inmates between 1964 and 1966. A five-year statute of limitations prohibited indictments for abuses prior to 1964. In jury trials held in November 1969, Bruton and five others were acquitted, with the exception of one charge against Bruton in which the jury was unable to reach a verdict. The jury evidently refused to believe former inmates' allegations of torture, and it complied with the closing argument request of Bruton's attorney not to let the federal government tell state employees what they could and could not do.[65] Of the other two men indicted, one former trusty guard pleaded guilty and another pleaded *nolo contendere*. In January 1970, at a retrial of the one outstanding charge against Bruton, the former superintendent also pleaded *nolo contendere*, fearing that a guilty plea or verdict would result in the loss of his state pension. Judge Henley gave Bruton the maximum sentence allowed under the federal civil rights

statutes—a thousand-dollar fine and one year in prison. He sus-
pended the prison term, however, calling it a "death sentence,"
since Bruton could not spend "sixty days" in prison before past
inmates of the Arkansas Penitentiary would kill him. Henley also
stated that, as far as he was concerned, the plea was a conviction
and that after hearing the evidence at the first trial he regretted
"that the punishment is not more severe."[66]

While the Penitentiary's past problems made headlines, Sarver
and the legislature headed for a new showdown over prison
finances. In June 1969 Corrections Commissioner Sarver declared
the financial situation in the department "critical," that reforms
were not being made because there was barely enough money to
hold "our heads above water and that's all." Money would not be
available until the prison crops were harvested in September.[67]
After a tour of the prisons by the legislative council's Committee
on Charitable, Penal, and Correctional Institutions, the committee members blamed the Department of Corrections for the fiscal
crisis and urged that the farms be made self-supporting. Their
report said that all other programs at the prisons should be
adjusted "so as not to interfere with the successful farmings operations at the Penitentiary."[68] The legislature had obviously not
accepted the goal of rehabilitation as superior to that of making a
profit. As one editorial charged: "Running a prison is one business where profit cannot be all-important. It is self-destructive if
it is. Consider ours, for example."[69]

Bickering over finances between the Board of Corrections
and the legislature continued throughout 1969. In December, 23
of the prison system's 110 employees were dismissed in an
attempt to save money. This measure inevitably led to an
increased dependence on armed inmate trusties, a practice that
prison reformers had long condemned and that Rockefeller was
trying to eliminate.[70]

Beginning in January 1970, hearings were held in Judge
Henley's court on the constitutionality of Arkansas's prison system. Twenty-four inmates had filed suit contending that the
trusty system and forced labor without pay violated their constitutional rights. Editorials indicate that elimination of the armed
trusty system had the support of everyone except the state legis-

lature, and federal action would apparently be necessary to convince it.[71] On February 18 that federal action came when Henley ruled that existing conditions at Cummins and Tucker constituted cruel and unusual punishment prohibited by the United States Constitution. Henley called the prisons a "dark and evil world." The judge listed guidelines for the Board of Corrections in making changes in the trusty system, calling the guidelines "minimum requirements if persons are going to continue to be confined in the Penitentiary." He insisted that trusties would "have to be stripped of their authority over the lives and living conditions of other convicts." Henley did not set a deadline for completing the necessary reforms because he recognized converting to free-world personnel would take time and that improvements over the past several years indicated an awareness on the part of the state government that the prisons were deficient.[72]

Henley's decision came only weeks before the scheduled special session of the legislature. It certainly was a powerful lever for Rockefeller in getting more money for the prisons. The governor's staff expressed their delight with Henley's ruling. Rockefeller's legal advisor, Marion Burton, stated for the press: "Maybe this is the turning point in developing a prison system that produces something other than hardened criminals."[73] Though the session was a dismal failure in most respects, the prisons were allocated $2.3 million. The necessity of additional funds served, on the other hand, as a lever for the legislature to use in convincing the Board of Corrections to agree to an appeal of Henley's decision. While both the legislative council and Joe Purcell, the attorney general, wanted to appeal the decision, Sarver and the Board of Corrections at first publicly stated their reluctance to permit an appeal, permission that was legally necessary for an appeal to be filed. On the same day that the legislature passed the $2.3 million appropriation, Purcell announced that an appeal of Henley's decision would take place. Board of Corrections chairman John Haley had informed Purcell earlier that day "to use your own judgement in the matter of appealing the decision," providing the appeal was not used to delay action toward prison reform.[74]

Reforms did continue while an appeal was filed, although not at a pace Henley found adequate. In April the judge issued a court order requiring immediate increased protection in the barracks area and the disarming of inmates.[75]

Throughout 1969 and the first half of 1970, Rockefeller remained relatively aloof from prison problems. While he worked toward passage of bills benefiting the prisons, he let Sarver and the Board of Corrections handle the running of the prisons both before and after Henley's decision. Despite the governor's obvious distancing of himself from prison operations, John Ward reported in a July 1970 memo that "negatives in terms of our prisons" were "shaping up to be perhaps the 'number one' [political] issue." Ward listed the pardons and parole program, escapes, and administrative errors as issues attracting "uncommon political interest."[76] This memo was written at a time when Sarver was taking increased criticism from legislators and prosecuting attorneys for the "leniency" he and the Board of Paroles showed toward prisoners.[77] Rockefeller evidently decided at this point to involve himself in the matter, sending a letter to county judges, prosecuting attorneys, and sheriffs. In the letter, the governor cited Act 50 of 1968, requiring courts to "supply adequate background materials on each inmate for use in making release decisions." Rockefeller wrote that "it has come to my attention that prison files now contain virtually no information of value from court officials," and urged the addressees, "as public officials, to comply with the intentions of the Legislation, and assume your responsibility concerning parole decisions."[78] Response to Rockefeller's letter was resentful, accusing the governor of trying to pass blame for parole problems to the courts and prosecuting attorneys. While the governor's office pointed out that information was provided to the parole board in only about 15 percent of the cases, Rockefeller's letter does appear to have been both politically motivated and a political disaster.[79]

On November 2, 1970, the day before the general election, eight inmates at Cummins prison farm took two "free world" and two trusty guards hostage. Two of the hostages were later exchanged for Sarver and Cummins superintendent Bill Steed. The inmates at first demanded their freedom but later turned to complaints about poor conditions at the prison, such as unsanitary conditions and a shortage of clothing and eating utensils. Rockefeller issued a statement saying: "We do not make deals with prisoners. We will not do so today."[80] After thirteen hours, the inmates surrendered and the hostages were freed. Sarver claimed that no deals had been made with the inmates.[81]

Three weeks later trouble again erupted at Cummins, and this time the cause was racial tension. Tucker was integrated in 1969 with few problems, but Cummins was not fully integrated until April 1970, on an order from Judge Henley. On November 20 fights broke out between black and white inmates. Prisoners of both races began demanding a return to segregation. Fighting continued over the next few days, and the state police were called in to stand guard and counteract the imbalance between eleven hundred inmates and thirty free-world employee guards. By November 23 the prisons were quiet again and the state police left.[82]

The racial disturbances were symptomatic of the times and tame compared to prison riots in other states.[83] But the two incidents in November were used by state legislators to denounce the Rockefeller administration's entire prison reform program and to launch a drive to oust Sarver and the Board of Corrections from their jobs. Sen. Virgil T. Fletcher of Benton stated: "It's a typical example of the era of excellence. We didn't use to have things like this at the prison."[84]

Despite the sniping of his critics, Rockefeller's two terms in office brought substantial change in prison conditions in the state. Diet and living conditions were improved, barracks were racially desegregated and then resegregated according to age and behavior, corporal punishment was outlawed, vocational training was begun, and so was the process of replacing armed trusties with hired personnel. Prisoners began receiving treatment as persons capable and worthy of rehabilitation. But Judge Henley's court orders and inmate complaints painted a picture of prison conditions that was still far from what most would call acceptable. And violence was still rampant in the prisons. In a single summer month in 1970, Cummins officials recorded nineteen stabbings, assaults, and attempted rapes. The armed trusty system made elimination of weapons almost impossible. Most of the blame for the continuation of these atrocities must lie with the legislature and the public for their apathy and shortsightedness. But Rockefeller and his prison appointees share the blame for the slow pace at which reforms progressed. An *Arkansas Democrat* editorial in March 1970 addressed this problem:

> And while the legislature has not appropriated enough money to do a great deal, it seems to us that more improvements could have been made with what was available. . . . The legislature provided money for a maximum security building more than a year ago, but work on it has still not begun. Too often, we think, the Rockefeller administration has wanted to wait until it could create the perfect prison.[85]

Rockefeller must, however, be given at least some high marks for prison reform. Politically, he would have been far better off had he left the prisons alone. His humanitarianism forbade this. His successor, Dale Bumpers, continued the reforms Rockefeller started. Bumpers too met fierce resistance from the legislature when attempting to attain more money for the prisons but, as a Democrat, was able to overcome much of the opposition. Federal intervention and violence continued at the prisons throughout the 1970s, but so too did reform.[86]

The prisons were not the only agency of state government to see reform or require the attention of the governor. Reform continued in the insurance industry with little fanfare or controversy under Insurance Commissioner Allan Horne and later, when Rockefeller appointed Horne to a vacant municipal judgeship, under A. Gene Sykes.[87] The Game and Fish Commission, on the other hand, continued to occupy both the governor's time and newspaper headlines.

Rockefeller's crusade against the Game and Fish Commission began in 1967, after a member of the governor's staff was denied access to Commission records. In the summer of 1968, Rockefeller formally leveled charges against three commissioners for alleged misuse of state equipment and employees for their own benefit. It was not until April 1969 that the governor appeared to be getting anywhere. On April 21 the state supreme court ruled unanimously that Rockefeller had the authority to hear charges against Game and Fish Commission members. In May Rockefeller dropped the single charge against Ernest Hogue because Hogue's term was expiring and the charge appeared to be an isolated incident. What started in 1967 as an attempt to oust all seven members of the commission was now limited to only two men, Raymond Farris and Newt Hailey. The hearing commenced on July 15 and ended on August 19, 1969. On November 4 Rockefeller issued his findings on Farris, who was found guilty of "gross misconduct" in office and was removed from the commission. A decision on Hailey was postponed. Farris died shortly after suffering a stroke in January 1970, and at that point Rockefeller dropped the case against Hailey.[88]

In retrospect, Rockefeller's crusade against the Game and Fish Commission appears to have been an enormous and futile waste of manpower and money. But in a 1972 interview, Rockefeller justified the hearings.

> Because I was fighting the dishonesty and corruption of years, for me to take an arbitrary position would have undermined many of the things that I was attempting to do. So I went through this extraordinarily expensive and painful exercise to achieve the results needed, even though time and normal attrition were working in my favor.
>
> From the time I instituted these proceedings, the commission did more constructive things. . . .
>
> The only thing that disappointed me in terms of the public was the fact that they could not understand the standards of integrity or justice that I was attempting to demonstrate. . . . They got impatient with me, not indignant with the law which gave the commission immunity and insulation from the people. They lost sight of this.[89]

The hearings did establish the fact that the Game and Fish Commission was not above the law, that its members could be held accountable for their actions.

Staffing state government with qualified people was a problem all governors had to contend with. As mentioned previously,

Rockefeller partially countered Arkansas's extremely low state salaries by supplementing the salaries of key employees. The practice continued in spite of an opinion by the state's attorney general that it was illegal, and despite press condemnation of it. In March 1969 Rockefeller announced "with pride" that he was supplementing the salaries of thirteen employees and for the first time disclosed who were receiving the supplements.[90]

Problems arose in 1969 between Rockefeller and Ralph Scott, director of the state police. Scott was unique, however, in that he was a Rockefeller appointee. On March 17 Scott sent the governor a letter resigning as director, citing as the cause a dispute with Rockefeller that had been smoldering since the previous May. Scott had then fired Highway Patrol director Kenneth McKee after McKee was arrested on a drunken driving charge in Missouri. Rockefeller wanted McKee to be granted a six-month leave of absence—and the governor and Scott compromised by placing McKee on indefinite leave. Scott told Rockefeller at the time that "McKee could not serve in the Arkansas State Police as long as I am the director."[91] McKee did not return to the state police. Instead, Rockefeller hired McKee as part of his private security force. In his letter of resignation, Scott wrote:

> It seems likely that we have both known since last May that this action was inevitable. It was clear at that time that we are not in accord in our concepts of moral and ethical conduct for police officers. . . .
> . . . Except for the security guards, it seems likely that we could have had a harmonious relationship and despite the constant attacks upon the morale of the organization, we have accomplished much. I think you should know that I leave disillusioned and disappointed and with deep regret.[92]

Reaction from both Republicans and Democrats was swift. Attorney General Joe Purcell wrote Rockefeller: "I have been disappointed and concerned by the circumstances surrounding the resignation. . . . I urge you not accept Colonel Scott's letter of resignation."[93] Republican leader Henry Britt wrote Scott: "You may rest assured that the Governor keeps his own counsel and does not act on the nit-picking of some of the palace guard.

. . . I think the two of you should resolve your differences."[94] Unfortunately, some viewed the issue from a more partisan standpoint. One Republican wrote: "We here in Phillips county are 100 percent behind the firing of Col. Scott. . . . We can never get anywhere in the building of strength in our party . . . unless we have complete loyalty to the Governor and to the Republican party."[95]

On April 2 Rockefeller wrote Scott, advising him that his letter of resignation was not accepted. The governor wrote that, after several meetings with Scott, "it was clear to me that we both share a serious concern over the future of the State Police program." Rockefeller further stated, "It should be perfectly clear to everyone that you are the Director of the Arkansas State Police and will continue to be so with full authority to execute your responsibilities as Director." Scott responded that he had a "sincere desire" to continue as director, and he did so for the rest of Rockefeller's term.[96] Rockefeller had clearly "bungled in handling his differences with Scott."[97] But it was to the governor's credit that, when faced with Scott's resignation, he was able to retain the police director with assurances of Scott's ultimate authority in that agency.

Rockefeller's closest advisors underwent a number of significant changes during his second term. In May 1969 the governor's personal legal advisor, G. Thomas Eisele, resigned to resume private law practice. The next month, Marion Burton, Rockefeller's executive secretary, resigned that position to fill the vacancy left by Eisele. Robert Faulkner, an assistant campaign director and legislative assistant to the governor, was named to Burton's former job.[98]

In August 1969 the presence of a Republican administration in both Little Rock and Washington afforded a rare opportunity when one of Arkansas's federal judges died. On the list of names the Republican State Committee submitted to the Justice Department for consideration was G. Thomas Eisele. Eisele had worked with Rockefeller since the early 1960s, and the governor wrote Nixon and Attorney General John Mitchell to urge Eisele's appointment, pointing out both his third-generation Arkansas Republican roots and his two Harvard law degrees. In

January 1970 Nixon appointed Eisele, but the appointment was not confirmed until August 5, having been held up by two controversial Nixon appointments to the Supreme Court.[99]

Rockefeller faced troubling and complex issues during his second term in office. He served as a calming influence during civil rights disturbances. Prison reform and school integration both continued, with the assistance of the federal courts. But politics intruded over the governor's busing stand, and the conflict with Ralph Scott further damaged Rockefeller's reputation. The year 1970 was a very difficult one for the governor, and, as the election approached, the problems multiplied.

SEVEN

Leaving
a Mixed Legacy

Tensions within the Arkansas Republican party had taken on new dimensions after Rockefeller's first gubernatorial victory in 1966. "Old Guard" conservatives, while resenting Rockefeller's attempts to change the party, were anxious to make full use of the new governor's patronage power. Republican officials at the county level were eager to influence appointment decisions without surrendering their autonomy to the state organization. The governor's staff had occasionally found itself at odds with the state party organization. This condition worsened after Richard Nixon's election in 1968 brought only rare opportunities for federal patronage. Rockefeller's reform program drew increased numbers of college students into the Young Republicans, who found themselves ideologically miles apart from county Republican officials and, at times, the state organization. These tensions grew during Rockefeller's two terms as governor, peaked over his controversial decision to seek a third term, and culminated in a bitter struggle for control of the party after his defeat. Growing tensions in the Republican party mirrored Rockefeller's declining popularity among the general population. After his defeat in 1970, Rockefeller retreated substantially from politics, as his dream of a true two-party system in Arkansas faded.

The 1966 election resulted in the need for the Arkansas Republican party to elect a new state chairman. John Paul Hammerschmidt, chairman since 1964, resigned following his election to the United States House of Representatives. Two men initially announced their intention to seek the position—Odell Pollard, the state committee's general counsel, and Dr. Wayne Babbitt, vice chairman during Hammerschmidt's tenure. However, Babbitt withdrew four days before the December 10 election. His letter of withdrawal stated:

> It saddens me greatly to witness the strife and controversy that has been created by the race for chairmanship of our Party. . . . We can ill afford the price of such unnecessary fighting among ourselves. If this doesn't cease at once, a sharp division in our ranks will be created that could last for years to come.
>
> After great deliberation and thought, it is apparent to me that the best course of action I can take for the benefit of the Party is to withdraw my candidacy.[1]

The causes of this controversy are unclear. According to Everett Ham, one of Rockefeller's aides, there was no real ideological split between Pollard and Babbitt. Rockefeller wanted Pollard because Babbitt "rubbed Win the wrong way," and "that's who got the election."[2] The *Gazette* called Pollard "the voice of compromise," noting that while he considered himself aligned with the more liberal factions of the party, Pollard worked well with both groups, as evidenced by his election by acclamation.[3]

Upon his election, Pollard cautioned fellow Republicans not to push too hard in patronage demands. Pollard warned, "Let us be sure that we do not ask the governor to appoint people who would not be good public servants."[4] Hammerschmidt also admonished the group: "Dispensing patronage can break up a political organization if it's not wisely done. Don't fall out over this item."[5] Pollard and Hammerschmidt were correct in recognizing the divisiveness of patronage. Unfortunately for the party, many Republicans were more interested in self-aggrandizement. The situation was further complicated by the demands of Democratic legislators and the necessity of working with them.[6]

Pollard and the Republican State Committee instructed Republican county chairmen to set up special committees to handle recommendations for state job appointments at the county level. These County Republican Recommendation Committees, or CRRCs, were designed to represent all of Rockefeller's supporters, including Democrats. The composition of these committees sometimes became a bone of contention between the state committee and county Republicans who wanted to dominate the CRRCs. In January 1967 Pollard notified Conway County's Republican committee that the CRRC they had submitted was unacceptable because it "did not represent the best interests of the Republican Party nor the campaign organizations who worked for Governor Rockefeller." The state committee instead appointed its own CRRC for Conway County and informed the county committee that "your County Chairman has not worked in the best interest of the Republican Party" and that the state-named CRRC "will be the body with which this State Committee will confer concerning job applications and job recommendations."[7] The opportunities these committees provided Democrats who supported Rockefeller was evident in a February 1967 memo reporting, "Ninety-two people have been put in jobs throughout the state at the request of the Republican Party, and 41 of these were in Pulaski County. More than half of the 92 are Democrats."[8]

Republicans in some counties never reconciled themselves to dispensing patronage to Democrats. One supporter, upset about an apparent "deal" the governor made with a Democratic legislator over an appointment to the Game and Fish Commission, wrote Marion Burton: "I assure you that if this deal goes through as it now stands; in the future I will work just as hard against Republican candidates in Arkansas as I have for them in the past two elections."[9] A complaint over an appointment from the Baxter County Republican committee prompted a reply from Van Rush, the party's executive director, that Rockefeller's selection was meant to "eliminate any further complicated political maneuvering" on the part of two Democratic legislators. Rush admonished the county committeeman that "the sooner we get more Republican legislators elected, the sooner we will eliminate complications like those which arose in the filling of this appointment."[10] Ralph Scott, director of the state police, responded to a complaint over an appointment by the Boone County Republican committee, stating:

> It might interest you to know that this selection was made by me personally in an effort to improve the caliber of the leadership of this organization which, for years, has been subjected to the type of political influence which, in my judgement, is being resorted to by the Boone County Republican Committee in this case. One of the most gratifying experiences in my life has been the relative freedom from political pressure which I have enjoyed under the administration of Governor Rockefeller.[11]

Colonel Willard Hawkins, Arkansas's Selective Service director, felt compelled to write Truman Altenbaumer about pressures Hawkins received from some county Republicans. Hawkins wrote:

> It is becoming increasingly obvious that some of our county chairmen and others have a mistaken idea of what the role of the county organization is as it relates to Selective Service. . . .
> It is the hope of both of us [Hawkins and G. Thomas Eisele] our county leaders will also recognize the problems of being so badly outnumbered as the minority party of the legislature.[12]

The realities of dealing with a Democratic legislature and finding sufficient numbers of competent Republicans made it impossible for Rockefeller to satisfy Republicans who wanted to "fire every state employee, fill every job with a Republican or supporter." John Ward reported that there was a "strong patronage group" within the party that would "still argue that one of his greatest mistakes was that he didn't do so."[13] Following Rockefeller's 1970 defeat, Neal Sox Johnson, Van Rush's successor as executive director of the Republican party, issued a statement to party officials across the state that the election might have turned out differently if Rockefeller's administration had given fewer appointments to "hard-core Democrats." According to Johnson, of the 476 Rockefeller appointees to state boards and commissions as of May 1970, only eighty-six had contributed money to the state Republican party. Johnson's justification for his correlation between these figures and Rockefeller's defeat was that "by appointing more Republicans and independents who might be inclined to go that way, the Party enthusiasm is raised and the base of supporters broadened."[14] Everett Ham agreed that Rockefeller "certainly" should have appointed more Republicans.[15] This is a traditional but simplistic view of the vote-getting process. There were not nearly enough Republicans in the state to elect a governor by themselves. Rockefeller's victories were owed, in large part, to dissatisfied Democrats. Republicans were unwilling to face the reality that Rockefeller's victories in 1966 and 1968 were personal ones and did not indicate widespread shifts of party allegiance within the electorate.

One segment of the electorate that gave an overwhelming percentage of its votes to Rockefeller in 1966 and 1968 was blacks. Republican state chairman Odell Pollard worked hard, in the months following Rockefeller's first inauguration, to transfer that loyalty to the Republican party. In May 1967 Pollard spoke at the thirtieth annual meeting of the Urban League of Greater Little Rock. Pollard pointed out steps the Republicans were taking to increase black participation in the party, including the establishment of a committee on human resources and the inclusion of one or more blacks on all seventy-five CRRCs. While criticizing "big brotherism" and coercion by the federal government, he acknowledged the necessity of federal legislation "to remove certain barriers." Pollard asserted that the Republican party was pledged "by precept and example" to help end racial discrimination.[16]

In the fall of 1967, Pollard issued several "progress reports" on the advancement of blacks in politics. His November report revealed the wishful thinking that existed in his May speech. While he pledged in May to put a black on each CRRC, by November only thirty-five of the state's seventy-five CRRCs included any blacks. Black participation in the Republican party improved in February 1968, when Minnie Pearl Ross was elected to the Republican State Committee by Pulaski County Republicans. In contrast, black Republicans fought hard at the

1972 Republican National Convention for better representation, settling on a compromise under which a black would be
appointed to the executive committee of the Republican National
Committee.[17]

Attempts to move black voters *en masse* into the ranks of
the Republican party were not successful during Rockefeller's
governorship. Rockefeller's huge black vote did not transfer to
other Republican candidates. There were many factors contributing to this vote splitting. Blacks had felt a strong allegiance to the national Democratic party ever since the New
Deal programs of Franklin Roosevelt. Nixon's Southern strategy of conservative Court appointments and moderation in civil
rights enforcement alienated most blacks and increased skepti-
cism toward Southern Republicans. The scarcity of Republicans
in Arkansas sometimes led to lower quality candidates, discour-
aging black and white voters. And it was unusual for any
Arkansas candidate, Republican or Democrat, to be as outspoken as Rockefeller on the civil rights issue.

The 1968 election was a turning point for Arkansas's
Republican party. For the first time since the presidency of
Ulysses S. Grant, Republican administrations sat in both Little
Rock and Washington. Rockefeller had supported his brother
Nelson at the Republican National Convention. According to the
Ripon Forum, the publication of the Ripon Society, a moderate
Republican research organization, Nixon punished Rockefeller
for this transgression by knighting John Paul Hammerschmidt
"as the state's chief dispenser of federal patronage." The journal
reported that "Rockefeller seems to have received short shrift
from certain segments of the GOP, particularly that segment
headquartered in the White House."[18] Rockefeller replied to the
article's report of strained relations between himself and Nixon
by claiming, "Fortunately, the national administration and my
office have been working closely together in ways that the author
was not familiar with." But Rockefeller did not deny that
Hammerschmidt controlled federal patronage in Arkansas.[19]
According to Hammerschmidt, it was "usual and traditional" for
federal patronage to be handled "by a senior elected federal-level
official." He added that "Governor Rockefeller welcomed my

input on state patronage matters, as I did his on the federal level."[20] Marion Burton also asserted that Rockefeller and Hammerschmidt were "very, very close," so patronage decisions were not a problem.[21]

Some Arkansas Republicans were dissatisfied with Rockefeller's allegiances at the national convention. Ulysses Lovell accused Rockefeller of "taking" the Arkansas delegates to the convention and called the governor's favorite-son nomination "a wild eyed tangent to satisfy the vanity of the 'golden toed cowboy.'"[22] But the state committee backed Rockefeller. In his reply to Lovell, Pollard noted that both the state executive committee and the state committee "unanimously passed resolutions" to support the governor as a favorite-son candidate months before Nelson Rockefeller declared his candidacy. Pollard went on to admonish his "old professor" that "if some of the older Republicans in Arkansas would learn to be just a little bit flexible, it would be much easier to elect the national ticket as well as Republican candidates in state races."[23]

The 1968 election was also a turning point for Arkansas's Republican party because of Charles Bernard's unsuccessful campaign for J. William Fulbright's Senate seat. Bernard's bitterness caused him to blame his defeat on Rockefeller, based on the governor's less-than-enthusiastic backing. After Rockefeller's 1970 defeat, Rockefeller and Bernard were on opposite sides of a bitter election fight for the state chairmanship of the Republican party. Bernard emerged victorious over William Kelly, whom Rockefeller actively supported.[24]

In the spring of 1969, Arkansas's Republican State Committee took steps to dispel the image of the party as a one-man operation. In anticipation of the end of Rockefeller's governorship, the party began a fund drive to "relieve" the governor "of some of the finance [sic] burden he has borne for the Party since 1960."[25] In April the party moved its headquarters from the Rockefeller-owned Tower Building to more modest surroundings. The move was symbolic because rent in the new building was higher than what the Republicans paid in the Tower Building. Odell Pollard pointed out, however, that the old rent would have been much higher if Rockefeller had charged what the office space was worth. Pollard also disclosed that Rockefeller was financing a third of the party's 1969 budget and had given more than that in the past. Both Rockefeller and the Republican leadership consistently refused to disclose the exact extent of the governor's financial aid.[26]

In his desire to dispel the Republican party's one-man-rule image, Pollard may have been attempting to quiet divisiveness within the party. No major political party is ever a coalition of totally like-minded people. It was inevitable that Arkansas Republicans would cover a wide spectrum of political ideologies, just as they had many different reasons for becoming Republicans. But Rockefeller was a polarizing force, a concrete symbol around which differing factions could congregate. A political party as weak as Arkansas's Republicans could not afford this polarity, especially after Rockefeller was no longer a candidate. The cost, continued ineffectiveness of the party, was too high.

This conflict between Rockefeller's support and unity within the party was apparent in discussions over recommendations for the federal judge vacancy that G. Thomas Eisele would eventually fill. In addition to Eisele, three other Republicans wanted the job—Odell Pollard, state Circuit Judge Henry Britt, and Ronald May, the state committee's general counsel. When the state executive committee met to vote on their recommendation, several members, including Charles Bernard, tried to convince the committee to send in only one name—Pollard's. One member, Dick Sturgis, pointed out "that a 'no' vote to Tom Eisele . . . would do irreparable damage to our relationship with the Governor."[27] A compromise was reached. All four names were submitted to Attorney General John Mitchell, but they were ranked in order of preference with Pollard first and Eisele second. Concerning the outcome, Young Republican chairperson Judy Petty stated that Van Rush, executive director of the party,

> told me he had talked with the Governor and the Governor was
> very displeased—apparently more so with Odell for pushing his
> recommendation than with the Party as a whole or the Executive
> Committee. Van did mention to me that he had been trying
> to get another installment of the Governor's pledge to the

Party—and that he had made sure he had it before the
Committee met to decide on their recommendation for Federal
Judge.[28]

This account says much about the relationship between
Rockefeller and Arkansas's Republican party. Evidently,
Rockefeller felt that, as governor, he had the right to expect
support of the state committee for his candidate. And the state
committee saw the governor as a big piggy bank.[29]

Stirrings of the discontent that would erupt in the 1970
state chairmanship fight began in October 1969. Dr. Wayne
Babbitt, vice chairman of the state committee, resigned to
accept a federal job. Two persons declared themselves candidates to fill the remainder of his term. One of them was Charles
Bernard. The *Gazette* reported that Bernard attracted "Party
conservatives and elements that are discontented with the control of the Party by Mr. Rockefeller."[30] Bernard won the election and in an interview asserted that the state Republican party
was "making the transition from this Rockefeller image . . .
toward a party that has a broad base."[31] Bernard, also the party's
finance chairman, worked toward that goal by mailing requests
for contributions to thirty thousand Arkansans. In his letter,
Bernard noted that fifteen hundred people were currently contributing to the party and that, while Rockefeller's contributions
were still substantial, "we've got to look beyond the governor's
participation in the Party . . . if we're going to be a realistic and
sound second party we've got to fund ourselves with a broad
base of support."[32]

Neal Sox Johnson touched on this same theme in a March
1970 memo to Rockefeller and other Republican leaders.
Johnson felt that, for the party to grow, more "prestigious and
upstanding citizens" needed to become involved as officers and
members of Republican county committees. This would not
happen, Johnson believed, until county committee positions
were "the most influential offices to hold in the county . . . particularly in regard to the many forms of patronage." In contrast,
Johnson accused both the governor's and state committee's
staffs of preferring "to work with or seek the advice of 'Big Jim'
who is a good Democrat, Independent or so-so Republican who

we consider more intelligent or influential in the county, than
'Little Joe,' who is a nice or naughty Republican county chairman."[33] But Johnson failed to address an important dilemma;
what was best for the growth of the Republican party was not
necessarily what was best for Arkansas government. Johnson's
plan would require a transition period in which admittedly inferior county chairmen would have tremendous influence over
patronage. The plan would also require a Republican governor
for an extended period of time. Rockefeller had only nine more
months in office.

If Republicans were hoping for new, unified leadership to
come from their youth, then Arkansas's Young Republican
League must have made them very nervous. Dissension and controversy surrounded the league's May 1970 convention. A fight
for control erupted between two factions, one led by Tom
Dillard and the other by Richard Drake. Dillard reputedly had
the support of outgoing chairperson Judy Petty and Rockefeller.
Drake alleged that the governor's public relations staff controlled the league. Both factions reportedly established new local
clubs just in time for the convention, with Drake admitting in
the press that he had worked hard to organize new clubs for the
support he would get. After bitter campaigning, Dillard was
elected chairman and Drake co-chairman. Once the voting was
over, but before consideration of the platform, fourteen black
delegates walked out of the convention, claiming "the involvement of blacks in the convention was not legitimate."[34]

The platform, or resolutions, adopted by the Young Republicans caused considerable consternation among state Republican
leaders as well as causing quite a stir in the press. They included
a call for Nixon to drop Spiro Agnew as his running mate in
1972, resolutions on the legalization of marijuana, abortion, and
gambling, and the repeal of both censorship laws and laws prohibiting the free expression of all sexual activities between con-
senting adults.[35]

Neal Sox Johnson, executive director of the state party,
issued a statement disavowing any connection between the resolutions and party leadership. Johnson, however, did not con-

demn the resolutions, stating instead that "a young person has the right to his own opinion."[36] In a letter to a faculty member at Arkansas A&M College, Johnson elaborated:

> We trust that you have observed by now that the "senior" GOP Party leadership does not condone the resolutions recently adopted by the Young Republicans; however, we recognize that we as parents and party leaders must assume a more concerned and positive approach in providing leadership to our youth. . . . As an auxiliary which utilizes the Republican name, the youthful members should recognize and avoid taking extreme positions that might be interpreted as "bad news" in reflecting an unpopular image on the Republican Party or its elected officials and public servants.
>
> . . . We should now devote our attention to closing the obvious "communication gap" that we recently experienced.[37]

Johnson could not afford to spend too much time worrying about the Young Republican League. By May 1970 the state's Republican leadership was consumed with whether or not Rockefeller should seek a third term as governor and what the consequences of his decision would be.

In March 1969 John Ward prepared a memo for Rockefeller outlining the assets and liabilities the governor would face if he decided to seek a third term. There were equal numbers of liabilities and assets listed, but the assets were less tangible. Among the assets were Rockefeller's image as an honest, courageous professional and an underdog in relation to the legislature. Ward also mentioned the governor's professional, experienced campaign organization, his strength in the black community, and the image of his being able to "get something" from Washington. But the liabilities were formidable. They included Rockefeller's narrow victory in 1968, his "inability to make progress with the legislature," weakening support among liberal Democrats who were finding new candidates to support, "waning strength in the Republican Party as the Bernard effort to take over progresses," Rockefeller's promises not to seek more than two terms, his "growing image as an impractical 'dreamer' about state government," and his "insistence on imposing tax burdens on the people." Ward concluded that the Republican party's chances for a 1970 gubernatorial victory were "slimmer than we had hoped for." While Rockefeller was the only candidate with a chance of winning, "even he would have a very difficult time."[38]

Throughout 1969, uncertainty over Rockefeller's plans led to speculation concerning his successor for the Republican nomination. Three men dominated these conversations—Lt. Gov. Maurice "Footsie" Britt, state representative George Nowotny, and Charles Bernard. Britt had planned to seek the governorship when Rockefeller stepped down. Britt considered himself Rockefeller's "heir apparent," recalling years later that Rockefeller "had pledged to me on several occasions that he wanted me to follow him in office, carry through on his remaining legislative program, continue to build a competitive political system, and make Arkansas a legitimate two-party state."[39] Britt made it clear that he would only consider being a candidate if Rockefeller chose not to run, but both Nowotny and Bernard stressed differences between themselves and the incumbent.[40]

The pros and cons of a third-term bid by Rockefeller were debated by the governor's staff and supporters. John Ward's book *The Arkansas Rockefeller* refers to an October 1969 memo prepared by Ward and "some of WR's staff" that, while recognizing the obstacles, concluded that "the best interests of Arkansas and the Republican Party would be served if you do seek a third term."[41] But Ward also acknowledged that a rift had developed within the governor's staff over the advisability of his running again.[42] On April 1, 1970, an opposing group of Rockefeller's associates met. The result was a memo to the governor that observed that Rockefeller's standing was "the lowest it had ever been in previous campaigns." Regarding a third term, the group concluded that while "WR is the only Republican candidate who has an opportunity to win. . . . It seemed to be a consensus that if the Governor's chances of winning a third term were remote, they would prefer he step out undefeated rather than be defeated in a third-term race."[43]

On April 9 Rockefeller sent a letter to all elected Republicans and county GOP officers in the state. The letter began "I have not decided whether to seek a third term," but went on to list all the justifications for seeking one. It was obviously an

attempt to prepare Republicans for the announcement that
Rockefeller would run again, breaking his promise to serve only
two terms. He continued:

> It is painful to admit an error, and reverse oneself, but my com-
> mitment to the Republican Party and to my own convictions are
> more important than my one statement. . . .
>
> Yes, we have made great progress, but we have not yet disman-
> tled the Old Guard! I didn't realize how touchy it would be to
> force out the stagnant and self-serving ideas and philosophies and
> install new blood, new faces and new ideas. . . .
>
> I have been honored that your support has enabled me to help
> in getting the two-party system underway. I hope I can continue
> to have the benefit of your advice and counsel, as well as your
> support in making this important decision.[44]

Though this letter reads as if written by a candidate,
Rockefeller still did not make any public announcements.
Charles Bernard did, however, responding to Rockefeller's letter by telling the press that "the state Republican Party would
be strengthened if Mr. Rockefeller bowed out of the race." As
for his own political ambitions, Bernard claimed that it was
"very doubtful" he would run for governor, whether Rockefeller
entered the race or not.[45] Apparently Bernard had decided to
concentrate on winning the state chairmanship instead.

On June 9 Rockefeller finally announced that he would seek
a third term. His statement explained his reasons for breaking his
two-term promise: "To quit now, I know in my heart, would
impose on me a feeling of guilt all of the rest of my days."[46]
There was not much surprise over Rockefeller's announcement.
The previous December, Karr Shannon, a not-too-sympathetic
columnist for the *Arkansas Democrat*, had speculated that
Rockefeller would run and the real reason behind the decision
would be the insecurity of the two-party system and the governor's desire to preserve what Shannon called the "Rockefeller
Republican Party."[47] But Robert Faulkner, Rockefeller's executive
secretary, said the primary reason for the third-term bid was
Orval Faubus's announcement that he would run. Faulkner told
Rockefeller that Faubus had entered the race. The governor's
response was: "Well that's it. I can't hand it back to him."
Faulkner's opinion was that "without any question, if Faubus

would not have run, [Rockefeller] wouldn't have run."[48] Certainly, Rockefeller was justified in his fear that his reform programs would die if Faubus won the election. And no other Republican had a chance of beating the former governor.

Both Republican and Democratic organizations were fully engaged in the 1970 election by the time Rockefeller made his formal announcement. The race started early on the Democratic side because of uncertainty over who the candidate would be. The field was wide open. Ward's March 1969 memo listed ten possibilities, noting "it is highly likely that one of them will be the nominee."[49] Only three of the ten—Attorney General Joe Purcell, House Speaker Hayes McClerkin, and Bill Wells, the 1968 Democratic candidate for lieutenant governor—ran in the August 1970 Democratic primary, and none of them made it to the runoff election.

By March 1970 two men with vastly different backgrounds had entered the Democratic race for governor. One was ex-governor Orval Faubus and the other was Dale Bumpers, a political unknown, a lawyer whose only office-holding experience was on the Charleston, Arkansas, school board. Rockefeller's staff expected Faubus to be the Democratic nominee. Ward wrote, "It seemed obvious that Faubus was in the Democratic driver's seat."[50] Rockefeller's public appearances prior to the Democratic primary were aimed at comparing his achievements with those of the "previous administration."[51]

The primary election was held on August 25. In addition to Purcell, McClerkin, Wells, Faubus, and Bumpers, three others—James Malone, Robert Compton, and William Cheek—also competed for the Democratic nomination. Faubus led with 156,578 votes, almost twice as many as his closest competitor, but he did not win a majority, thus necessitating a runoff election. Dale Bumpers narrowly won the right to oppose Faubus in the runoff, garnering 85,909 votes, just 4,343 more than the third-place candidate, Joe Purcell. Faubus's commanding lead was deceiving as it represented only 35 percent of the total vote.[52]

During the two weeks prior to the runoff, both Bumpers and Faubus charged that Rockefeller had put the other in the race on the presumption that the governor wanted the most "beatable" candidate as his opponent. In the September 8 runoff, Bumpers easily defeated Faubus, receiving 58.7 percent of the vote to Faubus's 41.3 percent. Both Purcell and McClerkin, who had come in third and fourth in the primary, endorsed Bumpers, and he received slightly more votes than he and all six of Faubus's opponents combined had received in the primaries.[53] The *New York Times*, calling the vote a "bad day for nonsense," noted: "When Orval Faubus retired in 1966 after six terms as Governor of Arkansas, most Americans were more than content to see and hear the last of him, but there was no way of telling for certain whether his fellow Arkansans shared that view. On Tuesday evening he found out that they do."[54]

As early as the fall of 1969, the press speculated on Democratic plans to defeat Rockefeller in the Republican primary. Jim Johnson, Rockefeller's 1966 segregationist Democratic opponent, announced in October that he was considering running against the governor in the primary, counting on low Republican voter turnout (compared to Johnson's expected bloc vote) to win. Republican and Democratic primaries were held simultaneously, but at different locations. Arkansas voters were free to vote in either primary, but not both. Most voters cast ballots in the far more influential Democratic primary. A candidate who could draw on a large bloc vote could therefore hope to unseat Rockefeller in the primary while most of his Democratic supporters were voting elsewhere. In the 1968 primaries, the Democrats had attracted approximately 475,000 voters, the Republicans fewer than 28,000. In October 1969 Rev. R. J. Hampton also announced that he was considering opposing Rockefeller in the Republican primary. Hampton, a black who switched parties in late 1968, criticized the governor for not hiring more blacks in his private enterprises. Johnson did not formally enter the primary race, but Hampton did, the first black gubernatorial candidate in Arkansas since 1920, amid speculation that he was planted there by Faubus supporters. If Hampton could draw black voters away from the Democratic primary and into the Republican, Faubus's chances of winning would presumably increase significantly. Hampton vigorously denied these charges but did admit receiving support from Jess P. Odom, the owner of the amusement park Dogpatch U.S.A., where Faubus had been employed for the last four years. Odom was also one of Faubus's major backers.[55]

Republican state Rep. George Nowotny, Jr., who had announced his intention to seek the Republican nomination for governor on March 26, 1970, reversed that decision on June 10. But Hampton was not Rockefeller's only primary opponent. Two other men entered the race: Lester Gibbs, a state Revenue Department employee who resigned his job in order to run, and James "Uncle Mac" MacKrell. Gibbs's campaign centered on two themes, taxes and prisons. Tax increases were not needed, Gibbs claimed, and were pushed by Rockefeller so that the governor could "buy up all the land in public sales."[56] On the subject of prisons, Gibbs advocated reinstating corporal punishment. MacKrell's campaign focused on what he labeled Rockefeller's abuse of the governor's emergency fund.[57]

The *Gazette* noted that none of Rockefeller's three Republican opponents were "worth serious consideration." The primary results verified this observation. Rockefeller received an overwhelming 58,197 votes compared to 829 for Hampton, 681 for MacKrell, and 423 for Gibbs. The primary vote total of 60,130 was more than twice the Republican primary vote in 1968, indicating that Rockefeller's opponents did draw voters over to the Republican primary, but the crossovers voted for the governor. Hampton in particular did not receive the bloc vote he hoped for. Most blacks apparently followed advice such as that given by a Blytheville black leader, Emmanual Lofton, who had advised Mississippi County blacks to vote for local candidates in the Democratic primary. Hampton received six votes in that county.[58]

The GOP candidate for lieutenant governor was Sterling Cockrill, Jr., who became a Republican in April 1970. Cockrill had served in the state house of representatives since 1957 and was one of the legislature's leaders, having served as speaker in 1967 and majority leader in 1969. These leadership positions highlighted philosophical differences between Cockrill and Old Guard Democrats. As Cockrill later recalled, "Being a supporter of Rockefeller, being from Pulaski County, being from Little Rock which the rest of the state doesn't really appreciate anyway and that's putting it kindly, I found I had a lot of problems in a leadership role that I didn't have when I was not a leader."[59] Cockrill received considerable criticism from fellow Democrats during the 1969 legislative session for his opposition to several bills supported by county Democratic leaders.

Unlike the party switches by Rockefeller's 1970 primary opponents, Cockrill had the enthusiastic backing of Rockefeller. John Ward and G. Thomas Eisele had approached Cockrill about switching parties. Cockrill later acknowledged that he was "real flattered" by this and that ego played a part in his decision. Before deciding, he met with Rockefeller, who promised Cockrill an active role as lieutenant governor and the role of "Republican heir apparent to the governorship" in 1972.[60] Cockrill's explanation to the press was that he wanted Arkansas's two-party system to continue, a desire that played no small part in his decision. Also in April, Maurice "Footsie" Britt announced that he would not seek reelection, opening the way for Cockrill to run for the number two slot. According to Britt, he did not run for a third term as lieutenant governor because "I knew deep down in my heart and from my exposure to the convictions of people not associated with government that he [Rockefeller] could not possibly win. I not only did not want to serve a third term myself, I likewise felt that I would go down in defeat with him if I did run again for that office." Britt also recalled that when he heard Cockrill would be the candidate, he was "elated."[61]

Cockrill announced for the position on June 13. He faced opposition in the primary from Gerald Williams, MacKrell's running mate. Cockrill easily defeated Williams, 49,869 to 6,598. Considering that Williams did not actively campaign, and MacKrell received only 681 votes, Williams's relatively large vote must be attributed to the reluctance of some Republicans to accept Cockrill.[62]

The only other constitutional office the Republicans filed for was secretary of state. They did not have a candidate for attorney general. All three Democratic congressmen were unopposed. The Republican party concentrated instead on the legislature, fielding fifty-four candidates, forty-three in house races and eleven in the senate. Five of the candidates were black. The

rationale behind concentrating on legislative races was to build
the party's strength in the legislature in order to ease the passage
of Republican measures. Neal Sox Johnson predicted that
Republicans would win in at least twenty of the fifty-four races.[63]

When Rockefeller entered the race for a third term, it was
with the knowledge that winning would be difficult. The governor's approval rating in April 1970 was the lowest of his two
terms—39 percent in contrast to a 50 percent approval rating in
December 1969. The pollster attributed the decline to the dissension in the unproductive March 1970 special session of the
legislature. The governor's popularity among blacks had
dropped to 71 percent. When Dale Bumpers, a Democrat with
no ties to the Faubus machine, became his Democratic opponent, Rockefeller's chances of winning dropped even further. A
post-runoff election poll showed Bumpers leading Rockefeller 70
to 20 percent with the remaining 10 percent undecided. The
pollster noted, "It seems to me that the governor is faced with
the most difficult candidate so far."[64]

This declining popularity could be attributed to a number
of factors. One explanation was Rockefeller's inability to get his
programs passed through the legislature. Each successive legislative session produced less significant legislation than the last,
culminating in the disastrous March 1970 special session. The
people of Arkansas were tired of this. It appeared that only a
Democratic governor would be able to work with the legislature.

Another factor in Rockefeller's declining popularity was
his apparent shift toward conservatism. The governor's retreat
on the busing issue was a prime example. Through January 1970
Rockefeller called the busing of students to achieve integration
"useful" if used with discretion. But a month later he claimed
that he had not and was not recommending busing.

The governor's appearance of growing conservatism was
enhanced by the controversy over the road leading to the Christ
of the Ozarks statue, a major tourist attraction at Eureka Springs
built by the right-wing, anti-Semitic Gerald L. K. Smith. In late
1969 the Ozarks Regional Commission announced that some
$226,000 in federal and state funds would be used to pave the
road. Rockefeller, a member of the four-state commission, sup-

ported the project, but opposition to the road was intense. In a letter to the *Arkansas Gazette*, the governor defended his position on the basis that the road was a postal route and that the taxpayers who visited Smith's attractions (one million people in 1968 and two million were estimated in 1970) "are entitled to have that money applied to improvement and maintenance of the roads which they drive, regardless of whether I or any other government official agrees with where they're going."[65] An American Civil Liberties Union investigation disclosed that the route of the new road did not go near three of the seven houses on the postal route the road supposedly covered, and that the new section of road would not only improve access to the statue, but divert traffic and noise from Smith's nearby Passion Play.[66] In June 1970 federal Secretary of Transportation John A. Volpe canceled approval of the $188,000 in federal funds slated for the project, ruling that construction of the road could not be justified. But even after this, Rockefeller continued to defend his support for the road.[67]

A December 1969 *Gazette* article commented on Rockefeller's "drift to the right," speculating that the governor, if he ran for a third term, would probably try to "associate himself more strongly with the conservatism of the national administration." The *Gazette* pointed to the Smith road—plus Rockefeller's increasing association with Republican conservatives such as Ronald Reagan, Spiro Agnew, and John Mitchell—as evidence of this "drift." The paper warned, however, that "it is not at all certain that the issues will produce a net gain for the governor politically."[68] John Ward stated that actions such as these were attempts by Rockefeller to appease conservative elements in Arkansas's Republican party and thus strengthen the party.[69] But in hindsight, the *Gazette* was correct. Rockefeller received no net gain from these actions. Had he run against a Jim Johnson or someone else equally inconceivable to white liberals and blacks, the conservative stance may have broadened his electoral base. But against Dale Bumpers, who had no ties to the Faubus machine, that approach drove Rockefeller's largest blocs of voters, urban liberal Democrats and blacks, to vote for the governor's opponent.

Other factors relating to the governor's declining popularity concerned his image. Staff problems continued, stemming
from the fact that Rockefeller was, as John Ward claimed, a "terrible" administrator.[70] The governor's image as a heavy drinker
continued and was a source of concern to his campaign staff,
who worked hard to keep the campaigns "dry."[71] Rockefeller also
drew increasing criticism during his second term for not being in
Little Rock enough. One "key Republican appointee" was
reported as saying in December 1969: "The man [Rockefeller] is
never around. I don't know what he's doing and he doesn't know
what I'm doing."[72] Complaints such as these prompted his staff
to compile lists of trips the governor had made, and to issue
justifications for each trip.[73]

The impact of Rockefeller's declining popularity was increased
because Bumpers did not provide the opportunity for traditional
attacks on the conservative Democratic machine. The state Democratic convention and platform indicated the extent of Bumpers'
control over the party. The convention elected Bumpers' choice
for state chairman, Joe Purcell, as well as many of his choices for
state committeemen. The platform reflected Bumpers' stand on
the issues. It included some items that Rockefeller had tried
unsuccessfully to get through the legislature, such as teacher
tenure, free high-school textbooks, state support of kindergartens, repeal of fair-trade liquor laws, and additional revenues.
In addition, the platform called for a "favorable vote" on the new
constitution, statewide use of voting machines, a code-of-ethics
bill, and opposition to casino gambling. Regarding prisons, the
platform endorsed rehabilitation, but emphasized that "prisoners
should be required to work, but should not be abused." A more
effective parole system was needed "and not abused by the executive." The platform "opposed busing to achieve racial balance in
public schools."[74]

The Republicans met two weeks after the Democrats. Their
platform was very similar to their opponents', and reflected
Rockefeller's unfulfilled goals. The planks on education were
almost identical. The Republicans called for reorganization of the
state government and higher salaries for state employees. They

advocated a "carefully drawn program of new revenues through tax reform." Regarding the prisons, the platform called for increased education and training, noting, "Prevention of crime, not profit through criminal labor, should be the goal of our prisons." The Republicans, like the Democrats, opposed busing. And they "wholeheartedly endorsed" the proposed new state constitution.[75] In his speech to the convention, Rockefeller attempted to tie Bumpers to Faubus, "Mutt" Jones, and the Democratic "Old Guard." While this was stretching credibility, it was the only attack Rockefeller could make on a candidate whose program was remarkably similar to his own.[76]

The 1970 campaign was relatively insipid. There were few issues over which the candidates disagreed. The *Gazette* noted that Rockefeller and Bumpers were "not too far apart in philosophy," and that this had "obviously . . . complicated the campaign plans of both men."[77] One segment of the voting public that did see a significant difference between the two candidates was labor. J. Bill Becker, president of the Arkansas AFL-CIO, had been critical throughout Rockefeller's administration of the governor's support of the state "right-to-work" law. The political branch of the AFL-CIO, the Committee on Political Education (COPE), endorsed Dale Bumpers on October 10. Even a Rockefeller-affiliated labor newspaper refused to endorse the incumbent. The *Arkansas Union Labor Bulletin* was published by Robert E. Fisher, an aide of Rockefeller's. But the paper did not endorse either candidate for governor.[78]

In Rockefeller's September 19 speech opening the campaign, he called for a debate between himself, Bumpers, and Walter Carruth, the gubernatorial candidate of the American Independent party. On September 29 Rockefeller repeated his debate challenge to Bumpers in a letter. On October 5 "Footsie" Britt, the governor's campaign manager, met with representatives of both Bumpers and Carruth to decide on a format "if and when" a debate took place. Bumpers did not "accept the challenge" to debate until October 28, by which time it was technically impossible for the television stations to arrange one before the election. It was to Bumpers' advantage not to debate, placing himself in a situation where he would be forced to be more specific concerning his goals. Also, since he was leading in the polls, Bumpers had the most to lose.[79]

Rockefeller's campaign for reelection suffered a serious setback early in the race, on October 8, when Vice Pres. Spiro Agnew, at the governor's request, spoke in Hot Springs. Agnew's speech was an attack against Sen. J. William Fulbright, Fulbright's "radiclib" (radical liberal) friends, the *Arkansas Gazette*, eastern newspapers, university faculties, and black militants. The *New York Times* reported on Agnew's speech that while the vice president "undoubtedly" inspired some conservative whites to vote for Rockefeller, Agnew "seriously embarrassed Mr. Rockefeller's black and white liberal workers."[80] The *Gazette* observed: "There are two Winthrop Rockefellers campaigning for governor, it seems. One of them brought in Spiro Agnew. . . . The other went on television Monday night with a dignified and reasoned resume of his case for re-election."[81] Newspaper reports were uncertain as to the circumstances regarding Agnew's visit, with some of Rockefeller's aides saying Agnew was invited, while others claimed his visit was at the request of the Nixon administration. John Ward claimed that Agnew was invited by the governor "at the insistence of Jermstad [Glen Jermstad, a Republican party stalwart] and over the objections of other members of the governor's staff." Ward also reported that Rockefeller knew the visit would "alienate some Negro voters."[82] Like other attempts to pacify and appeal to conservative Republicans, Agnew's visit appears to have hurt the governor more than it helped.

At the time of Agnew's visit, Rockefeller's campaign had already been damaged by another administration official—Atty. Gen. John Mitchell. Mitchell stated in *Women's Wear Daily* that Rockefeller could defeat Bumpers "by buying the votes of the far left or the hard right or the black vote." Mitchell denied the quote, but the damage had been done. Rockefeller's "excessive campaign spending" was a major theme of Bumpers' speeches.[83]

Rockefeller's "unprecedented spending" was one reason the *Gazette* gave when it endorsed Bumpers for governor. Another reason was Rockefeller's inability to pass his program through the legislature, because of his Republicanism and also because of a "certain innate inability in legislative relationships." The paper, which had endorsed Rockefeller in his previous races, noted, "Arkansas is the most Democratic of states by tradition and, with Dale Bumpers as nominee, all of us who are Democrats by instinct and by persuasion have the welcome opportunity for a grand homecoming."[84] The *Democrat* endorsed Rockefeller, wanting to give him a chance to fulfill his goals, but criticized the governor for his massive campaign expenditures.[85]

Rockefeller's October 6 poll showed that Bumpers, if the election were held then, would win with about 60 percent of the vote. A few days later, Bumpers' majority was not quite as heavy, but he was still winning 56 percent to 30 percent. The final poll, taken on October 31, concluded, "The overall guess is that Rockefeller will be elected." The figures showed Bumpers still leading 51 percent to 45 percent, but observed that Bumpers was losing ground and "may very probably keep losing through Tuesday's election."[86]

Rockefeller's pollster was far off the mark. Bumpers not only won, he did so overwhelmingly, 375,648 votes to Rockefeller's 197,418. Carruth received 36,132 votes. Sterling Cockrill lost his race for lieutenant governor, but by a slimmer margin, 232,429 to his Democratic opponent's 334,379 votes. The Republican effort to win seats in the legislature was a disaster; two of the four Republican incumbents in the house were defeated, and no new Republicans were elected to either branch of the General Assembly.[87]

An internal memo listing factors that contributed to Rockefeller's defeat included the people's knowledge of the governor's desire to raise taxes, the pre-election prison revolt, involvement of Arkansas's congressional delegation in Bumpers' campaign, the visit of Spiro Agnew, controversy between Rockefeller and the legislature, Bumpers' personality, and white backlash to Rockefeller's civil rights activities.[88] The memo did not mention the loss of black votes to Bumpers resulting from Rockefeller's attempts to get white conservative votes. The extent of the loss of black votes is debated. One set of statistics showed that Rockefeller retained 88 percent of the black vote,[89] while another showed that among Pulaski County blacks, Rockefeller's vote percentage dropped to 46 percent in 1970.[90] The single largest factor in Rockefeller's loss was the "white moderate's return to the Democratic party."[91] Rockefeller owed his victories in 1966 and 1968 largely to urban liberal Democrats who had tired of the Democratic "Old Guard" machine. These voters, in 1970, saw Bumpers as a fresh face and the better alternative.

Rockefeller's loss was part of a national trend. In the 1970 elections, the Democrats gained a majority of the nation's governorships for the first time since 1964. In the eleven states of the former Confederacy, Republican governors were reduced from four to two. In addition to Arkansas, Republican gubernatorial candidates lost in Georgia, Florida, and South Carolina. Florida's defeated Republican, Claude R. Kirk, Jr., was the incumbent. Only in Tennessee was a Republican elected governor. In Alabama, Democrat George Wallace ran unopposed. Nationwide, eleven of the thirty-five gubernatorial races were won by Republicans, all but two of them by incumbents, including Nelson Rockefeller in New York.[92]

In addition to striking a blow against Nixon's Southern strategy, Bumpers' victory was part of another Southern trend— a turn to fresh, new faces. Relative unknowns defeated die-hard segregationists. In addition to Bumpers' defeat of Faubus, Jimmy Carter defeated former governor Carl Sanders in Georgia in the Democratic primary, and in Florida, conservative Republican Claude Kirk lost in the general election.[93]

In the 1970 election, Arkansans also rejected a new state constitution. The holding of a constitutional convention had been approved by the voters in 1968, but by a slim margin, 227,429 votes to 214,432. Rockefeller had pushed hard for the convention, hoping to replace the state's reactionary 1874 constitution. The Seventh Arkansas Constitutional Convention convened on May 27, 1969, and by August 21 had a first draft ready for public examination. The convention met again from January 12, 1970, until February 10 to compose the final document. On February 10 the hundred delegates voted. Ninety-eight approved the document, with one negative vote and one abstention.[94]

In a speech to the convention delegates, Rockefeller asked that they, in their deliberations, not "overemphasize the current, the temporary, or the transitory."[95] For the most part, the convention delegates adhered to this advice. However, the new constitution contained Arkansas's right-to-work law, causing organized labor to oppose its passage. Other "current" issues included in the new constitution were a prohibition against the licensing of firearms, a ten-year prohibition on raising property tax assessments above 20 percent, and a prohibition on all gambling except pari-mutuel wagering on horse racing at Hot Springs and on greyhound racing at West Memphis. The proposed constitution did address many weaknesses in the 1874 constitution, permitting annual sessions of the General Assembly, requiring a three-fifths vote to override a gubernatorial veto instead of a simple majority, streamlining the executive branch, providing for four-year terms for constitutional officers, and eliminating salary ceilings for many positions. Tax increases would be only slightly easier to obtain. The new constitution called for a three-fifths majority vote on all tax measures rather than a three-fourths vote on some and a simple majority on others.[96]

The 1970 constitution was rejected by the voters, 301,195 to 223,334. This was in spite of strong endorsements by many of the state's newspapers and the efforts of a bipartisan committee, Arkansans for the Constitution of 1970, led by Republican "Footsie" Britt and former Democratic governor Sid McMath. The *Democrat* called the constitution's defeat a "backward step" and "more of a bitter disappointment than a surprise."[97] There were a number of factors contributing to the defeat. One was public opinion, which ranged from apathy to fear of anything new to ignorance of the contents of the new constitution. Many people feared higher taxes would result. Dale Bumpers' support for the new constitution was less than enthusiastic. Voting on the document in a general election, rather than in a special one, took much-needed attention away from the constitution. Approximately one hundred thousand people who voted in the governor's race did not bother to vote for or against the document. McMath wrote Rockefeller shortly after the election that "the issue is not dead," but it was.[98]

    Following the election, Rockefeller had one last significant contribution to make to the state. On December 29, 1970, two weeks before he would leave office, he commuted the death sentences of all fifteen men awaiting execution in Arkansas. During Orval Faubus's twelve years as governor, sixteen men had died in Arkansas's electric chair, but shortly after taking office in 1967, Rockefeller had imposed a moratorium on executions, and the electric chair was dismantled.

    On November 17, 1970, Rockefeller received a letter from Rev. J. F. Cooley, the Forrest City civil rights activist who was now dean of men at North Little Rock's Shorter College. Cooley reported that "after the election of November 3, the inmates on death row became (and still are) greatly disturbed. They feel their lives are finished with your going out of office." Cooley asked Rockefeller to consider commuting the sentences.[99] Rockefeller was already doing so. When he announced the commutations at a news conference, the governor gave as his rationale: "What earthly mortal has the omnipotence to say who among us shall live and who shall die? I do not. . . . I cannot and will not turn my back on life-long Christian teachings and beliefs, merely to let history run out its course on a fallible and failing theory of punitive justice."[100]

    Of the fifteen men whose sentences Rockefeller commuted, eleven were black. Six blacks were on death row for rape. The other blacks and the four whites had been convicted of murder. Rockefeller later further commuted two of the sentences from life imprisonment to forty-eight years.[101]

    Reaction to Rockefeller's announcement was understandably mixed. Rockefeller's staff received 324 letters and telegrams in favor of the commutations, and only seventy-three opposing them. But condemnation of Rockefeller's action was strong from prosecutors, circuit judges, and legislators. One prosecutor, a Republican appointed by Rockefeller to fill an unexpired term, wrote the governor: "I am greatly disturbed by the final action you took yesterday. . . . My personal standards of morality or your personal standards of morality concerning capital punishment are immaterial—we are public officials who have sworn to obey the duly enacted laws of the state."[102]

After leaving office, Rockefeller published an article justifying the use of executive clemency. He wrote in part:

> The truth is, in this country we have never established the use of executive clemency in capital cases for its own rightful consideration. . . .
>
> It is incomprehensible that the "cruel and unusual" aspect of the death penalty in our system of dealing with capital offenders can be denied. . . .
>
> Historically, the exercise of executive clemency has provided a form of moral leadership that has brought about substantive changes in the law. . . .
>
> . . . essential at our moment in history is a greatly broadened understanding and acceptance of the fact that executive clemency, far from being an extra legal device, is an intricate and necessary part of a fair and impartial system of justice.[103]

Regarding the commutations, Dale Bumpers stated: "I know he acted in accordance with his personal philosophy. I am sure he had sufficient information to justify in his own mind the action that he took."[104] Rockefeller's assertion that executive clemency provided moral leadership was borne out by the fact that no Arkansas governor after Rockefeller executed anyone until June 1990. Arkansas was one of only two Southern states to forego executions after the Supreme Court reinstated the death penalty in 1976. A 1987 *Gazette* article cited Rockefeller's commutations as a major factor, noting that his action "was a hard act to follow for the three governors who came after him—men of compassion and higher political ambitions who didn't want to preside over the first legal execution since 1964."[105]

As Rockefeller's term as governor drew to a close, he attempted to ensure that the Republican party would remain strong and ideologically moderate. The fight to replace Odell Pollard as state chairman of the party began in July 1970, with

Charles Bernard, William T. Kelly, and Everett Ham all running for the position. Rockefeller announced in August that he supported Kelly, the Pulaski County GOP chairman, for the position. Kelly was also chairman of the Governor's Council on Human Resources and considered the most liberal of the three candidates. The chairmanship election was originally scheduled for the state convention in October but was postponed until after the general election.[106]

Shortly after Rockefeller's defeat, a movement to draft him for the state chairmanship began. The campaign was led by a Republican businessman, Cass Hough. Rockefeller originally announced that while he would not actually seek the position, he would accept it if offered to him by acclamation. But on November 18 Rockefeller announced that he did not want the position, stating, "I believe I can better serve Arkansas in other ways and as National Committeeman." Rockefeller also reaffirmed his support for Kelly.[107]

Charles Bernard was elected state chairman by an overwhelming margin on November 21, 1970. The vote was 137 for Bernard, 28 for Kelly, and 27 for Ham. In the next round, Ham won the vice-chairmanship. According to John Ward, Rockefeller's "aides felt like Bernard and the party had kicked Rockefeller's teeth in."[108] The *Gazette* editorialized that, under Bernard, "it is hard to imagine [the state GOP] continuing along the same philosophic path that Winthrop Rockefeller has led it." The paper went on to speculate that "the liberalism of recent years may on hindsight be an aberration that traditional Republicans tolerated. Given the choice, as the governor's defeat in the general election furnished, they returned to their natural leanings."[109] Almost twenty years later, Robert Faulkner echoed this opinion. Faulkner said of Bernard's election, "A lot of them [Republicans] couldn't wait to throw out the Rockefeller influence and pick their own, more conservative, traditional Republican."[110]

Rockefeller retained his post as Arkansas's national committeeman until his death. But with Bernard as state chairman, Rockefeller's contributions to the party dropped dramatically.

John Ward suggested this in a November 24 memo, "I feel very strongly that you should NOT participate financially in the party under Charles Bernard to the extent that you have done in the past several years." His rationale was that "the party needs to revert to whatever it will be without your help."[111]

In September 1971 Charles Bernard made the mistake of announcing that the Republicans would probably not oppose Bumpers' reelection in 1972. The Arkansas GOP was a deeply troubled party, without even an appearance of cohesiveness. A Republican did oppose Bumpers—Len Blaylock, Rockefeller's welfare commissioner. The number of Republican legislative candidates in 1972 was half the number that had run in 1970. Rockefeller's only involvement in the campaign was to attend the national convention in Miami. By the fall of 1972, his health problems prevented any active campaigning. In the 1972 election, Nixon won a landslide in Arkansas, the first Republican presidential candidate to win the state since Reconstruction. But GOP state and local candidates met little success. John Paul Hammerschmidt was reelected, but Republican representation in the state legislature dropped to only two. Bumpers defeated Blaylock by more than three hundred thousand votes. More than a decade after Rockefeller first involved himself in the struggle to build a two-party system in Arkansas, it was still far from a reality.[112]

After his defeat, Rockefeller returned to Winrock Farms. In February 1971 he and his wife Jeannette separated. They divorced on April 30. By all accounts, the divorce was amicable; the two had simply grown apart. Shortly after the separation, Rockefeller's son, Winthrop Paul, married, and he and his wife came to Winrock to live.[113]

In July 1971 Rockefeller hosted a meeting at Winrock attended by five former Republican governors—Dewey Bartlett of Oklahoma, David F. Cargo of New Mexico, Frank Farrar of South Dakota, Harold LeVander of Minnesota, and Raymond P. Shafer of Pennsylvania. The purpose of the meeting was to discuss what contributions they could still make in public service.

In an interview with the press, Rockefeller made it clear that he was not running for any office, but that the United States wasted the talents and training of its former governors.[114]

Rockefeller had little time to put his talent and experience to use. In September 1972 a small cyst was removed from his armpit and a biopsy showed it was malignant. Rockefeller flew to New York for exploratory surgery, which revealed that the cancer had spread throughout his body and was inoperable. He underwent chemotherapy, but to no avail. In February 1973 he flew to his home in Palm Springs to escape the cold weather and the well-wishers. He died in the Desert Hospital in Palm Springs on February 22.[115]

A memorial service was held on Petit Jean Mountain on March 4, attended by approximately three thousand people, including Rockefeller's four brothers, his two ex-wives, and Vice Pres. Spiro Agnew. But the wide variety of Arkansans present showed how much respect he had commanded in the state. Dale Bumpers was there, as were former governors Orval Faubus and Sid McMath. One of the eulogies was delivered by William L. "Sonny" Walker, the first black man to head a state agency in Arkansas. All the eulogists concentrated on Rockefeller's desire to see racial equality. Walker, who was by then regional director of the Office of Economic Opportunity in Atlanta, told the assembled crowd that it took Rockefeller "to lead Arkansans to the constitutional and religious tenents [sic] that all men are equal and should love one another."[116]

EIGHT

In Perspective

On June 20, 1964, upon the opening of headquarters for his first unsuccessful gubernatorial campaign, Winthrop Rockefeller issued a sixteen-point "Statement of Beliefs." This manifesto was reissued when he ran again in 1966 and might serve as a foundation for evaluating his accomplishments. In summary form, the sixteen points were:

1. That Rockefeller would not, "under any circumstances," serve more than two terms.

2. That he would work to eliminate election frauds and abuses.

3. That he would "make a careful study of our entire educational system" and implement the reforms recommended by the study.

4. That he would eliminate illegal gambling and the illegal sale of liquor in Hot Springs. "I am morally opposed to organized gambling, and therefore would not support its legalization."

5. That, in a vague reference to civil rights, he believed that "human relations problems" should be solved on the local level "by voluntary action through faith, integrity, understanding and good will rather than through litigation and legislation."

6. That he would institute "businesslike accounting and reporting procedures" in state government.

7. That he would oppose the exertion of political pressure on state employees.

8. That he would strive to establish a two-party system.

9. That he would support health and welfare programs to assist the sick, handicapped, and elderly.

10. That he would establish rehabilitation programs in the prisons. "We must make the protection of society and the salvaging of human lives the chief goals of our penal system."

11. That he would help develop and support "cultural and intellectual activities."

12. That he would strive to "conserve and manage" the state's natural resources.

13. That he believed that "all relationships between private citizens and business on the one hand, and state government on the other, should be cordial, above-board and fair."

14. That he favored government closest to the people. "I believe in States Rights, and that such rights can best be preserved and protected through the exercise of States Responsibilities."

15. That he held it to be the responsibility of the state "to ensure the creation of full and rewarding jobs for all."

16. That it was his conviction that only "positive leadership and broad vision in these changing times can move Arkansas into an era of unprecedented economic and cultural growth."[1]

Obviously, this "Statement of Beliefs" was not simply Rockefeller's goals for the state, but was also a campaign document written with an election in mind and, as such, was meant to win support from all sectors of the voting public. But the goals are justified and can serve as a basis for evaluation.

Rockefeller achieved only limited success in his desired political reforms. To curb election frauds and abuses, he and the Republican party bankrolled forty-seven lawsuits challenging election results in various Arkansas counties, and every suit was eventually upheld by the state supreme court.[2] Although his "little Hatch Act," freeing state employees from much political pressure, failed to pass, his new Department of Administration, combining the Purchasing Department and the Comptroller's Office, did streamline accounting procedures in government offices. His Freedom of Information Act, mandating public access to state records, helped assure that relations between state government and the public were "above-board and fair." But the governor's pledge to seek no more than two terms was probably most unfortunate. After Governor Faubus's six terms, it assured the voters that he was not interested in establishing a political dynasty, but it also probably relegated him to lame-duck status during his final two years and gave his opponents an important campaign issue in 1970 when he eventually changed his mind.

Conservation had been a long-term interest of the Rockefeller family, and, accordingly, the governor promised in his "Statement of Beliefs" to "conserve and manage" the state's natural resources. Before and after his election, he enlisted the services of a groundwater biologist, Leslie E. Mack, as an advisor. Mack served as Rockefeller's representative "at any and all meetings involving the State of Arkansas regarding water resources," indicating the governor's concern.[3] Rockefeller also helped support the establishment of the Buffalo River as a national park.[4]

Another promise that the governor fulfilled was his veto of a bill to legalize gambling in Hot Springs and his crackdown on illegal gambling there. The problem of illegal liquor sales ended with passage of a Rockefeller-backed mixed-drink law, permitting the sale of mixed drinks in those areas where it was approved by the voters.

Economic reform was another part of the Rockefeller agenda. From 1955 until 1964, Rockefeller served as chairman of the Arkansas Industrial Development Commission, recruiting new industry to the state. As governor, he worked "to ensure the creation of full and rewarding jobs for all" by obtaining passage of Arkansas's first minimum wage law.

Many of Rockefeller's campaign promises concerned social reforms, and these concerns flowed in part from his lifelong predilection for helping those less fortunate than himself. As his legal advisor, G. Thomas Eisele, explained:

> Those are some marks of the degree of your civilization; how you treat people who are in prison, how you treat the mentally ill, how you treat the poor and neglected. I think Win was kind of a champion of the underdog . . . so he was very concerned and interested in all these things.[5]

Once elected, Rockefeller made his most lasting and significant contributions in these areas. He had been interested in educational opportunities even before his move to Arkansas. As governor, he worked hard for public school kindergartens, teachers' raises, and free textbooks, although he did not get everything he wanted, failing to convince the legislature to pass a teacher tenure bill or to allow state support of kindergartens. Rockefeller's pledge to support health and welfare programs was only moderately fulfilled. His welfare commissioner, Len Blaylock, worked to eliminate partisan meddling in the Welfare Department, but state welfare services for the sick, handicapped, and elderly were not significantly improved. The governor also helped develop and support "cultural and intellectual activities," but as a private citizen more so than in his official capacity. He was the principal force and contributor behind the establishment of the Arkansas Arts Center.

Rockefeller clearly made his greatest impact in prison reform and in civil rights. Arkansas's prisons in 1966 were violent work farms, guarded by armed prisoners entrusted with the power of life and death over their fellow inmates. Vocational and rehabilitative training did not exist. Prisoners suffered from a poor diet, and corruption was widespread. Rockefeller started Arkansas's prisons on the road to reform. Corporal punishment was eliminated, and sanitation and diet were improved. While a lack of funds prevented the complete elimination of the armed trusty system, the prisoner-staff ratio went from the worst in the nation, fifty-eight to one, to eight to one in 1970. The Rockefeller administration initiated the classification of prisoners according to the risk they posed, and ended racial segregation. High school classes were begun at Tucker, and vocational training facilities were constructed at both prisons. Rockefeller capped his prison reform agenda with his eleventh-hour commutations of the sentences of all fifteen men on Arkansas's death row. The commutations took place after the governor's unsuccessful third-term bid. He stood to gain no political advantage from his actions. He acted solely according to his personal beliefs. More than fifteen years later, a journalist who had been a newspaper reporter in Arkansas in 1970 wrote of the commutations, "He managed to overcome the awful moral burden of immense wealth and lesser burdens of personal weaknesses to become a genuine moral leader."[6] The most moving tribute to the governor's clemency came from one of the death row inmates. When Rockefeller died, the convict sent a letter to civil rights activist Rev. J. F. Cooley, who submitted it to the *Arkansas Gazette*. The unidentified inmate wrote:

> From you I learned that "color" has no merit in judging men, and from him [Rockefeller] I learned that it is "God" that gives men power over other men and not the efforts of man:
>   You gave me the education and wisdom to become a man, and Mr. Rockefeller gave me back my life to have a chance to perfuse [*sic*] it.[7]

Rockefeller's achievements in the area of civil rights were, in some respects, less tangible. He came to Arkansas in 1953, already an active member of the National Urban League and a firm believer in equal opportunity for blacks. But, when he ran for governor in 1964 and 1966, segregationists still appeared the more popular candidates. To avoid alienating white voters, Rockefeller did not emphasize his civil rights record.

In the context of the 1960s, Rockefeller was not a "liberal." He opposed the 1964 Civil Rights Act, branding it an unnecessary expansion of the police powers of the executive branch of the federal government. He believed in volunteerism, example, and persuasion rather than coercion. Once elected, he worked to increase black participation in state government. He oversaw the integration of Arkansas's draft boards and, whenever possible, appointed blacks to state boards and commissions. When the legislature refused to establish a state human resources council, Rockefeller created one by executive order. Approximately half of the council's forty-eight members were black, including, at one point, its director, Ozell Sutton. And in November 1969 William "Sonny" Walker became the first black department

head in Arkansas when Rockefeller named him to run the state
Office of Economic Opportunity.

But Rockefeller did much more in Arkansas to promote
racial equality than the numbers indicate. As a former Democratic legislator put it, "Probably his greatest accomplishment
was to make racial toleration acceptable and respectable in
Arkansas."8 After the assassination of Martin Luther King, Jr.,
Rockefeller stood on the steps of the state capitol hand in hand
with black leaders and sang "We Shall Overcome." He consistently met with spokesmen for the black community, attempting
to work out compromises whenever problems arose. Twenty
years later, an *Arkansas Gazette* editor wrote that while many
Arkansans have "made much of the fact that Arkansas never experienced the violence that occurred in so many other American
cities during the civil rights struggle. . . . The credit for this goes
to Winthrop Rockefeller, who brought blacks into the mainstream of our society for the first time."9 His only apparent lack
of moral courage was his waffling over the busing issue prior to
the 1970 election.

While the governor made significant strides in civil rights,
his administration was inconsequential in women's rights.
Despite the fact that this was an issue receiving considerable
attention across the nation, women were noticeably absent from
the upper echelons of state government. Rockefeller also failed
in his attempts to reorganize the executive branch of the government, enact income-tax increases and reform, repeal the "fair-
trade" liquor laws, and eliminate armed trusties in the prisons by
increasing the paid staff.

The source of at least some of these failures was the friction
between the Republican governor and the Democratic legislature. Much of this ineffectiveness was inevitable given the political situation. Rockefeller was the first Republican governor in
Arkansas in the twentieth century, and legislators were not used
to cooperating with the opposition. After twelve years of Faubus's
rather autocratic tenure, legislators were eager to exhibit and
experience a degree of independence. And Rockefeller was no
ordinary Republican. He had personally financed the campaigns
of Republican candidates who had opposed many of the legisla-

tors, and the victorious Democrats resented Rockefeller's forcing them into the expense of a campaign in the general election. Many had never before faced Republican opposition—their races traditionally ended after the Democratic primary.

But Rockefeller himself must share the blame for the problems between governor and legislature. As John Ward summed up Rockefeller's relationship with the legislators, "He just never understood those people."[10] Historian Neil R. Peirce wrote:

> It may be that WR never had a chance with the Democratic legislature, but on the other hand, he did little personally to rectify the situation. Never was he willing to engage in the kind of cajoling and favor-swapping that most governors, especially those from the South, must engage in to get their programs approved. Privately, Rockefeller was contemptuous of the legislators, whom he described to me as shortsighted, petty men, the passers of frivolous resolutions, unwilling to face up to the state's gut problems.[11]

Whether or not this is an accurate representation of Rockefeller's view of the legislature, it does describe the view shared by some observers. A 1971 study by the Citizens Conference on State Legislatures ranked Arkansas's legislature forty-sixth in the nation. But the *New York Times*, reflecting on this ranking, noted changes in the makeup and attitude of the legislature: "There is still a strong rural flavor, a strong conservative current and an obvious willingness to defer to special interests. But, compared to the late 1950's and the early 1960's, the Arkansas legislature of today is remarkably progressive."[12]

Regardless of the General Assembly's composition, Rockefeller frequently could not convince its members to vote with him. He was unable to deal with them effectively as individuals. One former Little Rock legislator recalled, "Rockefeller didn't spend time to talk to the legislators. He didn't remember their names."[13] Sterling Cockrill agreed that Rockefeller "was distant, he appeared to be aloof . . . he really did not know how to wine and dine. He didn't know how to create a power group of his own."[14] The gentle art of persuasion is an essential tool for a politician, and Rockefeller could not persuade. He expected legislators to embrace his program because of its obvious value. Passage of

Rockefeller's agenda was possible since much of it became law during Dale Bumpers' administration. Bumpers secured an income-tax increase and reform package similar to the one Rockefeller could not pass. He also won passage of an executive branch reorganization bill based on a plan originally proposed by Rockefeller, and the General Assembly approved significant salary increases for many department heads. Arkansas's Fair Trade Liquor Law was repealed, and additional prison reforms were enacted.[15] Bumpers' success with Rockefeller's program could not be attributed solely to the fact that the new governor was a Democrat. The consensus among legislators and observers was that Bumpers was also "an incredibly skilled governor and a politician."[16] Bumpers himself agreed that he and Rockefeller "shared a number of aspirations for the state and were certainly not far apart philosophically." Bumpers felt that "a number of factors" influenced his success with the legislature, including their pleasure at having "a Democratic governor to work with again." He went on to say: "On a personal level, I treated the legislators as I would want to have been treated had I been a member of the legislative branch. . . . I respected the legislators and understood their need to serve their individual constituencies, but I also expected their help for the programs I felt strongly about."[17]

One stumbling block to legislative success that Rockefeller could not control was the two-year gubernatorial term. There was only one regular legislative session between elections. Many legislators saw no reason to cooperate with the Republican governor when there was a good chance he would not be in office for another term. They merely had to stall for sixty-odd days and work toward his defeat in the upcoming election. During his first term, the governor enjoyed considerable success in getting his program passed through the General Assembly, but his influence diminished considerably in the second term. For his part, the two-year term meant Rockefeller had constantly to consider his actions in terms of electoral consequences.[18]

Rockefeller's performance as governor was further hampered by his poor administrative skills and by his drinking. According to John Ward, Rockefeller's public relations director, the governor was a "terrible" administrator.[19] And Robert Faulkner recalled that Rockefeller "wouldn't come in for weeks at a time to the governor's office—he didn't want to be bogged down . . . with every guy who had a special axe to grind." Faulkner added that Rockefeller's absences did not mean he was ignoring his duties. The governor spent "every waking minute" thinking about "mankind and Arkansas mankind." But still, Rockefeller had Faulkner do "a jillion telephone calls that it would've been much more powerful and meaningful if he [Rockefeller] would've done them."[20] Any organization needs direction. The complexities of state government and the sensitive nature of politics required more direct supervision from Rockefeller. The governor's drinking also detracted from his effectiveness by damaging both his performance and his image. Though the governor of a predominantly "dry" state, he made no secret of his drinking.

Other aspects of his lifestyle and background damaged his image and effectiveness as well. Rockefeller was not an Arkansan by birth, he was a multimillionaire from New York. This meant he was not only an outsider, but the most alien and suspicious of outsiders. John Ward wrote a New York journalist during the 1964 campaign: "Anything that appears in print implying that Mr. Rockefeller is really a New Yorker transplanted into the state will damage us. Mr. Rockefeller is an Arkansan."[21] Rockefeller's opponents used both his birthplace and his inheritance against him. Dale Bumpers successfully made a campaign issue of the amount of money Rockefeller's staff spent on the election in 1970. Nelson Rockefeller's national exposure and presidential ambitions also damaged Winthrop's popularity. In Arkansas, a liberal Republican like Nelson Rockefeller had very few supporters. Republicans and Democrats alike feared Winthrop would, once elected, prove to be as liberal as Nelson. Despite denials and proof that the brothers were not ideological soulmates, Nelson Rockefeller's ambitions and programs were a continual problem for Winthrop. Everett Ham, Rockefeller's political assistant from 1961 until 1966, claimed that "every time Nelson opened his mouth, he cost Win 10,000 votes or support or whatever."[22]

Considering both his personal shortcomings and the handicaps endemic to being a Republican governor in a thoroughly Democratic state, Rockefeller achieved an extraordinary amount of success during his four years in office. This success was not limited to concrete advances and social reforms. Orval Faubus observed that because "Rockefeller was honest, [his administration] was an asset to the state and not the detriment that it could have been because of the partisan differences." Faubus opined that, under Rockefeller, "honesty from the head man on down through the different agencies was good."[23]

Rockefeller helped move Arkansas into a new era. Following the 1970 defeat, Nelson Rockefeller consoled his brother.

> You personally and alone have taken a great southwestern state that was run by a reactionary structure that gave very little attention and concern to the people and lifted it into the 20th Century.
>
> . . . As a result of your prominence and ability to be elected Governor two times, you forced the Democratic party and the people to pick a young, bright, attractive, progressive candidate in that predominantly Democratic State. And in so doing, you rendered a uniquely creative and constructive service to the people of the State of Arkansas. All of us in the family are very proud of you.[24]

This sentiment was echoed by a Democratic state representative who told the defeated incumbent, "I agree with the proposition that we Democrats owe to you the fact that we finally have a nominee for Governor that we can be proud of."[25] John Ward reluctantly acknowledged that Rockefeller "did more good for the Democratic party than he did for the Republican party."[26] G. Thomas Eisele agreed that "one of his greatest contributions . . . was that he essentially brought about the reformation of the Democratic party."[27] Rockefeller's tenure made it possible for the Democratic party to break away from the Faubus machine. The Democrats defeated Rockefeller only with a candidate with no ties to the old ways. Rockefeller forced politicians in the state to change, to put the needs of the people ahead of maintaining a political infrastructure.

Dale Bumpers, the Democrat who defeated Rockefeller,

agreed that Rockefeller helped move Arkansas and its Democratic party into a new era.

> I think Governor Rockefeller was a fairly good politician and a good governor—considering the political difference he had with the legislature—and those abilities stemmed from the fact that he was sincerely motivated to move Arkansas forward. Arkansas was his adopted home; he loved it; and I believed he wanted to give something back to the state and its people which had accepted him and allowed him to live the kind of life—so different from his [sic] life his brothers and cousins were living—he had chosen. Governor Rockefeller made Arkansans feel good about themselves because he was from such a prominent family and had chosen to put his roots down here and make Arkansas his home. I also think Governor Rockefeller was a bridge between the "old-style" politics and government in Arkansas and the new. If there had not been a Winthrop Rockefeller, I am not sure there would have been a Governor Dale Bumpers, a Governor David Pryor or a Governor Bill Clinton.[28]

In his farewell address to Arkansas's General Assembly, Rockefeller stated, "When the history of the past four years is written, I hope the historian may think of me as something more than a political phenomenon; but as a catalyst who hopefully has served to excite in the hearts and minds of people a desire to shape our own destiny."[29] Rockefeller was a catalyst. His uniqueness as a Republican New York multimillionaire made it possible for him to ignore convention, to serve as a bridge between old and new, and to spur on social, political, and economic reform in Arkansas.

An important part of his initial "Statement of Beliefs" that Rockefeller failed to realize was his ambition of building a permanent two-party system in the state. His elections were personal victories and were in no way indicative of growing Republican party strength. Philosophical differences between Rockefeller and many state Republicans always existed. These differences were exacerbated by the controversies that arose over the governor's appointments. Resentment grew among county Republicans whenever Rockefeller appointed a Democrat to a state board or commission, but appointments of Democrats were necessary not only because Rockefeller owed his election to crossover voters, but also because there were not enough qualified Republicans available.[30] When Rockefeller failed to give his wholehearted support to Charles Bernard in his 1968 race against J. William Fulbright, it caused resentment that eventually led to a rift among Arkansas's Republicans. The governor's 1970 invitation to Vice Pres. Spiro Agnew may have been good for the morale of the state Republican party, but it was disastrous for Rockefeller's reelection campaign.

In most matters in which the needs of the state and the needs of the Republican party clashed, party needs were sacrificed. This was inevitable because, while governor, Rockefeller's closest advisors were not, for the most part, party stalwarts. G. Thomas Eisele, Marion Burton, Robert Faulkner, and John Ward were more interested in reforming the state than in building the GOP. They seemed to work under the assumption that, by doing so, more people would recognize the superiority of the Republican party and flock to it. But the Democratic tradition was too strong in Arkansas. Rockefeller's election forced the Democrats to reform their own party, and when they did, the voters willingly returned to that fold.

Arkansas voters were not averse to voting a split ticket, and Rockefeller's election was not indicative of increased Republican membership. For instance, in 1972 Richard Nixon carried all of Arkansas's seventy-five counties with 69.1 percent of the vote, but in that same election, the Republican gubernatorial candidate, Len Blaylock, lost all seventy-five counties with only 24.6 percent of the vote.[31] Only two years after Rockefeller's unsuccessful bid for a third term, Arkansas's Republican party was, in voting strength, back where it started before his governorship.

Despite this apparent lack of electoral strength, Rockefeller's activities and influence left Arkansas's Republican party stronger. Referring to the state GOP, Marion Burton said that Rockefeller "made something out of nothing."[32] He left behind a Republican party with a newfound "respectability."[33] There may not have been many more party members in 1970 than there were in 1960, but the party was no longer dominated by men interested chiefly in federal patronage. While it is true that the party after 1970 took a much more conservative path than Rockefeller would have preferred, it was, nonetheless, a party striving for electoral success. John Ward summarized Rockefeller's legacy to the state Republican party.

> He had lost his leadership power in the party pretty much by the time he lost the '70 election because the rewards had not gone on a patronage basis. . . . His idea of a two-party system did not incorporate the concept of patronage and political payoff which in some respects made it weak as a concept. . . . The legacy . . . is the Republican party today is a much better, a much more competent group of people, has a lot more integrity and is more nearly a viable second party. I give Rockefeller credit for that.[34]

Rockefeller's victories in 1966 and 1968 were part of a regional increase in Southern Republican election successes. But Rockefeller's winning margin came in large part from urban liberals and blacks. Most other Southern Republican office-holders were conservatives who owed their victories to white backlash to the civil rights movement. This trend had begun in earnest at the presidential level in 1948. The death of the solidly Democratic South was owed in large part to Harry S. Truman's civil rights stance that threatened white supremacy, and Southern voters deserted him in droves.[35] In 1948, of the eleven former Confederate states, none gave its electoral votes to the Republican candidate, Thomas Dewey, but four, Alabama, Louisiana, South Carolina, and Mississippi, voted for the Dixiecrat, or States Rights Democratic candidate, Strom Thurmond.[36] In 1952 the Deep South returned to the Democratic fold, while Tennessee, Virginia, Florida, and Texas voted for Eisenhower. These four states, with the addition of Louisiana, again went with Eisenhower in 1956. In 1960 the name of Texan Lyndon Johnson on the Kennedy ticket and Eisenhower's intervention in Little Rock lured white Southerners back to the Democratic fold. Only Virginia, Tennessee, and Florida voted for Nixon. But by 1964 Johnson was *persona non grata* in much of the South for one reason—his work for passage of the Civil Rights Act of 1964. The federal government was destroying the South's segregationist Jim Crow laws, and the national Democratic party was leading the destruction. In 1964 Georgia, Alabama, Louisiana, South

Carolina, and Mississippi voted for conservative Republican Barry Goldwater. Through all of these defections, Arkansas was the only Southern state to go consistently, if not always enthusiastically, with the Democratic candidate. This changed in the 1968 three-way race between Hubert Humphrey, Richard Nixon, and George Wallace. In that election, only Texas stayed with Humphrey. Arkansas, Louisiana, Mississippi, Alabama, and Georgia voted for Wallace, while Virginia, Tennessee, North and South Carolina, and Florida all went with Nixon.[37]

It is too simplistic to assert that the growth of presidential Republicanism in the South was based exclusively on the race issue. There were certainly other factors, including increased migration of Northerners into the region, the post–World War II growth of suburbs, and the increase in "Sunbelt" industries. But the growth of Southern presidential Republicanism was rooted primarily in reaction to national Democratic support of the civil rights movement.[38] This was particularly true beginning in 1964. The Southern presidential Republicanism of 1952, 1956, and 1960 "was in its most solid gains and its most durable form an urban phenomenon."[39] Economics played an important part in Eisenhower's and Nixon's strength in the region. However, between 1960 and 1964, "the right-wing movement which Goldwater represented altered the party's character in the southern states."[40] The sit-ins, freedom rides, and the 1964 Civil Rights Act all helped to reassert race as the dominant theme in Southern presidential politics.

Presidential Republicanism did not automatically lead to a corresponding growth in the Republican party at the state level. But where the GOP did gain in size and electoral success, it usually did so by portraying itself as the defender of "states' rights," the most common euphemism for an anti-integrationist stance. Southern Republican parties were normally to the ideological right of the local Democratic organizations. In 1966, the year Rockefeller won the governorship of Arkansas, Florida also elected a GOP governor for the first time since Reconstruction. But Claude Kirk was a conservative who won against a liberal Democrat. And as governor, he stood firmly on the side of segregationists. In that same year, Howard "Bo" Callaway, another conservative Republican, won a plurality in Georgia's gubernatorial campaign. However, the Democratic state house of representatives elected his arch-conservative Democratic opponent, Lester Maddox. The epitome of conservative Southern Republicans was not a governor, but Sen. Strom Thurmond of South Carolina, who joined the GOP in 1964. The Republican parties of Alabama, Mississippi, and Louisiana also attracted voters dissatisfied with the civil rights movement in the 1960s, although in these three states the GOP remained inconsequential.[41]

Tennessee voters elected a Republican governor, Winfield Dunn, in 1970. Dunn ran on a conservative platform. And in North Carolina, which like Arkansas and Tennessee had always had a substantial Republican minority in its mountain regions, the GOP finally achieved electoral success in 1972 when Sen. Jesse Helms and Gov. James E. Holshouser were elected. Both were considered very conservative.[42]

The Republican party in Virginia, to some extent, also appeared to follow this traditional route to the right of the state's Democratic party. In the 1960s many conservative Democrats switched to the GOP. But when Virginians, in 1969, elected their first Republican governor since Reconstruction, he was a racial moderate. Linwood Holton lost his first campaign in 1965 because he was considered too liberal. Holton and Rockefeller were often lumped together as exceptions in the South—Republicans with reform agendas and moderate racial views who did not subscribe to the Southern strategy in which Democratic opponents were depicted as "captive of a liberal national party that has trampled on Southern interests."[43] To the contrary, Holton and Rockefeller "were more progressive on civil rights than most of the [Southern] Democrats who were elected governor."[44]

If the size and strength of a party can be measured by the number of candidates it puts in office, then Arkansas's Republican party most closely resembled that of a Deep South state during Rockefeller's tenure. Between 1966 and 1972, only Alabama, Louisiana, and Mississippi had Republican representation in their state legislatures at a level as low as Arkansas's. Florida and Tennessee had the largest GOP delegations in their legislatures—Florida's averaged approximately 35 percent while Tennessee's hovered around 50 percent. In Congress, only Florida, South Carolina, Tennessee, and Texas had any Republican senators during these years. As of 1970, both of Tennessee's senators were Republican. In the House, Arkansas again ranked near the bottom proportionately, along with Georgia, Louisiana, Mississippi, South Carolina, and Texas. Considering the relatively weak nature of Arkansas's Republican party, it is a testimony to Rockefeller's abilities that he was one of the first Republican governors in the South in modern times.[45]

Rockefeller was an anomaly in Southern Republicanism. Hence, his influence on the GOP in Arkansas and in the rest of the South was relatively small. One study called the Rockefellers "progressive old money" within the Republican party.[46] As such, they were part of a dying breed. Influence within the GOP during Richard Nixon's presidency was shifting away from the Northeast urban elite and toward grass-roots conservatism in the Midwest and West. Nixon's "Southern Strategy" was part of that trend. Southern Republican growth came from the racially and economically conservative elements in the South. Rockefeller and Virginia's Linwood Holton were not indicative of a trend; they were exceptions to it.

Rockefeller's two terms as governor were influential in Southern politics, but not because of any lasting effect on the GOP. Winthrop Rockefeller was one of the first of a new breed of Southern political leaders—men who looked beyond racial issues and toward economic growth and social reform. Rockefeller's election indicated that pro-segregationism was no longer a prerequisite for victory. This was verified in 1970 with the elections of Dale Bumpers in Arkansas, Jimmy Carter in Georgia, Ruben Askew in Florida, and John West in South Carolina; all Democrats, but also politicians who were "ready to move past the traditional racial politics of the region to deal with their actual problems—health, education, the environment, housing."[47]

Winthrop Rockefeller was unique. His former aides all agree that he was not personally ambitious. He ran for governor because he saw it as the only way to realize his dreams for his adopted state of Arkansas. His words and actions continually indicated an aversion to the limelight. His only personal motive may have been to achieve respect—not for the name Rockefeller, but for himself as a man. This appears to have been a lifelong quest. Marion Burton reflected, "He was a guy with his own resources . . . who permitted the use of those resources . . . he was a true philanthropist in every respect."[48] As a result, Arkansas government became more respectable, more responsible. Proponents of each of the causes Rockefeller fought for will always say more could and should have been done. But given both his own personal shortcomings and the difficulties endemic to Arkansas politics, he accomplished a great deal. Rockefeller's governorship was a watershed in twentieth-century Arkansas history.

Notes

1. Heir to a Legacy
of Wealth and Public Service

1. Peter Collier and David Horowitz, *The Rockefellers: An American Dynasty* (New York: Holt, Rinehart and Winston, 1976), 29; Alvin Moscow, *The Rockefeller Inheritance* (Garden City, N.Y.: Doubleday, 1977), 71.

2. Quoted in Collier and Horowitz, *The Rockefellers*, 86.

3. John D. Rockefeller died in 1937 at the age of ninety-seven. His son died in 1960. Both homes on West Fifty-fourth Street were torn down in 1938 to make room for the Museum of Modern Art.

4. Winthrop Rockefeller, "A Letter to My Son," 10–12, unpublished manuscript, Winthrop Rockefeller Collection, University of Arkansas at Little Rock Archives and Special Collections, University of Arkansas at Little Rock Library (hereafter cited as WR Papers); Collier and Horowitz, *The Rockefellers*, 219; Ferdinand Lundberg, *The Rockefeller Syndrome* (Secaucus, N.J.: Lyle Stuart, 1975), 273; William Manchester, *A Rockefeller Family Portrait: From John D. to Nelson* (Boston: Little, Brown, 1958), 52; Moscow, *The Rockefeller Inheritance*, 52–53, 197. "A Letter to My Son" is not dated. A 1970 letter from John Ward, Governor Rockefeller's public relations director, states it was written in 1950 "from the Governor's dictated notes by David Camelon," and presented to Winthrop Paul Rockefeller on his twenty-first birthday. John Ward to Don Gonzales, 15 January 1970, WR Papers, Record Group IV, Box 87, Folder 1.

5. Mary Ellen Chase, *Abby Aldrich Rockefeller* (New York: Macmillan, 1950), 43.

6 Collier and Horowitz, *The Rockefellers*, 219.

7. Lundberg, *The Rockefeller Syndrome*, 273.

8. Rockefeller, "A Letter to My Son," 10–12.

9. WR Papers, Record Group III, Box 96, File 4.

10. By 1921 John D., Sr., who was America's first billionaire, had already given away another $550 million to various philanthropies. At the

time of his death, his taxable estate was worth $26,410,837.10. Federal and state taxes took 60 percent of that amount. Collier and Horowitz, *The Rockefellers*, 135; Moscow, *The Rockefeller Inheritance*, 101.

11. Rockefeller, "A Letter to My Son," 26; Joe Alex Morris, *Those Rockefeller Brothers: An Informal Biography of Five Extraordinary Young Men* (New York: Harper and Brothers, 1953), 16–17; Moscow, *The Rockefeller Inheritance*, 40–41; Collier and Horowitz, *The Rockefellers*, 182–83.

12. Rockefeller, "A Letter to My Son," 27.

13. Moscow, *The Rockefeller Inheritance*, 56; Collier and Horowitz, *The Rockefellers*, 192.

14. Rockefeller, "A Letter to My Son," 7; Moscow, *The Rockefeller Inheritance*, 56.

15. Rockefeller, "A Letter to My Son," 24; Moscow, *The Rockefeller Inheritance*, 127.

16. *New York Times*, 7 June 1931.

17. Rockefeller, "A Letter to My Son," 29.

18. Rockefeller, "A Letter to My Son," 33.

19. *New York Times*, 6 February 1934.

20. Rockefeller, "A Letter to My Son," 34; Moscow, *The Rockefeller Inheritance*, 199; Joe Alex Morris, "The Rockefellers," part 2, *Saturday Evening Post*, 6 January 1951, 56.

21. Rockefeller, "A Letter to My Son," 35–72; *New York Times*, 9 February 1935, 30 April 1936, 19 January 1937.

22. John D. Rockefeller, Jr., to Raymond B. Fosdick, president, Rockefeller Foundation, 17 September 1936, Rockefeller Family Archives, Rockefeller Archive Center, North Tarrytown, New York (hereafter cited as Rockefeller Family Archives), Record Group 2, Office of the Messrs. Rockefeller (OMR), Rockefeller Boards, Box 26, Folder 261.

23. Rockefeller, "A Letter to My Son," 74–78; Winthrop Rockefeller to John D. Rockefeller, Jr., 4 September 1936, John D. Rockefeller, Jr., to Raymond B. Fosdick, president, Rockefeller Foundation, 17 September 1936, Rockefeller Family Archives, Record Group 2, OMR, Rockefeller Boards, Box 26, Folder 261.

24. Rockefeller, "A Letter to My Son," 89; *New York Times*, 19 January 1937.

25. Rockefeller, "A Letter to My Son," 89–90.

26. *New York Times*, 25 January 1939.

27. Rockefeller, "A Letter to My Son," 115–16.

28. *New York Times*, 6 July 1940, 2 January 1941.

29. Rockefeller, "A Letter to My Son," 116; *New York Times*, 8 October 1941, 24 January 1942, 7 January 1944, 18 April, 27 November 1945, 6 December 1946; Capt. Thomas M. Rivers to John D. Rockefeller, Jr., 10 April 1945, WR Papers, Record Group IV, Box 69, File 3; Moscow, *The Rockefeller Inheritance*, 201–04; Morris, *Those Rockefeller Brothers*, 116–24.

30. Rockefeller, "A Letter to My Son," 90–91; *New York Times*, 28 February, 16 June 1938.

31. Nelson Rockefeller to Winthrop Rockefeller, 3 May 1938, Rockefeller Family Archives, Record Group 2, OMR, Welfare—General, Box 14, Folder 23.2.

32. John D. Rockefeller, Jr., to Winthrop Rockefeller, 18 May 1938, Rockefeller Family Archives, Record Group 2, OMR, Welfare—General, Box 14, Folder 23.2.

33. Memo, Arthur Jones to Arthur Packard, 12 August 1940, Rockefeller Family Archives, Record Group 2, OMR, National Urban League, Box 39, Folder 111.4.

34. *New York Times*, 26 September 1946, 18 April 1947.

35. Winthrop Rockefeller to Robert W. Dowling, president, National Urban League, 24 December 1952, Rockefeller Family Archives, Record Group 2, OMR, National Urban League, Box 40, Folder 111.4; memo, David F. Freeman to Dana S. Creel, 27 April 1960, Rockefeller Family Archives, Record Group 2, OMR, National Urban League, Box 41, Folder 111.43; *New York Times*, 19 June 1956. Information concerning Rockefeller's private activities after 1960 is available only to the extent that it was made public in newspaper accounts. The records are still closed.

36. Oral history interview conducted by the Rockefeller Archive Center with James Hudson, 1 May 1973, at 30 Rockefeller Plaza, New York, New York, Rockefeller Archive Center, Rockefeller Family Tape; Moscow, *The Rockefeller Inheritance*, 204; *New York Times*, 6 December 1946.

37. Oral history interview with James Hudson, 1 May 1973, Rockefeller Archive Center.

38. *New York Times*, 5 September 1952, 22 December 1948, 2 January 1949; (New York) *Amsterdam News*, 1 January 1949.

39. Richard Bush, Colored Orphan Asylum, to Winthrop Rockefeller, 13 January 1941, Margaret B. DeVecchi, Riverdale Childrens Association, to Arthur Jones, Room 5600, 30 Rockefeller Plaza, 5 November 1951, Rockefeller Family Archives, Record Group 2, OMR, National Urban League, Box 39, Folder 111.2.

40. Industrial Relations Counselors, Inc., brochure, Rockefeller Family Archives, Record Group 2, OMR, Economic Interests, Box 16, Folder 129.

41. *New York Times*, 13 January, 1 November 1949, 9 March 1950, 23 November 1951, 15 May 1952.

42. *New York Times*, 12 January 1949, 11 August 1950; Joe Alex Morris, "The Rockefellers," conclusion, *Saturday Evening Post*, 13 January 1951, 30; Moscow, *The Rockefeller Inheritance*, 205.

43. *New York Times*, 1 June 1951; Collier and Horowitz, *The Rockefellers*, 261.

44. *New York Times*, 14 February, 18 September 1948, 16 June 1952.

45. *New York Times*, 7 June 1953. The only ground for divorce in New

York State at this time was adultery.

46. Moscow, *The Rockefeller Inheritance*, 268.

47. Oral history interview with James Hudson, 1 May 1973, Rockefeller Archive Center.

48. Memo, Raymond H. Wilkins to John D. Rockefeller, Jr., John D. Rockefeller III, Nelson A. Rockefeller, Laurance S. Rockefeller, and David Rockefeller, 9 June 1954, memo, Dana S. Creel to John D. Rockefeller III, Nelson A. Rockefeller, Laurance S. Rockefeller, and David Rockefeller, 6 June 1955, Rockefeller Family Archives, Record Group 2, OMR, Welfare Interests—Greater New York Fund, Box 15, Folder 23.2.

49. Winthrop Rockefeller to New York State Chamber of Commerce, 25 June 1953, Robert W. Gumbel to Winthrop Rockefeller, 17 November 1953, Thelma Irby to Robert W. Gumbel, 9 December 1953, Rockefeller Family Archives, Record Group 2, OMR, Economic Interests, Box 6, Folder 37.

50. Moscow, *The Rockefeller Inheritance*, 269.

51. Collier and Horowitz, *The Rockefellers*, 257; Lundberg, *The Rockefeller Syndrome*, 284; Moscow, *The Rockefeller Inheritance*, 211, 268.

52. Oral history interview with James Hudson, 1 May 1973, Rockefeller Archive Center.

53. Winthrop Rockefeller to Dana Creel, 6 August 1955, Rockefeller Family Archives, Record Group 2, OMR, Welfare Interests—Youth, Box 7, Folder 1; Moscow, *The Rockefeller Inheritance*, 269; John Ensor Harr and Peter J. Johnson, *The Rockefeller Century* (New York: Charles Scribner's Sons, 1988), 545.

54. *New York Times*, 28 April 1953; Moscow, *The Rockefeller Inheritance*, 211–12; Manchester, *A Rockefeller Family Portrait*, 53–54; Harr and Johnson, *The Rockefeller Century*, 544.

55. *New York Times*, 27 December 1953; Moscow, *The Rockefeller Inheritance*, 269–74, 278–79; Collier and Horowitz, *The Rockefellers*, 257–58.

56. Quoted in Harr and Johnson, *The Rockefeller Century*, 359.

57. In addition to these trusts, the elder Rockefeller sold Rockefeller Center and Pocantico Hills to his five sons. He also gave the Rockefeller Brothers Fund (RBF) the $58 million mortgage on Rockefeller Center. The RBF was incorporated in 1940 as a means of coordinating the brothers' philanthropic activities. By the time of his death, John D. Rockefeller, Jr., had given a total of $240 million to his family and $550 million to charity. Moscow, *The Rockefeller Inheritance*, 110, 167, 416; Harr and Johnson, *The Rockefeller Century*, 358–61, 522.

58. *Arkansas Gazette*, 21 April 1954, 6 May 1956; *New York Times*, 7 May 1956, 11 December 1960; Moscow, *The Rockefeller Inheritance*, 274; William C. Havard, ed., *The Changing Politics of the South* (Baton Rouge: Louisiana State University Press, 1972), 15.

59. *New York Times*, 11 December 1960.

60. *Arkansas Gazette*, 9 February 1986.

61. John D. Rockefeller III had begun integrating dining and housing facilities at Williamsburg in 1949. Manchester, *A Rockefeller Family Portrait*, 54; Harr and Johnson, *The Rockefeller Century*, 494.

62. "Remarks by Winthrop Rockefeller, National Urban League Annual Conference Dinner: September 11, 1958, Omaha, Nebraska," Rockefeller Family Archives, Record Group 2, OMR, National Urban League, Box 39, Folder 111.4.

63. *New York Times*, 6, 9 January, 18, 20 June, 4 August 1954, 12 June 1956; *Arkansas Gazette*, 12 June 1956.

64. Moscow, *The Rockefeller Inheritance*, 275.

65. Interview with Orval E. Faubus, Conway, Arkansas, 14 March 1988.

66. Harry S. Ashmore, *Arkansas: A History* (New York: W. W. Norton, 1978; reprint, 1984), 176–78.

67. *Arkansas Gazette*, 18 June 1955; Neal R. Peirce, *The Deep South States of America: People, Politics, and Power in the Seven Deep South States* (New York: W. W. Norton, 1974), 137.

68. Interview with Orval E. Faubus, 14 March 1988.

69. Orval Faubus to Winthrop Rockefeller, 19 November 1956, Orval E. Faubus Papers, Special Collections, David W. Mullins Library, University of Arkansas, Fayetteville, Arkansas (hereafter cited as the Faubus Papers), Series 7, Subseries 2, Box 244, Folder 4; Moscow, *The Rockefeller Inheritance*, 276.

70. *Arkansas Gazette*, 13, 23 April 1956.

71. Tony Freyer, *The Little Rock Crisis: A Constitutional Interpretation* (Westport, Conn.: Greenwood Press, 1984), 21.

72. Numan V. Bartley, "Looking Back at Little Rock," *Arkansas Historical Quarterly* 25 (Summer 1966): 103; David R. Goldfield, *Promised Land: The South since 1945* (Arlington Heights, Ill.: Harlan Davidson, 1987), 73.

73. Ashmore, *Arkansas*, 149–50; Freyer, *The Little Rock Crisis*, 42–58, 67–68; Robert Sherrill, *Gothic Politics in the Deep South: Stars of the New Confederacy* (New York: Grossman, 1968), 84.

74. Robert R. Douglas at a symposium marking the Crisis's thirtieth anniversary. Reprinted in the *Arkansas Gazette*, 27 September 1987.

75. Dan Durning, "Arkansas 1954 to Present," in *Historical Report of the Secretary of State of Arkansas* (Little Rock: 1978), vol. 3, *A History of Arkansas*, 188; Ashmore, *Arkansas*, 150; Freyer, *The Little Rock Crisis*, 74–81; Sherrill, *Gothic Politics in the Deep South*, 86. Faubus himself has consistently disagreed with this assessment. At the symposium marking the thirtieth anniversary of the crisis, he said: "I didn't need the Little Rock Crisis of 1957 to help me win a third term. I would have won hands down. . . . I took the action I did . . . to keep disorder at a minimum, to prevent property damage, or injury and death to individuals." *Arkansas Gazette*, 30 September 1987.

76. *Arkansas Gazette*, 15 February 1957; Freyer, *The Little Rock Crisis*, 89.

77. Ashmore, *Arkansas*, 150.

78. Federal Bureau of Investigation Interview Report, interview with William R. Ewald, 9 September 1957, FBI–Little Rock Crisis Reports, FBI #44-12284-937, University of Arkansas at Little Rock Archives and Special Collections, University of Arkansas at Little Rock Library, Series III, Box 1, File 4; memorandum of telephone call, Dwight D. Eisenhower and Herbert Brownell, Jr., 11 September 1957, DDE Diaries Series, Box 27, "September 1957 Telephone Calls," Papers of Dwight D. Eisenhower as President of the United States, 1953–61, Eisenhower Library, Abilene, Kansas.

79. Orval Eugene Faubus, *Down from the Hills*, (Little Rock: Pioneer, 1980), 207–08.

80. *Arkansas Gazette*, 3 September 1957; Freyer, *The Little Rock Crisis*, 117.

81. Ashmore, *Arkansas*, 151; Brooks Hays, *A Southern Moderate Speaks* (Chapel Hill: University of North Carolina Press, 1959), 136–38.

82. *New York Times*, 6 October 1957; Ashmore, *Arkansas*, 151–52.

83. Freyer, *The Little Rock Crisis*, 148.

84. Ashmore, *Arkansas*, 155; Goldfield, *Promised Land*, 76.

85. *Arkansas Gazette*, 5 October 1957; *New York Times*, 6 October 1957.

86. Harold S. Caplin, vice president, Seamprufe Inc., to Winthrop Rockefeller, 17 September 1957, Harold S. Caplin to Orval Faubus, 17 September 1957, Faubus Papers, Series 16, Box 562, Folder 3.

87. Sherrill, *Gothic Politics in the Deep South*, 75.

88. *Arkansas Gazette*, 3 October 1957; Ashmore, *Arkansas*, 152; Orval Eugene Faubus, *Down from the Hills Two* (Little Rock: Democrat Printing and Lithographing, 1986), 5.

89. *Arkansas Gazette*, 22 January 1960.

90. Orval Faubus to Winthrop Rockefeller, 9 March 1960, WR Papers, Record Group IV, Box 122, Folder 2; *Arkansas Gazette*, 5 March 1960.

91. *Arkansas Gazette*, 12 November 1962; *Arkansas Democrat*, 14 November 1962; Orval Faubus to James C. Leake, 16 November 1962, Faubus Papers, Series 7, Subseries 2, Box 246, Folder 3.

92. Faubus, *Down from the Hills Two*, 228.

93. *Arkansas Democrat*, 25 November 1962.

94. William P. Rock to Winthrop Rockefeller, 10 January 1963, Faubus Papers, Series 7, Subseries 2, Box 246, Folder 5; *Arkansas Democrat*, 10 February 1963.

95. *Arkansas Democrat*, 20 February 1963; *Arkansas Gazette*, 20, 23, 24 February 1963.

96. *Arkansas Democrat*, 25 February, 2 March 1963; *Arkansas Gazette*, 27–28 February 1963; *North Little Rock Times*, 28 February 1963; *Fort Smith Times Record*, 28 February 1963.

97. *Arkansas Democrat*, 5 March 1963; *Arkansas Gazette*, 7–8 March 1963.

98. Winthrop Rockefeller to Orval Faubus, 28 March 1964, Faubus

Papers, Series 7, Subseries 2, Box 247, Folder 4.

    99. Tom W. Dillard, "Winthrop Rockefeller," in Timothy P. Donovan and Willard B. Gatewood, Jr., eds., *The Governors of Arkansas: Essays in Political Biography* (Fayetteville: University of Arkansas Press, 1981), 229.

    100. Peirce, *The Deep South States of America*, 138.

    101. Interview with Orval E. Faubus, 14 March 1988.

    102. *New York Times*, 5 April 1964.

2. Taking Control of Arkansas's Republican Party

    1. V. O. Key, Jr., *Southern Politics in State and Nation* (New York: Alfred A. Knopf, 1949), 183.

    2. Key, *Southern Politics in State and Nation*, 184.

    3. Key, *Southern Politics in State and Nation*, 185–201.

    4. Key, *Southern Politics in State and Nation*, 277–92.

    5. Dillard, "Winthrop Rockefeller," 229; Collier and Horowitz, *The Rockefellers*, 440; Peirce, *The Deep South States of America*, 138; Jack Bass and Walter DeVries, *The Transformation of Southern Politics: Social Change and Political Consequence since 1945* (New York: Basic Books, 1976), 34; Michael S. Lottman, "The GOP and the South," *Ripon Forum* 6 (July–August 1970): 23.

    6. Billy Burton Hathorn, "The Republican Party in Arkansas, 1920–1982," (Ph.D. diss., Texas A&M University, 1983), 1: 120–26.

    7. Hathorn, "The Republican Party in Arkansas, 1920–1982," 1: 67, 112–14, 120–25.

    8. *Arkansas Gazette*, 6 October 1957.

    9. *Arkansas Gazette*, 11 October 1960.

    10. *New York Times*, 19 October 1960; *Arkansas Gazette*, 9, 11, 12 October 1960; Committee for the Two-Party System questionnaire, WR Papers, Record Group III, Box 15, Folder 5.

    11. Winthrop Rockefeller to John D. Rockefeller III, 5 November 1960, WR Papers, Record Group III, Box 15, Folder 5.

    12. George H., Room 5600, Rockefeller Plaza, to David Hunter, 3 November 1960, WR Papers, Record Group III, Box 13, Folder 5b.

    13. Press release by Winthrop Rockefeller, 22 September 1960, WR Papers, Record Group III, Box 2, Folder 1.

    14. Memo, David Hunter to Winthrop Rockefeller, 13 September 1960, memo, David Hunter to Winthrop Rockefeller, 18 September 1960, WR Papers, Record Group III, Box 13, Folder 5b.

    15. Memo, David Hunter to Winthrop Rockefeller, 28 September 1960, WR Papers, Record Group III, Box 14, Folder 5b.

    16. *Arkansas Gazette*, 12 October 1960.

17. Memo, David Hunter to Winthrop Rockefeller, 28 September 1960, WR Papers, Record Group III, Box 14, Folder 5b.

18. Kershaw Burbank to Winthrop Rockefeller, 25 October 1960, WR Papers, Record Group III, Box 13, Folder 1.

19. "1960 Republican Program for Arkansas," WR Papers, Record Group III, Box 2, Folder 1.

20. "1960 Republican Program for Arkansas," WR Papers, Record Group III, Box 2, Folder 1.

21. Hathorn, "The Republican Party in Arkansas, 1920–1982," 1: 191–92.

22. Memo, "Problems of Republican Organizations—1960–1962," Don Hall to Winthrop Rockefeller through David Hunter, 25 November 1960, WR Papers, Record Group III, Box 14, Folder 5b.

23. *Arkansas Gazette*, 25 May 1961; *New York Times*, 28 May 1961.

24. Interview with Everett A. Ham, Jr., North Little Rock, Arkansas, 27 November 1987.

25. *Arkansas Gazette*, 17 September 1961.

26. *Arkansas Gazette*, 30 August 1962.

27. Quoted in *Arkansas Gazette*, 30 August 1962.

28. Henry M. Britt to David L. Hunter, 7 December 1960, WR Papers, Record Group III, Box 13, Folder 5a.

29. *Arkansas Gazette*, 30 August, 2 September 1962.

30. *New York Times*, 16 September 1962.

31. Belden Associates, "A Study of Voter Opinion in Arkansas, September 1–14, 1962," viii, xi, WR Papers, Record Group IV, Box 72.

32. Hathorn, "The Republican Party in Arkansas, 1920–1982," 1: 199–200.

33. Walter L. Stouffer, Jr., to fellow Republicans, 13 October 1963, WR Papers, Record Group III, Box 10, Folder 1b; William L. Spicer to John Paul Hammerschmidt and Gene Holman, 13 January 1964, WR Papers, Record Group III, Box 15, Folder 1; Winthrop Rockefeller to members of the executive committee, state committeemen, and county chairmen, 31 January 1964, WR Papers, Record Group III, Box 1, Folder 2; *Arkansas Gazette*, 18 August 1963; *Wall Street Journal*, 31 March 1964.

34. John L. Ward, *The Arkansas Rockefeller* (Baton Rouge: Louisiana State University Press, 1978), 10; interview with Everett A. Ham, Jr., 27 November 1987.

35. Interview with Everett A. Ham, Jr., 27 November 1987.

36. William L. Spicer to Winthrop Rockefeller, 10 May 1963, William L. Spicer to Everett Ham, 10 May 1963, WR Papers, Record Group III, Box 85, Folder 5. The ellipses in the second paragraph are in the original.

37. William L. Spicer to Winthrop Rockefeller, 26 June 1963, WR Papers, Record Group IV, Box 85, Folder 5.

38. Ward, *The Arkansas Rockefeller*, 9.

39. William L. Spicer to Marion Burton, 1 August 1963, WR Papers, Record Group IV, Box 85, Folder 5; interview with Marion Burton, Little Rock, Arkansas, 27 November 1987.

40. "Notice and Call of Special Meeting of State Executive Committee," 19 August 1963, WR Papers, Record Group III, Box 1, Folder 2; *Arkansas Gazette*, 26 September 1963.

41. Marion Burton to William L. Spicer, 19 September 1963, WR Papers, Record Group IV, Box 85, Folder 5; *Arkansas Democrat*, 24 September 1963.

42. *Wall Street Journal*, 31 March 1964; Winthrop Rockefeller to William L. Spicer, 27 October 1963, Winthrop Rockefeller to William L. Spicer, 13 December 1963, WR Papers, Record Group IV, Box 85, Folder 5; William L. Spicer to John Paul Hammerschmidt and Gene Holman, 13 January 1964, WR Papers, Record Group III, Box 15, Folder 1.

43. Interview with Marion Burton, 27 November 1987.

44. Interview with Everett A. Ham, Jr., 27 November 1987. County election commissions consisted of three members, two from the governor's party and one from the opposition. Election fraud was easier if all three members were Democrats.

45. Quoted in Ward, *The Arkansas Rockefeller*, 14.

46. *Arkansas Gazette*, 27 September 1963; Winthrop Rockefeller to members of the executive committee, state committeemen, and county chairmen, 31 January 1964, Martha Townsend to all county chairmen, 10 March 1964, WR Papers, Record Group III, Box 1, Folder 2; *Wall Street Journal*, 10 March 1964.

47. Bill Spicer to U. A. Lovell, et al., 12 May 1964, Bill Spicer to Friends, 12 May 1964, WR Papers, Record Group IV, Box 85, Folder 5.

48. Memo for files, transcript of phone conversation between Winthrop Rockefeller and William Spicer, from Jane Bartlett, 1 June 1964, WR Papers, Record Group III, Box 1, Folder 2.

49. Memo, Martha Townsend to news media, 27 June 1964, WR Papers, Record Group IV, Box 85, Folder 5.

50. Quoted in *Saturday Evening Post*, 19 November 1966; Helen M. Pate, Internal Revenue Service, to G. Thomas Eisele, 3 January 1963, WR Papers, Record Group III, Box 245, Folder 1; "Memorandum Re: Economics of Wirges' Pending Legal Matters" (unsigned, but contents indicate it is most likely from G. Thomas Eisele to Rockefeller), 9 December 1963, WR Papers, Record Group III, Folder 2; Ward, *The Arkansas Rockefeller*, 38–39.

51. G. Thomas Eisele to Hon. Russell Roberts, 1 August 1966, order, Circuit Court of Conway County, 19 September 1966, WR Papers, Record Group III, Box 241, Folder 4; press release, 500 Tower Building, Little Rock, 19 September 1966, WR Papers, Record Group III, Box 35, Folder 10a; *Arkansas Gazette*, 24 October 1963, 14, 16 February 1965; *Arkansas Democrat*, 21 October 1963.

52. Complaint at law, *C. C. Brewer, plaintiff,* v. *Gene Wirges, d/b/a Morrilton Democrat, defendant,* 10 June 1963, G. Thomas Eisele to Hon. Wiley W. Bean, 28 August 1963, 16 September 1963, 15 October 1963, notice of appeal, *C. C. Brewer* v. *Gene Wirges, d/b/a Morrilton Democrat,* 1 November 1963, G. Thomas Eisele to Nathan Gordon, 2 December 1963, WR Papers, Record Group III, Box 243, Folder 1a; *Arkansas Gazette,* 11 June 1967; *Saturday Evening Post,* 19 November 1966; Ward, *The Arkansas Rockefeller,* 39.

53. *Arkansas Gazette,* 6, 11 June 1968.

54. *New York Times,* 10 July 1968; G. Thomas Eisele to Truman Altenbaumer, 28 October 1965, Arkansas Republican Party Archives, University of Arkansas at Little Rock Archives and Special Collections, University of Arkansas at Little Rock Library (hereafter cited as Republican Archives), Series II, Box 2, Folder 3.

55. Judgment in the Matter of the Estate of Clyde Cecil Brewer, Sr., 22 October 1965, WR Papers, Record Group III, Box 243, Folder 2; G. Thomas Eisele to Hon. Russell Roberts, 28 January 1966, WR Papers, Record Group III Box 243, Folder 7; G. Thomas Eisele to Hon. Russell Roberts and Hon. Wiley Bean, 15 March 1965, G. Thomas Eisele to Tom Downie, 28 October 1965, G. Thomas Eisele to Anne H. Strickland, American Civil Liberties Union, 21 February 1966; complaint, *Gene Wirges, plaintiff,* v. *Marlin Hawkins, defendant,* no date, WR Papers, Record Group III, Box 244, Folder 4; *Arkansas Gazette,* 2, 9, 21, 28 October, 25 November 1964; *Arkansas Democrat,* 7 June 1965; *Saturday Evening Post,* 19 November 1966.

56. Statement of Judge Bean to the grand jury, 20 October 1964, WR Papers, Record Group III, Box 9, Folder 2.

57. *Arkansas Democrat,* 16 February 1965.

58. Quoted in Ward, *The Arkansas Rockefeller,* 38.

59. Memo, G. Thomas Eisele to Winthrop Rockefeller, 11 March 1965, WR Papers, Record Group III, Box 245, Folder 2.

60. Memo, Odell Pollard to members of the Conway County Republican Committee and members of the Conway County Republican Women's Club, 19 January 1967, Robert Holloway to Everett Ham, 27 February 1967, Republican Archives, Series II, Box 2, Folder 13; John Oliger to Winthrop Rockefeller, 7 August 1968, Winthrop Rockefeller to John Oliger, 18 September 1968, WR Papers, Record Group III, Box 552, Folder 5.

61. *Arkansas Gazette,* 10 October 1959.

62. *New York Times,* 28 July 1960.

63. Memo, David Hunter to Winthrop Rockefeller, 25 November 1960, WR Papers, Record Group III, Box 14, Folder 5b.

64. Mid South Opinion Surveys, 10 October 1960, Belden Associates, "A Study of Voter Opinion in Arkansas, February 8–15, 1961," WR Papers, Record Group IV, Box 72.

65. "Statement by Winthrop Rockefeller," 14 April 1962, WR Papers, Record Group III, Box 13, Folder 5a; *New York Times*, 15 April 1962.

66. Interview with Everett A. Ham, Jr., 27 November 1987.

67. Ward, *The Arkansas Rockefeller*, 21.

68. Moscow, *The Rockefeller Inheritance*, 287.

69. "Meet the Press" transcript, 3 May 1964, WR Papers, Record Group IV, Box 47, Folder 4.

70. Orval Faubus to Herbert A. Tellman, 8 May 1964, Faubus Papers, Series 17, Box 596, Folder 14; *Arkansas Gazette*, 16, 17 October, 1 November 1964.

71. Faubus, *Down from the Hills Two*, 309.

72. Ward, *The Arkansas Rockefeller*, 32–33; Belden Associates, "A Study of Voter Opinion in Arkansas, December 11–December 26, 1964," WR Papers, Record Group IV, Box 74.

73. *New York Times*, 7 May 1963, 8 November 1963, 5 May 1964.

74. *New York Times*, 22 May 1964; *Arkansas Gazette*, 12 July 1964.

75. Telegram, Winthrop Rockefeller to Nelson Rockefeller, 16 June 1964, WR Papers, Record Group III, Box 14, Folder 1; *Arkansas Gazette*, 22 July 1964; Hathorn, "The Republican Party in Arkansas, 1920–1982," 215.

76. Memo, G. Thomas Eisele to Win Rockefeller, 11 August 1964, WR Papers, Record Group III, Box 215, Folder 2.

77. Ward, *The Arkansas Rockefeller*, 23–26.

78. Memo, G. Thomas Eisele to Win Rockefeller, 11 August 1964, WR Papers, Record Group III, Box 215, Folder 2.

79. *New York Times*, 9, 13, 14 September 1964.

80. Hathorn, "The Republican Party in Arkansas, 1920–1982," 226–27; *New York Times*, 5 November 1964.

81. Belden Associates, "A Study of Voter Opinion in Arkansas, December 11–December 26, 1964," WR Papers, Record Group IV, Box 74.

82. *Arkansas Gazette*, 12 January 1965; *New York Times*, 1 March 1965; G. Thomas Eisele to Winthrop Rockefeller, 6 May 1965, WR Papers, Record Group IV, Clippings Files, Voter Registration 1965; statement by Winthrop Rockefeller, May 11, 1965, WR Papers, Record Group III, Box 35, Folder 10c.

83. Interview with Marion Burton, 27 November 1987.

84. Interview with Everett A. Ham, Jr., 27 November 1987. The man who recorded the phony votes told Ham the story several years later, after a falling out with his cohorts.

85. "The Election Research Council, Inc. Report February 21, 1965," WR Papers, Record Group III, Box 40, Folder 5; John Ward to Earl Mazo of the *New York Times*, 16 February 1965, WR Papers, Record Group IV, Box 71, Folder 4; *New York Times*, 20 September 1964; Ward, *The Arkansas Rockefeller*, 29–32.

86. Winthrop Rockefeller to Warren G. Magnuson, 18 March 1965,

WR Papers, Record Group IV, Box 31, Folder 2; Winthrop Rockefeller to Jack Miller, 17 March 1965, Winthrop Rockefeller to John F. Baldwin, 18 March 1965, Jacob K. Javits to Winthrop Rockefeller, 15 April 1965, WR Papers, Record Group IV, Box 43, Folder 5; *Voting Rights Act of 1965, Statutes at Large* 79, 437 (1965).

87. John Ward to Earl Mazo, 16 February 1965, WR Papers, Record Group IV, Box 71, Folder 4; Belden Associates, "A Study of Voter Opinion in Arkansas October 3–October 10, 1964," WR Papers, Record Group IV, Box 73; "Meet the Press" transcript, 3 May 1964, WR Papers, Record Group IV, Box 47, Folder 4.

88. Memo, John Ward to Winthrop Rockefeller, Jean Tool, Everett Ham, and Marion Burton, 3 May 1965, WR Papers, Record Group IV, Box 72, Folder 2.

89. John Ward to Earl Mazo, 16 February 1965, WR Papers, Record Group IV, Box 71, Folder 4.

90. Ward, *The Arkansas Rockefeller*, 40; John Ward to Wallace Seawell, 3 February 1966, WR Papers, Record Group IV, Box 84, Folder 9.

91. Faubus, *Down from the Hills Two*, 320.

92. Faubus, *Down from the Hills Two*, 414.

93. *New York Times*, 12 January, 22 March, 28 April, 27 July, 11 August 1966.

94. *New York Times*, 28 April 1966; *Arkansas Outlook*, July, August 1966; Ward, *The Arkansas Rockefeller*, 55–56.

95. *Arkansas Gazette*, 6 November 1966.

96. Ward, *The Arkansas Rockefeller*, 56; Mid-South Opinion Surveys, 24 October 1966, 1 November 1966, 6 November 1966, WR Papers, Record Group IV, Box 76.

97. Interview with John L. Ward, 8 September 1986, Little Rock, Arkansas; *Arkansas Gazette*, 2, 6 November 1966, 24 March 1968; Earl Black, *Southern Governors and Civil Rights: Racial Segregation in the South as a Campaign Issue in the Second Reconstruction* (Cambridge, Mass.: Harvard University Press, 1976), 267–71; Richard E. Yates, "Arkansas: Independent and Unpredictable," in Havard, *The Changing Politics of the South*, 279–80.

98. *New York Times*, 26 October 1966; Ward, *The Arkansas Rockefeller*, 55–56.

99. Maurice "Footsie" Britt to author, 24 November 1989.

100. Hathorn, "The Republican Party in Arkansas, 1920–1982," 266–71.

101. Memo, Irene G. Samuel to Edwin Dunaway, 17 November 1966, WR Papers, Record Group IV, Box 128, Folder 3.

102. *Pine Bluff Commercial*, 25 September 1966.

103. Quoted in Ward, *The Arkansas Rockefeller*, 65.

104. Interview with John L. Ward, 8 September 1986.

105. Stephen Hess and David S. Broder, *The Republican Establishment: The Present and Future of the G. O. P.* (New York: Harper and Row, 1967), 2–4.

3. A Legislative History
of Rockefeller's First Term

1. "Inaugural Address Delivered by the 37th Elected Governor of Arkansas Winthrop Rockefeller," 10 January 1967, 1, WR Papers, Record Group III, Box 35, Folder 2a.

2. Donald T. Wells, "The Arkansas Legislature," in *Readings in Arkansas Government*, Walter Nunn, ed., (Little Rock: Rose Publishing, 1973), 60.

3. Wells, "The Arkansas Legislature," 60–63.

4. In a 1988 interview, Orval Faubus argued that normally the legislature "would have permitted the new governor to have a look at [the appointments] at least." Interview with Orval E. Faubus, 14 March 1988.

5. *Arkansas Democrat*, 10, 15 January 1967; *Arkansas Gazette*, 14 January 1967; *New York Times*, 10 January 1967; *Memphis Commercial Appeal*, 10 January 1967.

6. *Arkansas Gazette*, 12 January 1967.

7. Morrell Gathright to Winthrop Rockefeller, 17 January 1967, WR Papers, Record Group III, Box 89, Folder 7.

8. Ward, *The Arkansas Rockefeller*, 69–70.

9. Oscar Fendler to Winthrop Rockefeller, 15 November 1966, WR Papers, Record Group III, Box 465, Folder 2.

10. *Arkansas Gazette*, 19 November 1966.

11. *Arkansas Gazette*, 29 November 1966; *Memphis Commercial Appeal*, 29 November 1966; Wells, "The Arkansas Legislature," 61.

12. *Pine Bluff Commercial*, 7 December 1966.

13. Legislative Calendar, 1967–70, WR Papers, Record Group IV, Clippings File, Legislative Calendar (hereafter cited as Legislative Calendar, 1967–70).

14. Legislative Calendar, 1967–70.

15. *Arkansas Democrat*, 4 April 1967; *Arkansas Gazette*, 17 January 1967.

16. Winthrop Rockefeller to Mr. Speaker and members of the Sixty-sixth General Assembly, Veto Message of House Bill 174, WR Papers, Record Group IV, Box 169, Folder 7; Winthrop Rockefeller to Alice Gover, AEA Department of Classroom Teachers, 17 January 1967, WR Papers, Record Group III, Box 476, Folder 2; *Arkansas Democrat*, 31 January 1967; *Arkansas Gazette*, 1 February 1967.

17. *Arkansas Gazette*, 1, 2 February 1967; *Memphis Commercial Appeal*, 4 February 1967.

18. Memo, Winthrop Rockefeller to Arkansas Classroom Teachers, 13 March 1967, WR Papers, Record Group III, Box 378, Folder 5; state Department of Education analysis of House Bill No. 162 of 1967, 24 January 1967, WR Papers, Record Group III, Box 217, Folder 4; telegram, Doris Glenn, Little Rock Central High, to Winthrop Rockefeller, 16 March 1967,

Paul Burge, elementary supervisor, Jonesboro Public Schools, to Winthrop Rockefeller, 17 March 1967, Betty Little, teacher, to Winthrop Rockefeller, 11 March 1967, Rep. Hayes McClerkin to Winthrop Rockefeller, 24 March 1967, WR Papers, Record Group III, Box 379, Folder 1. The Arkansas Teachers Association was the black teachers' organization. It merged with the AEA in 1969.

19. Memo, Winthrop Rockefeller to Arkansas Classroom Teachers, 13 March 1967, WR Papers, Record Group III, Box 378, Folder 5.

20. "Here's What Happened in the Legislature," *Journal of Arkansas Education* 39 (May 1967): 4.

21. *Arkansas Gazette*, 3 February 1967.

22. *Arkansas Gazette*, 3 February 1967.

23. Legislative Calendar, 1967–70; *Arkansas Gazette*, 2, 3 February, 10 March 1967.

24. Rep. Hayes McClerkin to Winthrop Rockefeller, 24 March 1967, WR Papers, Record Group III, Box 379, Folder 1; Arkansas State Chamber of Commerce, "Legislative Bulletin," 31 March 1967, WR Papers, Record Group III, Box 42, Folder 2; *Arkansas Gazette*, 5, 9, 26, 29 March 1967; *Arkansas Democrat*, 9, 29 March 1967.

25. According to Robert Faulkner, Rockefeller's liaison to the Constitutional Revision Study Commission, the governor wanted a commission before a constitutional convention was called in order to build public support for a new constitution. Interview with Robert Faulkner, Little Rock, Arkansas, 9 February 1988.

26. Interim report on the Governor's Program, 27 February 1967, WR Papers, Record Group III, Box 234, Folder 1 (hereafter cited as Governor's Program Report, 27 February 1967); *Arkansas Gazette*, 11 February 1967; *Arkansas Democrat*, 9 March 1967.

27. Rep. John E. Miller to Winthrop Rockefeller, 23 February 1967, WR Papers, Record Group III, Box 540, Folder 9; Governor's Program Report, 27 February 1967; Legislative Calendar, 1967–70; *Arkansas Gazette*, 19 November 1966, 28 February 1967.

28. Wright, Lindsey, and Jennings, attorneys at law, to G. Thomas Eisele, 3 January 1967, WR Papers, Record Group III, Box 230, Folder 3.

29. *Pine Bluff Commercial*, 29 December 1966.

30. *Arkansas Gazette*, 23 February 1967.

31. Governor's Program Report, 27 February 1967; *Arkansas Gazette*, 23 February 1967.

32. *Arkansas Gazette*, 9 March 1967; Governor's Program Report, 27 February 1967; G. Thomas Eisele to Richard B. McCulloch, 23 December 1966, WR Papers, Record Group III, Box 228, Folder 5.

33. *Arkansas Gazette*, 17 January 1967.

34. Winthrop Rockefeller to Max Howell, 17 February 1967, WR Papers, Record Group III, Box 217, Folder 4; Governor's Program Report,

27 February 1967; Legislative Calendar, 1967–70; *Arkansas Gazette*, 9 March 1967.

35. *Arkansas Gazette*, 19 November 1966.

36. *Arkansas Democrat*, 10 February 1967; *Arkansas Gazette*, 8 February 1967.

37. *Arkansas Gazette*, 27 January 1967; *Pine Bluff Commercial*, 28 January 1967.

38. Reprinted in *Arkansas Gazette*, 14 February 1967.

39. Transcript of conversation between Sen. Bill Ingram and Lt. Gov. Maurice "Footsie" Britt, undated, WR Papers, Record Group IV, Clippings File, W. K. Ingram File.

40. *Arkansas Gazette*, 24 February 1967; *Arkansas Democrat*, 24 February 1967; *Pine Bluff Commercial*, 24 February 1967.

41. *Arkansas Gazette*, 11, 15 February 1967; *Memphis Commercial Appeal*, 27 February 1967.

42. Jesse C. Hayes to Winthrop Rockefeller, 24 March 1967, WR Papers, Record Group III, Box 489, Folder 4.

43. *Arkansas Democrat*, 8 March 1967.

44. Bills Vetoed by Governor, "Legislative Digest, Acts of 1967," 15, WR Papers, Record Group III, Box 281, Folder 1. The law requiring voters to designate their political party affiliation was later defeated by Arkansas voters in a protest referendum. Diane D. Blair, *Arkansas Politics and Government: Do the People Rule?* (Lincoln: University of Nebraska Press, 1988), 3.

45. *New York Times*, 4, 5, 7 March 1967; *Arkansas Democrat*, 4, 5, 6 March 1967; *Arkansas Gazette*, 5 March 1967.

46. *New York Times*, 7 March 1967.

47. Oscar Alagood to Winthrop Rockefeller, 6 March 1967, WR Papers, Record Group III, Box 402, Folder 1.

48. Senate Journal 1967, Vol. 3, No. 85, 1956, Arkansas History Commission, Little Rock, Arkansas.

49. *Arkansas Gazette*, 9 April 1967.

50. Interview with Sterling Cockrill, Little Rock, Arkansas, 3 October 1989.

51. *Arkansas Gazette*, 19 March 1967.

52. Memo, Winthrop Rockefeller to all members of the General Assembly, 9 January 1968, WR Papers, Record Group III, Box 214, Folder 2; *Arkansas Democrat*, 25 August 1967.

53. Richard Griffin to Winthrop Rockefeller, 16 August 1967, WR Papers, Record Group III, Box 481, Folder 2.

54. Guy Jones to Winthrop Rockefeller, 19 September 1967, Winthrop Rockefeller to Guy Jones, 20 October 1967, WR Papers, Record Group III, Box 507, Folder 2; Richard Griffin to Winthrop Rockefeller, 20 October 1967, Richard Griffin to Winthrop Rockefeller, 13 January 1968, WR Papers, Record Group III, Box 481, Folder 2; Julian Hogan, state budget director to

Winthrop Rockefeller, 22 June 1967, WR Papers, Record Group III, Box 225, Folder 2; Len Blaylock, Department of Public Welfare to Winthrop Rockefeller, 20 October 1967, WR Papers, Record Group III, Box 242, Folder 2b; *Arkansas Gazette,* 26 November 1967; *Magnolia* (Arkansas) *Daily Banner-News,* 7 November 1967; *Arkansas Democrat,* 16 December 1967.

55. Memo, Winthrop Rockefeller to all members of the General Assembly, 9 January 1968, WR Papers, Record Group III, Box 214, Folder 2.

56. State Administration Department, Budget and Accounting Division, "State of Arkansas Budget Information and Proposed Bills Covering Items Which May Be Considered by the First Extraordinary Session of the Sixty-Sixth General Assembly," vols. A, B, and C, WR Papers, Record Group III, Box 214, Folder 1.

57. *Pine Bluff Commercial,* 5 February 1968.

58. *Arkansas Gazette,* 3 February 1968.

59. "Address by Governor Winthrop Rockefeller to the 66th General Assembly (Extraordinary Session) at 12:30 p.m., February 5, 1968," WR Papers, Record Group III, Box 335, Folder 1 (hereafter cited as Rockefeller Address, 5 February 1968).

60. Rockefeller Address, 5 February 1968; State of Arkansas Executive Department Proclamation, 5 February 1968, WR Papers, Record Group III, Box 42, Folder 5a (hereafter cited as Executive Proclamation, 5 February 1968); *New York Times,* 4, 6 February 1968; *Pine Bluff Commercial,* 6 February 1968.

61. "Unanimous Resolution of Entire Arkansas State Police Commission," 25 May 1967, WR Papers, Record Group III, Box 82, Folder 2; Joe Purcell, attorney general, to Winthrop Rockefeller, 30 June 1967, WR Papers, Record Group III, Box 82, Folder 4; *Arkansas Gazette,* 19 December 1967; *Arkansas Democrat,* 20 December 1967.

62. Winthrop Rockefeller to Rep. James L. Sheets, 14 February 1968, WR Papers, Record Group III, Box 282, Folder 2; "Special Legislative Report for Republican Leadership," 6, 8, 12, 15, 16, 21 February 1968, WR Papers, Record Group III, Box 389, Folder 4; *Arkansas Gazette,* 19 December 1967; 6, 17, 20 February 1968; *Arkansas Democrat,* 20, 21 December 1967, 20 February 1968; *Pine Bluff Commercial,* 6, 16 February 1968.

63. Rockefeller Address, 5 February 1968.

64. Legislative Calendar, 1967–70; *Pine Bluff Commercial,* 25 February 1968.

65. The other major recommendation, the creation of a Department of Correction, is discussed below.

66. Memo, state Administration Department to G. Thomas Eisele, 21 February 1968, WR Papers, Record Group III, Box 281, Folder 1; Legislative Calendar, 1967–70.

67. Winthrop Rockefeller to certain members of the House of Representatives, 20 February 1968, WR Papers, Record Group III, Box 282, Folder 2.

68. Winthrop Rockefeller to certain members of the House of Representatives, 20 February 1968, WR Papers, Record Group III, Box 282, Folder 2; Rockefeller Address, 5 February 1968; "AEA Legislative Bulletin," 9, 16 February 1968, WR Papers, Record Group III, Box 213, Folder 3; Special Legislative Report for Republican Leadership, 21 February 1968, WR Papers, Record Group III, Box 389, Folder 4.

69. Statement by Gov. Winthrop Rockefeller *re* prison reform proposals, 12 February 1968, WR Papers, Record Group III, Box 289, Folder 1.

70. Rockefeller Address, 5 February 1968; Executive Proclamation, 5 February 1968; *Magnolia Daily Banner-News,* 7 February 1968; *Arkansas Gazette,* 7, 14 February 1968.

71. Sen. Olen Hendrix to Winthrop Rockefeller, 14 February 1968, Winthrop Rockefeller to Olen Hendrix, 14 February 1968, WR Papers, Record Group III, Box 282, Folder 2; *Pine Bluff Commercial,* 15 February 1968; *Arkansas Gazette,* 16, 21 February 1968; *New York Times,* 22 February 1968; *Memphis Commercial Appeal,* 21 February 1968.

72. The controversy surrounding the prisons themselves is discussed in the next chapter.

73. *Arkansas Gazette,* 9 February 1968.

74. *Arkansas Gazette,* 22 February 1968; *Hot Springs Sentinel-Record,* 22 February 1968; *Pine Bluff Commercial,* 25 February 1968.

75. "Remarks by Governor Winthrop Rockefeller for the Opening of the Legislative Council Meeting at 10 a.m., Tuesday, April 30, 1968," WR Papers, Record Group III, Box 280, Folder 4.

76. State of Arkansas Executive Department Proclamation, 20 May 1968, WR Papers, Record Group III, Box 42, Folder 5a.

77. Statement by Winthrop Rockefeller, 28 May 1968, WR Papers, Record Group IV, Box 166, Folder 2; *Arkansas Gazette,* 29 May, 2 June 1968.

78. Interview with John L. Ward, 8 September 1986.

79. "Remarks Developed by Governor Winthrop Rockefeller for Delivery to the Special Session of the Arkansas General Assembly, May 20, 1968," WR Papers, Record Group III, Box 282, Folder 3 (hereafter cited as Governor's Remarks, 20 May 1968); memo, G. Thomas Eisele to Winthrop Rockefeller, 4 June 1968, WR Papers, Record Group IV, Box 62, Folder 6.

80. Memo, Winthrop Rockefeller to Arkansas Law Enforcement Officials, no date, WR Papers, Record Group IV, Box 156, Folder 4; *Arkansas Gazette,* 28, 30 May 1968.

81. Governor's Remarks, 20 May 1968; *Arkansas Gazette,* 19 May 1968; *Arkansas Democrat,* 19 May 1968.

82. John E. Miller to Winthrop Rockefeller, 29 January 1968, WR Papers, Record Group III, Box 540, Folder 9; memo, Reda to Mr. Eisele, 26 January 1968, Marcus Halbrook to G. Thomas Eisele, 1 December 1967, WR Papers, Record Group III, Box 214, Folder 3; *Texarkana Gazette,* 10 December 1967; *Memphis Commercial Appeal,* 26 January 1968.

83. Winthrop Rockefeller to Roy L. Murphy, Hot Springs Chamber of Commerce, 25 January 1968, WR Papers, Record Group III, Box 199, Folder 7.

84. *Arkansas Gazette*, 31 January 1968.

85. Mid South Opinion Surveys, 1 April 1968, WR Papers, Record Group IV, Box 78.

86. Governor's Remarks, 20 May 1968; *Arkansas Democrat*, 5 April; 9, 17 May 1968; *Arkansas Gazette*, 18 April, 10 May 1968.

87. Ward, *The Arkansas Rockefeller*, 91.

88. Legislative Calendar, 1967–70, WR Papers.

89. Quoted in *Arkansas Democrat*, 26 May 1968.

90. John Robert Starr, *Yellow Dogs and Dark Horses: Thirty Years on the Campaign Beat with John Robert Starr* (Little Rock: August House, 1987), 88.

91. *Arkansas Democrat*, 26 May 1968.

92. *Pine Bluff Commercial*, 26 May 1968; *Arkansas Democrat*, 26 May 1968.

4. A Reform Agenda and the Fight for Reelection

1. Starr, *Yellow Dogs and Dark Horses*, 88.

2. *Arkansas Gazette*, 18 February, 18 March, 22 May, 22 June 1966; *Memphis Commercial Appeal*, 2 June 1966; *Arkansas Democrat*, 5 June, 3 July 1966.

3. John Norman Harkey to Winthrop Rockefeller, 7 December 1967, WR Papers, Record Group III, Box 228, Folder 3.

4. *Arkansas Gazette*, 4 February, 14 July, 12 December 1967; *Arkansas Democrat*, 3, 8 March, 25 July 1968.

5. Len E. Blaylock to Winthrop Rockefeller, 4 April 1967, WR Papers, Record Group III, Box 100, Folder 7; memo, Margaret Kolb *re* Department of Welfare, 5 December 1966, A. J. Moss to Carl Stobaugh, Conway County Welfare Office, 21 February 1967, WR Papers, Record Group III, Box 242, Folder 2c; *Arkansas Democrat*, 24 June, 12, 18 October 1967; *Arkansas Gazette*, 19 August, 10, 19 October 1967, 22 June 1968; *Memphis Commercial Appeal*, 9 September, 10 October 1967.

6. *Arkansas Gazette*, 3 June 1967.

7. Winthrop Rockefeller to Stanley McNulty, 7 April 1967, T. S. McNulty to Winthrop Rockefeller, 11 April 1967, WR Papers, Record Group III, Box 87, Folder 4.

8. Ward, *The Arkansas Rockefeller*, 146.

9. Winthrop Rockefeller to Stanley McNulty, 26 May 1967, WR Papers, Record Group III, Box 87, Folder 4.

10. T. S. McNulty, Verl Hudspeth, Ernest Hogue, Newt L. Hailey, Raymond Farris, Ed Gordon, and Tom Pugh to Winthrop Rockefeller, 31 May 1967, WR Papers, Record Group III, Box 87, Folder 4; *Arkansas Democrat,* 4 June 1967.

11. Statement by Gov. Winthrop Rockefeller, 7 September 1967, WR Papers, Record Group III, Box 18, Folder 2; *Arkansas Gazette,* 8 September 1967.

12. Decree, Chancery Court of Pulaski County, Arkansas, 29 January 1968; notice of appeal, Chancery Court of Pulaski County, Arkansas, 29 January 1968; Edward L. Wright to Winthrop Rockefeller, 15 April 1968, H. W. McMillan to Winthrop Rockefeller, no date, Winthrop Rockefeller to Ernest Hogue, 12 August 1968, Winthrop Rockefeller to Newt Hailey, 12 August 1968, Edward L. Wright to Winthrop Rockefeller, 8 October 1968, WR Papers, Record Group III, Box 112, Folders 1a and 1b; *Arkansas Gazette,* 14 October, 22 November 1967, 13 January, 16, 18 July, 28 September 1968; *Arkansas Democrat,* 22 November 1967, 15 April 1968. No evidence of wrong-doing was ever found against the other commissioners. The hearing itself is discussed in greater detail in chapter 6.

13. Ward, *The Arkansas Rockefeller,* 71.

14. Ward, *The Arkansas Rockefeller,* 72.

15. Memo, Van Rush to Winthrop Rockefeller, 8 August 1967, Carmack Sullivan to G. Thomas Eisele, 17 August 1967, Col. C. C. King to Bob Scott, 23 January 1968, WR Papers, Record Group III, Box 232, Folder 3; memo, Truman Altenbaumer to Marion Burton, 17 July 1967, Tom A. Little, Jr., president, Arkansas Real Estate Association, to Winthrop Rockefeller, 14 August 1967, Aubrey Jackson, Sharp County Republican Committee, to Ola Farwel, 18 September 1967, resolution, Arkansas Real Estate Association, 22 September 1967, Henry Ginger, assistant attorney general, to O. D. Hadfield, Jr., Arkansas Real Estate Commission, 28 June 1968, Supreme Court of Arkansas, Opinion No. 5-5007, 15 September 1969, M. E. "Pete" Thornton to Ralph C. Miller, Springdale Board of Realtors, 25 November 1970, WR Papers, Record Group III, Box 125, Folder 10.

16. Marion Burton to Talbot Field, 20 December 1968, WR Papers, Record Group III, Box 335, Folder 1; Winthrop Rockefeller to Joe Purcell, no date, WR Papers, Record Group III, Box 82, Folder 4; *Arkansas Gazette,* 12 April, 5, 8 May, 20 July 1967, 18 January 1968; *Arkansas Democrat,* 21 April 1967.

17. Peirce, *The Deep South States of America,* 131.

18. Peirce, *The Deep South States of America,* 131.

19. *Pine Bluff Commercial,* 6 May 1967; *Milwaukee Sentinel,* 4 May 1967; *Arkansas Gazette,* 8 May 1967; *Topeka State Journal,* 8 May 1967.

20. *Arkansas Gazette,* 15, 16 January 1967; *New York Times,* 17 January 1967; memo, Col. Herman E. Lindsey to Winthrop Rockefeller, 6 February

1967, WR Papers, Record Group III, Box 99, Folder 5.

21. *Arkansas Gazette*, 16 January 1967; *Pine Bluff Commercial*, 15 January 1967.

22. "Police Report 9160166-66, Criminal Investigation Division [Arkansas State Prison], Arkansas State Police," in *A Documentary History of Arkansas*, ed. C. Fred Williams, et al. (Fayetteville: University of Arkansas Press, 1984), 262–63.

23. Reprinted in *Arkansas Gazette*, 18 January 1967.

24. Austin MacCormick to Winthrop Rockefeller, 30 November 1966, WR Papers, Record Group III, Box 483, Folder 4.

25. Ward, *The Arkansas Rockefeller*, 101.

26. *Arkansas Gazette*, 17, 18 January 1967; memo, Col. Herman E. Lindsey to Winthrop Rockefeller, 6 February 1967, WR Papers, Record Group III, Box 99, Folder 5.

27. Neither the Penitentiary Study Commission nor the legislative committee investigated conditions at the prisons to the extent that the state police had done. The Study Commission report described the prison facilities in the most antiseptic of terms, for example, giving the dimensions of a building without any detail as to its condition. "Report of the Arkansas Penitentiary Study Commission," 1 January 1968, WR Papers, Record Group IV, Box 109, Printed Reports.

28. Memo, Col. Herman E. Lindsey to Winthrop Rockefeller, 6 February 1967, memo, Winthrop Rockefeller to members of the legislative committee investigating the state prison system, 6 February 1967, WR Papers, Record Group III, Box 99, Folder 5; *New York Times*, 5 February 1967; *St. Louis Post Dispatch*, 19 February 1967.

29. *Arkansas Democrat*, 6 April 1967; *Arkansas Gazette*, 6 April 1967.

30. Memo, Tom Murton to the Arkansas Penitentiary Board, 27 June 1967, WR Papers, Record Group III, Box 342, Folder 4.

31. *Arkansas Democrat*, 5 July 1967.

32. Press release, governor's office, 23 August 1967, WR Papers, Record Group III, Box 92, Folder 3.

33. *Arkansas Gazette*, 24 August 1967; Thomas O. Murton, "Observations on the Correctional Needs of the State of Arkansas," 1 August 1967, WR Papers, Record Group III, Box 92, Folder 3.

34. Thomas O. Murton, "Observations on the Correctional Needs of the State of Arkansas."

35. Ward, *The Arkansas Rockefeller*, 104.

36. Tom Murton to Tom Eisele, 25 April 1967, WR Papers, Record Group III, Box 342, Folder 4.

37. Tom Murton to Sidney A. Kegeles, 26 April 1967, WR Papers, Record Group III, Box 342, Folder 4.

38. Bob Scott to Tom Murton, 18 August 1967, WR Papers, Record Group III, Box 547, Folder 4.

39. Tom Murton and Joe Hyams, *Accomplices to the Crime* (New York: Grove, 1970), 114.

40. Murton and Hyams, *Accomplices to the Crime*, 221.

41. *Arkansas Democrat*, 26, 27 October, 1 November 1967; *Arkansas Gazette*, 26 October 1967.

42. O. E. Bishop to the Arkansas State Penitentiary Board, 1 November 1967, WR Papers, Record Group III, Box 342, Folder 4.

43. *Arkansas Gazette*, 1 December 1967; *Arkansas Democrat*, 1, 12, 16 December 1967; *Memphis Commercial Appeal*, 16 January 1968; *New York Times*, 9 January 1968.

44. *New York Times*, 28, 31 January 1968; *Houston Chronicle*, 31 January 1968; *Washington Post*, 1 February 1968; *St. Louis Post-Dispatch*, 1 February 1968; *Los Angeles Times*, 4 February 1968; *Shreveport Journal*, 6 February 1968; *Racine* (Wisconsin) *Journal-Times*, 7 February 1968; *Arizona Republic*, 12 February 1968; *Newsweek*, 12 February 1968.

45. Murton and Hyams, *Accomplices to the Crime*, 3; *New York Times*, 31 January, 1 February 1968.

46. Reprinted in *Arkansas Gazette*, 19 May 1968.

47. *Arkansas Gazette*, 19 May 1968; *New York Times*, 9 June 1968; memos, Capt. Buck Halsell to Col. Carl Miller, Arkansas State Police, Penitentiary Investigation, Daily Reports, 8, 9 February 1968, WR Papers, Record Group III, Box 93, Folder 1.

48. *Arkansas Democrat*, 13 April 1972; *Arkansas Gazette*, 14 April 1972.

49. Memo, John Ward to Bill Conley, 18 April 1968, WR Papers, Record Group IV, Box 83, Folder 5; *Arkansas Gazette*, 19 May 1968.

50. Winthrop Rockefeller to Ramsey Clark, 26 March 1968, WR Papers, Record Group IV, Box 83, Folder 5; Ramsey Clark to Winthrop Rockefeller, 16 October 1968, WR Papers, Record Group III, Box 332, Folder 3.

51. *New York Times*, 20 May 1968.

52. Murton and Hyams, *Accomplices to the Crime*, 210.

53. *Arkansas Gazette*, 22, 23 November 1967.

54. Interview with John L. Ward, Little Rock, Arkansas, 8 September 1986.

55. Quoted in *New York Times*, 9 March 1968; *Los Angeles Times*, 11 March 1968; *New York Times*, 12, 13 February 1968.

56. Ward, *The Arkansas Rockefeller*, 105–06; *Arkansas Gazette*, 18 February 1968; *Arkansas Democrat*, 9 February 1968; *Los Angeles Times*, 11 March 1968; *New York Times*, 7 February 1968.

57. *Arkansas Democrat*, 9 February 1968.

58. Tom Murton to Winthrop Rockefeller, 28 February 1968, WR Papers, Record Group III, Box 52, Folder 2c.

59. Memo, Tom Eisele to Winthrop Rockefeller, 28 February 1968, WR Papers, Record Group III, Box 90, Folder 4.

60. Winthrop Rockefeller to Board of Corrections, 4 March 1968, WR Papers, Record Group III, Box 52, Folder 2c.

61. Winthrop Rockefeller to Victor Urban, 7 March 1968, WR Papers, Record Group III, Box 604, Folder 5; *Arkansas Gazette*, 9 March 1968; *Arkansas Democrat*, 6, 7 March 1968; *Pine Bluff Commercial*, 3, 12 March 1968.

62. *Arkansas Gazette*, 9 March 1968.

63. Murton and Hyams, *Accomplices to the Crime*, 236.

64. *New York Times*, 15 October 1968; *Arkansas Democrat*, 16 October 1968.

65. *New York Times*, 10 December 1968.

66. *Arkansas Gazette*, 9 November 1968.

67. Senate Journal, 1967, vol. 3, no. 83, 879–84, Arkansas History Commission, Little Rock, Arkansas; "Report of the Arkansas Penitentiary Study Commission," 1 January 1968, WR Papers, Record Group IV, Box 109, Printed Reports.

68. Arkansas Republican State Committee, "A Public Progress Report on Advancement of the Negro in State Government," September 1967, WR Papers, Record Group III, Box 316, Folder 3. In contrast, the only blacks on boards and commissions prior to Rockefeller's administration were those serving all-black institutions.

69. Memo, Willard A. Hawkins to Winthrop Rockefeller, 15 January 1968, WR Papers, Record Group III, Box 97, Folder 1; Winthrop Rockefeller to Lt. General Lewis B. Hershey, 19 June 1968, WR Papers, Record Group III, Box 492, Folder 3.

70. Willard A. Hawkins to Truman Altenbaumer, 6 December 1968, WR Papers, Record Group III, Box 233, Folder 2; Willard A. Hawkins to Edward M. Kennedy, 4 November 1969, WR Papers, Record Group III, Box 489, Folder 3.

71. Ward, *The Arkansas Rockefeller*, 165.

72. Arkansas Republican State Committee, "A Public Progress Report on Advancement of the Negro in State Government," September 1967, WR Papers, Record Group III, Box 316, Folder 3; memo, William T. Kelly, chairman, Governor's Council on Human Resources, to Winthrop Rockefeller, 29 April 1968, WR Papers, Record Group III, Box 52, Folder 2c; memo, Ozell Sutton to officials, civic leaders, and concerned persons, 13 September 1968, memo, Ozell Sutton to mayors, city managers, and chiefs of police, 13 September 1968, newsletter, Governor's Council on Human Resources, December 1968, WR Papers, Record Group III, Box 116, Folder 2; *Arkansas Democrat*, 16, 23 June 1968.

73. *Arkansas Democrat*, 8 April 1968.

74. George T. Smith to Winthrop Rockefeller, 8 April 1968, Republican Archives, Series II, Box 1, Folder 11; telegram, Winthrop Rockefeller to David Lawrence, editor, *U.S. News & World Report*, 18 April 1968, WR Papers, Record Group III, Box 98, Folder 2a; Ralph D. Scott,

Arkansas State Police, to Winthrop Rockefeller, 8 April 1968, WR Papers, Record Group III, Box 86, Folder 13; *Arkansas Democrat*, 8 April 1968; Ward, *The Arkansas Rockefeller*, 165–67; Stephen B. Oates, *Let the Trumpet Sound: The Life of Martin Luther King, Jr.* (New York: Mentor, 1982), 473–76.

75. Rev. C. B. Knox, Rev. Cecil Cone, and Rev. John H. Corbitt to Winthrop Rockefeller, 12 April 1968, WR Papers, Record Group III, Box 86, Folder 13.

76. *Arkansas Democrat*, 10, 11 April 1968; *Arkansas Gazette*, 10, 12, 16 April 1968; *Memphis Commercial Appeal*, 12 April 1968.

77. State of Arkansas, Executive Proclamation, 10 August 1968, WR Papers, Record Group III, Box 337, Folder 4; Ralph D. Scott to Winthrop Rockefeller, 12 August 1968, WR Papers, Record Group III, Box 579, Folder 5; *Arkansas Gazette*, 10, 12 August 1968; *Arkansas Democrat*, 10, 15 August 1968. A federal grand jury returned indictments in July 1969 against the two assistant wardens accused of beating the youth. The wardens were charged, under federal law, with violating his civil rights. *Arkansas Gazette*, 12 July 1969.

78. Faubus, *Down from the Hills Two*, 362.

79. Winthrop Rockefeller to certain law enforcement officials in Garland County and Pulaski County, 22 February 1967, WR Papers, Record Group III, Box 87, Folder 3; *Arkansas Gazette*, 18 January, 28 February, 18 August, 5, 8, 11 October, 8 December 1967, 24 February 1968; *Arkansas Democrat*, 19 April, 19 October, 7 December 1967; *Memphis Commercial Appeal*, 18, 27 August 1967; *New York Times*, 8 April, 6, 17 December 1967; *Pine Bluff Commercial*, 6 December 1967.

80. Winthrop Rockefeller to Spiro Agnew, 20 February 1968, WR Papers, Record Group III, Box 401, Folder 3; telegram, Nelson Rockefeller to Winthrop Rockefeller, 22 March 1968, WR Papers, Record Group III, Box 571, Folder 3; telegram, Winthrop Rockefeller to Thurston Morton, 10 April 1968, WR Papers, Record Group III, Box 545, Folder 5; *Christian Science Monitor*, 5 February 1968; *New York Times*, 1 March, 12 April 1968; *Arkansas Gazette*, 22 March, 5 April 1968; *Arkansas Democrat*, 28 March, 1 May 1968.

81. Richard Nixon to Winthrop Rockefeller, 8 July 1968, telegram, Richard Nixon to Winthrop Rockefeller, 26 July 1968, WR Papers, Record Group III, Box 550, Folder 2; Rogers C. B. Morton to Winthrop Rockefeller, 22 July 1968, WR Papers, Record Group III, Box 545, Folder 5; Ulysses A. Lovell to Odell Pollard, 12 August 1968, WR Papers, Record Group III, Box 524, Folder 6; *Arkansas Gazette*, 14 January 1968; *New Orleans Times-Picayune*, 15 July 1968.

82. Telegram, John Hay Whitney to Winthrop Rockefeller, 25 July 1968, WR Papers, Record Group III, Box 615, Folder 1; *New York Times*, 4, 21 July, 8 August 1968; *Cleveland Plain Dealer*, 21 July 1968; *Arkansas Democrat*, 5 August 1968; *Arkansas Gazette*, 7, 8 August 1968.

83. Resumes of 1968 Democratic opponents, WR Papers, Record Group III, Box 218, Folder 4.

84. *Arkansas Gazette*, 1, 14 August 1968; Hathorn, "The Republican Party in Arkansas, 1920–1982," 2: 289–90; *New York Times*, 14 August 1968.

85. Ward, *The Arkansas Rockefeller*, 115–17; *New York Times*, 7, 31 July 1968; *Arkansas Gazette*, 1 August 1968. Rockefeller supported Bernard but refused to attempt to influence the Democrats for Rockefeller organization, which consisted largely of Fulbright supporters, and this was what angered Bernard. Interview with Robert Faulkner, 9 February 1988.

86. *Arkansas Gazette*, 8, 21 September 1968.

87. Eugene Newsom, "Mid-South Opinion Surveys," 19 May, 6 October, 30 November, 5 December 1967, 1 February, 1 April, 5 September 1968, WR Papers, Record Group IV, Box 78.

88. Interview with John Ward, 8 September 1986.

89. Memo, John Ward and Tom Eisele to Winthrop Rockefeller, 12 August 1968, WR Papers, Record Group III, Box 642, Folder 1; *New York Times*, 25 July 1968; Ward, *The Arkansas Rockefeller*, 76–77, 94–95, 117.

90. In a 1989 interview, Sterling Cockrill confirmed Crank's association with the Old Guard, explaining that "when there was a need for Democratic leadership, Marion Crank was pushed into that role by the status quo Democrats, the county politicians, the Court House group, the whatever machine there was left." Interview with Sterling Cockrill, 3 October 1989; Ward, *The Arkansas Rockefeller*, 126–28; Starr, *Yellow Dogs and Dark Horses*, 98–99; *Arkansas Gazette*, 14 August 1968.

91. Eugene Newsom, "Mid-South Opinion Surveys," 4 November 1968, WR Papers, Record Group IV, Box 81; Ward, *The Arkansas Rockefeller*, 130; Starr, *Yellow Dogs and Dark Horses*, 100; *Arkansas Gazette*, 6, 7 November 1968.

92. *New York Times*, 3, 6, 7 November 1968; *Arkansas Gazette*, 7, 8 November 1968.

93. Jim Ranchino, *Faubus to Bumpers: Arkansas Votes, 1960–1970* (Arkadelphia, Ark.: Action Research, 1972), 53–54.

5. Minor Victories and Major Defeats in the Legislature

1. Memo, Tom Eisele to Winthrop Rockefeller, 1 November 1968, WR Papers, Record Group III, Box 238, Folder 2c.

2. Telegram, John Bethell, Harry Colay, Hugh Beasley, Lloyd McCuistion, Joel Ledbetter, and Sterling Cockrill to Winthrop Rockefeller, 18 November 1968, WR Papers, Record Group III, Box 230, Folder 4.

3. *Arkansas Gazette*, 1 December 1968.

4. "Address by Gov. Winthrop Rockefeller to the Arkansas Legislative Council," 10 December 1968, WR Papers, Record Group III, Box 286, Folder 3.

5. Interview with Robert Faulkner, 9 February 1988.

6. Memo, Winthrop Rockefeller to members of the General Assembly, 2 January 1969, WR Papers, Record Group III, Box 152, Folder 2; *Arkansas Gazette*, 11 December 1968; *Arkansas Democrat*, 11 December 1968; *Benton Courier*, 19 December 1968; *Pine Bluff Commercial*, 29 December 1968; Ward, *The Arkansas Rockefeller*, 132–33.

7. "Text of Governor Winthrop Rockefeller's Second Inaugural Address," 14 January 1969, WR Papers, Record Group III, Box 334, Folder 6.

8. *Arkansas Democrat*, 12, 13, 15 January 1969.

9. *Arkansas Gazette*, 31 May 1987.

10. *Arkansas Gazette*, 6 December 1968, 31 May 1987; *Pine Bluff Commercial*, 29 December 1968, 11 January 1969. The Futrell Amendment applied to state personal and corporate income taxes. None of Rockefeller's other proposed taxes were on the books in 1934. The Futrell Amendment is still in effect today.

11. Eugene Newsom, Mid-South Opinion Surveys, 21 January 1969, WR Papers, Record Group III, Box 316, Folder 1; Eugene Newsom, Mid-South Opinion Surveys, 24 February 1969, WR Papers, Record Group IV, Box 81.

12. "Text of Governor Winthrop Rockefeller's Address to the Joint Session of the Legislature," 19 February 1969, WR Papers, Record Group III, Box 289, Folder 1.

13. "Remarks by Governor Rockefeller to the Joint Session of the Legislature," 10 March 1969, WR Papers, Record Group IV, Box 195, Folder 1; *Arkansas Democrat*, 11 March 1969.

14. Legislative Calendar, 1967–70; *Arkansas Gazette*, 9, 10, 18 April 1969; *Arkansas Democrat*, 9, 10, 19, 20 April 1969; *New York Times*, 16 March 1969; *Kansas City Times*, 9 May 1969.

15. C. Calvin Smith, *War and Wartime Changes: The Transformation of Arkansas 1940–1945* (Fayetteville: University of Arkansas Press, 1986), 124.

16. Peirce, *The Deep South States of America*, 148.

17. Peirce, *The Deep South States of America*, 148; Ward, *The Arkansas Rockefeller*, 135–40; Durning, "Arkansas 1954 to Present," 196–97; *New York Times*, 16 March 1969; *Arkansas Democrat*, 12 January, 1, 12 May 1969; *Arkansas Gazette*, 18, 22 January 1969; Arkansas Education Association, *Legislative Bulletin*, 22 February, 1 March 1969.

18. G. Thomas Eisele to James McHaney, 21 November 1968, WR Papers, Record Group III, Box 213, Folder 2; James McHaney to G. Thomas Eisele, 17 December 1968, statement of position of the Little Rock Jaycees on the local option question, 13 December 1968, WR Papers, Record Group III, Box 230, Folder 5; *Arkansas Democrat*, 15 January, 9 February 1969; *Arkansas Gazette*, 11, 21 January 1969; *Fort Smith Times Record*, 19 January 1969.

19. *Arkansas Democrat*, 19 January 1969.

20. Reprinted in *Arkansas Democrat*, 8 February 1969.

21. Eugene Newsom, Mid-South Opinion Surveys, 24 February 1969, WR Papers, Record Group IV, Box 81; memo, William P. Bond, Jr., to Winthrop Rockefeller, 17 February 1969, WR Papers, Record Group III, Box 380, Folder 1.

22. *Arkansas Gazette*, 21 January, 21, 26 February 1969; *Arkansas Democrat*, 27 February, 1 March 1969; *Memphis Commercial Appeal*, 1 March 1969.

23. *Arkansas Gazette*, 21 January 1969; Starr, *Yellow Dogs and Dark Horses*, 108–15.

24. Faubus, *Down from the Hills Two*, 18.

25. Legislative Calendar, 1967–70; memo, Robert Faulkner to Marion Burton, 30 April 1969, WR Papers, Record Group IV, Box 195, Folder 2 (hereafter cited as Faulkner to Burton, 30 April 1969); *Arkansas Gazette*, 29 January, 25 March 1969; *Arkansas Democrat*, 12 February 1969.

26. Legislative Calendar, 1967–70; Faulkner to Burton, 30 April 1969; *Arkansas Gazette*, 7 February 1969; *Arkansas Democrat*, 21 February 1969.

27. Winthrop Rockefeller to Kelly Bryant, 28 May 1969, WR Papers, Record Group III, Box 290, Folder 3; Legislative Calendar, 1967–70; *Arkansas Gazette*, 7, 29, 30 May, 3 June 1969; *Arkansas Democrat*, 8, 29 May 1969.

28. Executive Order, Office of the Governor, March 1969, WR Papers, Record Group III, Box 106, Folder 4b; *Arkansas Gazette*, 27 March 1969.

29. Winthrop Rockefeller to David Mullins, 16 November 1967, David Mullins to Winthrop Rockefeller, 25 October 1967, WR Papers, Record Group III, Box 131, Folder 1; E. Grainger Williams to Winthrop Rockefeller, 10 November 1967, WR Papers, Record Group III, Box 616, Folder 7; members of Senate District 18 and House District 22 to Winthrop Rockefeller, 11 December 1967, WR Papers, Record Group III, Box 440, Folder 2.

30. *Arkansas Democrat*, 11 February 1969; memo, Tom Eisele to Winthrop Rockefeller, 7 February 1969, WR Papers, Record Group III, Box 290, Folder 2; memo, Bill Bond to Winthrop Rockefeller, 6 February 1969, WR Papers, Record Group III, Box 380, Folder 1; *Arkansas Gazette*, 29 January, 10 April 1969; *Arkansas Democrat*, 30 January, 3 February 1969.

31. *Arkansas Gazette*, 12 February 1969.

32. *Arkansas Democrat*, 18 March 1969; *Arkansas Gazette*, 20 March 1969.

33. Winthrop Rockefeller to Mr. President and members of the Sixty-seventh General Assembly, 11 March 1969, WR Papers, Record Group III, Box 290, Folder 3.

34. *Arkansas Gazette*, 19 March 1969.

35. Legislative Digest, Acts of 1969, A-V-3, WR Papers, Record Group IV, Box 88; *Arkansas Gazette*, 22 January 1969.

36. Winthrop Rockefeller to Mr. Speaker and members of the Sixty-seventh General Assembly, 24 March 1969, WR Papers, Record Group III, Box 290, Folder 3; Legislative Digest, Acts of 1969, A-V-14, WR Papers, Record Group IV, Box 88.

37. Winthrop Rockefeller to chairman, Joint Budget Committee, no date, WR Papers, Record Group III, Box 316, Folder 8; address by Gov. Winthrop Rockefeller to the Arkansas Legislative Council, 10 December 1968, WR Papers, Record Group III, Box 286, Folder 3; *Arkansas Gazette*, 25 March 1969; *Arkansas Democrat*, 25 March 1969.

38. *Arkansas Gazette*, 18, 20, 26 February, 4, 19 March 1969.

39. Interview with Robert Faulkner, 9 February 1988.

40. *Arkansas Gazette*, 9 May 1969.

41. *Arkansas Gazette*, 9 May 1969.

42. Grady P. Arrington to Winthrop Rockefeller, 9 July 1969, WR Papers, Record Group III, Box 204, Folder 7; *Arkansas Democrat*, 9 March 1969.

43. Winthrop Rockefeller to Grady P. Arrington, 28 July 1969, WR Papers, Record Group III, Box 204, Folder 7.

44. Winthrop Rockefeller to Hayes McClerkin, 31 October 1969, WR Papers, Record Group III, Box 334, Folder 6; *Arkansas Democrat*, 3, 6 November 1969.

45. *Arkansas Democrat*, 7 November 1969.

46. Worth Camp to Winthrop Rockefellow [*sic*], 5 January 1970, WR Papers, Record Group III, Box 432, Folder 1; *Arkansas Gazette*, 19 December 1969.

47. *Arkansas Democrat*, 8 January 1970.

48. John I. Purtle to Winthrop Rockefeller, 17 February 1970, WR Papers, Record Group III, Box 564, Folder 3; Winthrop Rockefeller to John E. Miller, 26 January 1970, WR Papers, Record Group III, Box 294, Folder 5; Winthrop Rockefeller to Jim Caldwell, 3 February 1970, WR Papers, Record Group III, Box 275, Folder 4.

49. Guy H. Jones to Winthrop Rockefeller, 4 February 1970, WR Papers, Record Group III, Box 507, Folder 2.

50. *Arkansas Democrat*, 1 March 1970; *Arkansas Gazette*, 3 March 1970.

51. *Arkansas Gazette*, 3 March 1970; *Arkansas Democrat*, 25 January, 1 March 1970.

52. "Address by Governor Winthrop Rockefeller to the Joint Session of the Arkansas General Assembly," 2 March 1970, WR Papers, Record Group III, Box 286, Folder 2.

53. State of Arkansas Executive Department Proclamation, 2 March 1970, WR Papers, Record Group III, Box 56, Folder 1; *Arkansas Gazette*, 1 March 1970.

54. "Address by Governor Rockefeller to the Joint Session of the Arkansas General Assembly," 2 March 1970, WR Papers, Record Group III, Box 286, Folder 2.

55. *Arkansas Gazette*, 1, 3 March 1970; *Arkansas Democrat*, 1 March 1970; *Pine Bluff Commercial*, 3 March 1970.

56. Legislative Calendar, 1967–70; *Arkansas Gazette*, 4, 6 March 1970.

57. "Address by Governor Rockefeller to the Joint Session of the

Arkansas General Assembly," 2 March 1970, WR Papers, Record Group III, Box 286, Folder 2.

58. *Arkansas Democrat*, 1 March 1970.

59. *Arkansas Gazette*, 6, 7, 8, 10 March 1970.

60. Legislative Calendar, 1967–70; *Arkansas Gazette*, 8, 10 March 1970.

61. *Arkansas Gazette*, 15 March 1970, *New York Times*, 9 March 1970.

62. *Arkansas Gazette*, 10, 13, 15 March 1970; *New York Times*, 9 March 1970.

63. Eugene Newsom, Mid-South Opinion Surveys, 20 April 1970, WR Papers, Record Group IV, Box 82.

64. Interview with Cal Ledbetter, Jr., Little Rock, Arkansas, 15 September 1987.

65. Interview with Sterling Cockrill, 3 October 1989.

6. Fighting for Progress and Keeping the Peace

1. *Arkansas Democrat*, 7 April 1969; Winthrop Rockefeller to C. E. "Mike" Frost, 3 July 1969, WR Papers, Record Group III, Box 471, Folder 1.

2. One exception was a trip to France in May 1970 in which Rockefeller headed a United States delegation of four governors. The trip was an exchange program with French prefects and was labeled a "considerable contribution to Franco-American relations" by the State Department. As chairman of the Southern Governors Conference, Rockefeller played host to the four French prefects for a portion of their trip to the United States in September, for which he also received high marks from the State Department. A. E. Manell, acting special assistant to the secretary of state, to Winthrop Rockefeller, 5 June 1970, memo, A. E. Manell to the secretary, 1 June 1970, telegram, Ambassador Watson to Secretary Rogers, 8 June 1970, WR Papers, Record Group III, Box 527, Folder 4; Charles R. Tanguy to Winthrop Rockefeller, 24 September 1970, WR Papers, Record Group III, Box 597, Folder 3.

3. Telegram, Winthrop Rockefeller to the president, 4 November 1969, Richard Nixon to Winthrop Rockefeller, 4 June 1970, WR Papers, Record Group III, Box 550, Folder 2.

4. Winthrop Rockefeller to Garry Langston, 17 October 1969, WR Papers, Record Group III, Box 518, Folder 1.

5. *New York Times*, 16 October 1969; *Arkansas Gazette*, 15, 16 October 1969.

6. Statement by Gov. Winthrop Rockefeller, 14 October 1969, WR Papers, Record Group III, Box 337, Folder 3.

7. *Arkansas Gazette*, 15 October 1969.

8. *Arkansas Gazette*, 16 October 1969.

9. *New York Times*, 12 May, 4 June 1970; *Arkansas Gazette*, 2 May 1970.

10. *Arkansas Democrat*, 11 November 1969; *Arkansas Gazette*, 31 December 1970.

11. Arkansas Employment Security Division, Report of Minority Group Activities, October–December 1968, Governor's Council on Human Resources, Newsletter, December 1968, memo, Ozell Sutton to Winthrop Rockefeller, Marion Burton, Tom Eisele, Pete Thornton, and Truman Altenbaumer, 6 January 1969, memo, Neal Sox Johnson to Johnny Lang and York Williams, 2 April 1970, WR Papers, Record Group III, Box 116, Folder 2; Winthrop Rockefeller to Adolph Holmes, economic director, National Urban League, 16 May 1969, Winthrop Rockefeller to Adolph Holmes, 23 October 1969, WR Papers, Record Group III, Box 496, Folder 1; memo, York W. Williams, Jr., to Pete Thornton, 16 January 1970, WR Papers, Record Group IV, Box 93, Folder 2.

12. *New York Times*, 7 April 1969; *Arkansas Gazette*, 7 April 1969. The *Gazette* reported the crowd at six hundred people. According to the *Times*, three thousand attended.

13. Patricia Washington McGraw, Grif Stockley, and Nudie E. Williams, "We Speak for Ourselves: 1954 and After," in Tom Baskett, Jr., ed., *Persistence of the Spirit: The Black Experience in Arkansas* (Little Rock: Arkansas Endowment for the Humanities, 1986), 40–43.

14. McGraw, Stockley, and Williams, "We Speak for Ourselves," 43; *New York Times*, 17, 29 August 1969; *Arkansas Gazette*, 21, 22 March, 8 April, 6 June 1969.

15. Quoted in McGraw, Stockley, and Williams, "We Speak for Ourselves," 43.

16. *Arkansas Gazette*, 21, 22 March 1969.

17. *Arkansas Gazette*, 8 April 1969.

18. *Arkansas Gazette*, 6 June 1969.

19. *Arkansas Gazette*, 2 July 1969.

20. *Arkansas Gazette*, 11 August 1969.

21. Telegram, Winthrop Rockefeller to Rev. E. A. Williams, 5 August 1969, WR Papers, Record Group III, Box 98, Folder 2a; "A Special Meeting in the Governor's Conference Room in Regard to the Racial Situation in Forrest City," 6 August 1969, WR Papers, Record Group III, Box 338, Folder 1; *Arkansas Gazette*, 2 July, 11, 14, 17 August 1969; *New York Times*, 17 August 1969.

22. Ralph D. Scott to Winthrop Rockefeller, 18 August 1969, WR Papers, Record Group III, Box 86, Folder 13; *Arkansas Gazette*, 2 July, 13 August 1969.

23. Memo, Charles Allbright to John Ward, 19 August 1969, WR

Papers, Record Group III, Box 116, Folder 2.

24. *Arkansas Gazette*, 20 August 1969; *New York Times*, 20 August 1969; Ward, *The Arkansas Rockefeller*, 170–74.

25. Ralph D. Scott to Winthrop Rockefeller, 19 August 1969, WR Papers, Record Group III, Box 86, Folder 13; *Arkansas Gazette*, 20 August 1969; *New York Times*, 25 August 1969.

26. Reported in a memo, Ralph Scott to Bill Miller, 19 August 1969, WR Papers, Record Group III, Box 86, Folder 13.

27. *Arkansas Gazette*, 20, 21 August 1969.

28. *Washington Post*, 23 August 1969; State of Emergency Proclamation, 22 August 1969, WR Papers, Record Group III, Box 205, Folder 10; *New York Times*, 22, 25 August 1969; *Arkansas Democrat*, 20, 21, 25 August 1969; *Arkansas Gazette*, 22 August 1969.

29. *New York Times*, 29 August 1969.

30. *Arkansas Gazette*, 28 August 1969; State of Arkansas Executive Proclamation, 27 August 1969, WR Papers, Record Group III, Box 207, Folder 5; *New York Times*, 29, 30 August 1969; *Memphis Commercial Appeal*, 27 August 1969; *Arkansas Gazette*, 27, 28 August 1969.

31. Memo, Winthrop Rockefeller to Ralph Scott, 19 September 1969, Ralph Scott to Winthrop Rockefeller, 22 September 1969, WR Papers, Record Group III, Box 341, Folder 4; *Arkansas Gazette*, 17, 19, 20 September, 1, 28 October 1969; *Memphis Commercial Appeal*, 18 September 1969; *Arkansas Democrat*, 20 September 1969; Ward, *The Arkansas Rockefeller*, 174–75.

32. Statement by Gov. Winthrop Rockefeller, 11 September 1969, WR Papers, Record Group III, Box 207, Folder 5; *Arkansas Democrat*, 9 September 1969.

33. Kenneth McKee and Robert E. Fisher, Report on Conditions at Carthage, no date, WR Papers, Record Group IV, Box 112, Folder 3; *Arkansas Democrat*, 5 November, 4 December 1969. McKee, a state police officer on indefinite leave, and Fisher, a journalist, were put on Rockefeller's personal payroll to investigate racially troubled areas for the governor.

34. Sam Watkins, principal, Carthage Public Schools, to Robert Faulkner, 6 October 1969, WR Papers, Record Group III, Box 199, Folder 1; *Arkansas Democrat*, 5 November, 4 December 1969; *Pine Bluff Commercial*, 3 June 1970.

35. Race Relations Information Center, "Racial Protest in the South—1969 Style," as reported in the *Christian Science Monitor*, 3 December 1969.

36. Gradualism was not successfully challenged until 1969, when the Supreme Court ruled in *Alexander* v. *Holmes County Board of Education* that segregation must end immediately.

37. *New York Times*, 28 September 1970.

38. Telegram, Winthrop Rockefeller to Richard Nixon, 26 June 1969, WR Papers, Record Group III, Box 550, Folder 2; *New York Times*, 28 June 1969; *Arkansas Gazette*, 28 June 1969.

39. *New York Times*, 30, 31 January, 4 July 1969.

40. *New York Times*, 13 September 1969.

41. *New York Times*, 30 October 1969.

42. *New York Times*, 14 December 1969, 15 January, 3 February 1970.

43. Jerris Leonard, assistant attorney general, to Winthrop Rockefeller, 14 April 1970, Winthrop Rockefeller to Jerris Leonard, 3 April 1970, WR Papers, Record Group III, Box 521, Folder 1; *Arkansas Gazette*, 4 April 1970.

44. Jerris Leonard to Arkansas State Board of Education, 14 April 1970, WR Papers, Record Group III, Box 521, Folder 1.

45. State Board of Education to T. E. Patterson, 9 September 1968, WR Papers, Record Group III, Box 323, Folder 1. The Arkansas Teachers Association was the black teachers' organization.

46. *Arkansas Gazette*, 4 April 1970.

47. *Arkansas Gazette*, 11, 13 May 1970.

48. *Arkansas Gazette*, 14 May, 6, 18 June, 28 July, 1, 30 August 1970. Racially identifiable schools were those that were more than 80 percent black or white.

49. *New York Times*, 18 September 1969; Ward, *The Arkansas Rockefeller*, 176.

50. The October decision *Alexander v. Holmes County Board of Education* ordered integration "at once." In December the Court used this ruling to order six school districts in four states to desegregate by 1 February 1970. *New York Times*, 30 October, 14 December 1969.

51. *Arkansas Gazette*, 24 January 1970.

52. Memo, Dona Williams to Robert Faulkner and John Ward, 20 February 1970, WR Papers, Record Group III, Box 324, Folder 1; *Arkansas Gazette*, 5 February 1970.

53. Statement by Governor Rockefeller, 21 February 1970, WR Papers, Record Group IV, Box 165, Folder 4; petition to Winthrop Rockefeller, 5 February 1970, WR Papers, Record Group III, Box 83, Folder 2b; *Memphis Commercial Appeal*, 19 February 1970.

54. *Pine Bluff Commercial*, 24 February 1970; *Arkansas Gazette*, 22 February 1970.

55. Interview with Robert Faulkner, 9 February 1988.

56. *New York Times*, 26 February, 15, 25 March, 26 August 1970, 21 April 1971; *Chicago Daily News*, 25 February 1970.

57. Silas Hunt, in 1948, became the first black to attend the University of Arkansas's law school. His classes were held one-on-one in the basement. Hunt died of tuberculosis in 1949. Jackie L. Shropshire, who became the first black to graduate, spent his first few days in class with a railing around his desk to separate him from the other students. *Arkansas Gazette*, 31 January 1988.

58. Leon Panetta to Winthrop Rockefeller, 1 August 1969, memo, Mary McLeod, education advisor for Winthrop Rockefeller, to news media, 4 August 1969, WR Papers, Record Group IV, Box 167, Folder 7; Baskett,

Persistence of the Spirit, 38–40; *The Chronicle of Higher Education*, 25 March, 12 August 1987; *Arkansas Gazette*, 5 August, 11 October 1969; *Arkansas Democrat*, 11 October 1969.

59. *Arkansas Gazette*, 5 March 1969; *New York Times*, 5 March 1969.

60. *Arkansas Gazette*, 6, 12 March 1969.

61. *Arkansas Gazette*, 13 March 1969.

62. Telegram, Winthrop Rockefeller to Thomas J. Dodd, 12 March 1969, WR Papers, Record Group III, Box 99, Folder 1b.

63. *Arkansas Gazette*, 21 March 1969.

64. Tom Murton on the "Dick Cavett Show," typed transcript of interview, 28 September 1970, WR Papers, Record Group III, Box 641, Folder 1; Jean K. Tool to Winthrop Rockefeller, 23 September 1970, WR Papers, Record Group III, Box 601, Folder 5.

65. *New York Times*, 12 July, 23 November 1969; *Arkansas Gazette*, 12 July, 22 November 1969; *Arkansas Democrat*, 15 July 1969.

66. *Arkansas Gazette*, 17 January 1970.

67. *Arkansas Gazette*, 12 June 1969.

68. Reprinted in the *Arkansas Gazette*, 16 July 1969; *Memphis Commercial Appeal*, 19 July 1969; *Arkansas Gazette*, 27 July 1969.

69. *Arkansas Democrat*, 17 July 1969.

70. *Arkansas Gazette*, 19 September, 15, 20 November, 3 December 1969; *Memphis Commercial Appeal*, 19 September 1969.

71. *Arkansas Gazette*, 31 December 1969, 8, 25, 27 January 1970; *Arkansas Democrat*, 18 January 1970.

72. *Arkansas Gazette*, 19 February 1970.

73. *Arkansas Gazette*, 20 February 1970.

74. *Arkansas Gazette*, 6 March 1970; *Arkansas Democrat*, 24 February, 6 March 1970; *Arkansas Gazette*, 22, 25, 26 February, 7 March 1970.

75. *Arkansas Gazette*, 16, 19 April, 15 September 1970; *Arkansas Democrat*, 14 September 1970.

76. Memo, John Ward to Marion Burton, 17 July 1970, WR Papers, Record Group IV, Box 69, Folder 1.

77. *Arkansas Gazette*, 31 May 1970; *Pine Bluff Commercial*, 9 July 1970; *Arkansas Democrat*, 17 July 1970.

78. Winthrop Rockefeller to all circuit judges and prosecuting attorneys, 7 August 1970, WR Papers, Record Group III, Box 339, Folder 4.

79. Robert H. Dudley to Winthrop Rockefeller, 10 August 1970, Bill F. Doshier to Winthrop Rockefeller, 20 August 1970, Robert Faulkner to Aubrey Jackson, 26 August 1970, WR Papers, Record Group III, Box 339, Folder 4.

80. *Arkansas Gazette*, 3 November 1970.

81. *Arkansas Gazette*, 3 November 1970; *Arkansas Democrat*, 2 November 1970; *Pine Bluff Commercial*, 3 November 1970.

82. *Arkansas Gazette*, 26 February, 22, 24 November 1970; *Arkansas Democrat*, 22, 23 November 1970.

83. The worst of the prison riots of these years occurred in September 1971, at Attica prison in New York. Gov. Nelson Rockefeller had a far more difficult time of it than his brother in Arkansas. Thirty-three inmates and nine guards were slaughtered by the New York State Police in violence worse than the prison riots that precipitated the massacre. James E. Underwood and William J. Daniels, *Governor Rockefeller in New York: The Apex of Pragmatic Liberalism in the United States* (Westport, Conn.: Greenwood Press, 1982), 223–36.

84. *Arkansas Gazette*, 24 November 1970.

85. *Arkansas Democrat*, 5 March 1970; Peirce, *The Deep South States of America*, 143–44; Ward, *The Arkansas Rockefeller*, 111–14.

86. *Arkansas Democrat*, 31 December 1970; *Pine Bluff Commercial*, 11 December 1970.

87. Allan W. Horne to Marion Burton, 26 December 1968, WR Papers, Record Group III, Box 331, Folder 5; *Arkansas Gazette*, 11 February 1969, 6 March, 9 June, 14 October 1970; *Arkansas Democrat*, 25 February, 12 June, 9 July 1970.

88. State of Arkansas Executive Proclamation, 4 November 1969, WR Papers, Record Group III, Box 87, Folder 4; Edward L. Wright to Winthrop Rockefeller, 21 April 1969, WR Papers, Record Group III, Box 329, Folder 1; *Arkansas Democrat*, 21 April 1969; *Arkansas Gazette*, 19 August, 5 November 1969; Ward, *The Arkansas Rockefeller*, 149–53.

89. Ward, *The Arkansas Rockefeller*, 153–54.

90. *Arkansas Gazette*, 5 March 1969.

91. *Arkansas Gazette*, 19 March 1969.

92. Ralph D. Scott to Winthrop Rockefeller, 17 March 1969, WR Papers, Record Group III, Box 341, Folder 4.

93. Joe Purcell to Winthrop Rockefeller, 18 March 1969, WR Papers, Record Group III, Box 341, Folder 5.

94. Henry M. Britt to Ralph Scott, 19 March 1969, WR Papers, Record Group III, Box 341, Folder 5.

95. Bankston Waters to Marion Burton, 20 March 1969, WR Papers, Record Group III, Box 341, Folder 5.

96. Winthrop Rockefeller to Ralph Scott, 2 April 1969, Ralph Scott to Winthrop Rockefeller, 3 April 1969, WR Papers, Record Group III, Box 341, Folder 5.

97. *Arkansas Gazette*, 20 March 1969.

98. *Arkansas Gazette*, 6 June, 13 August 1969.

99. Winthrop Rockefeller to Richard Nixon, 16 September 1969, WR Papers, Record Group IV, Box 61, Folder 1; Winthrop Rockefeller to John N. Mitchell, 14 November 1969, WR Papers, Record Group III, Box 324, Folder 3; *Arkansas Democrat*, 29 September 1969, 30 April 1970; *Arkansas Gazette*, 18 August 1970.

7. Leaving a Mixed Legacy

1. Dr. Wayne Babbitt to fellow Republicans, 6 December 1966, WR Papers, Record Group IV, Box 124, Folder 1.

2. Interview with Everett A. Ham, Jr., 27 November 1987.

3. *Arkansas Gazette*, 18 December 1966.

4. *Arkansas Gazette*, 11 December 1966.

5. *Arkansas Gazette*, 11 December 1966.

6. See chapters 3 and 5 for a discussion of patronage and the state legislature.

7. Memo, Odell Pollard to members of the Conway County Republican Committee and members of the Conway County Republican Women's Club, 19 January 1967, Republican Archives, Series II, Box 2, File 13; *Arkansas Gazette*, 11 December 1966.

8. Memo, John Ward to Winthrop Rockefeller, 27 February 1967, Republican Archives, Series I, Box 1, File 2.

9. Gus Albright to Marion Burton, 16 May 1969, WR Papers, Record Group III, Box 343, Folder 1.

10. Van Rush to T. W. Carr, 7 February 1969, Republican Archives, Series II, Box 1, Folder 9.

11. Ralph D. Scott to F. S. Garrison, 20 March 1970, WR Papers, Record Group III, Box 341, Folder 3.

12. Willard A. Hawkins to Truman Altenbaumer, 6 December 1968, WR Papers, Record Group III, Box 233, Folder 2.

13. Ward, *The Arkansas Rockefeller*, 71.

14. *Arkansas Gazette*, 11 November 1970.

15. Interview with Everett A. Ham, Jr., 27 November 1987.

16. Remarks by Odell Pollard to the Urban League of Greater Little Rock, 12 May 1967, WR Papers, Record Group III, Box 43, Folder 3; *Arkansas Gazette*, 13 May 1967.

17. "A Public Progress Report," Arkansas Republican State Committee, September 1967, WR Papers, Record Group III, Box 43, Folder 3; "A Public Progress Report," Arkansas Republican State Committee, November 1967, WR Papers, Record Group III, Box 341, Folder 2; *Arkansas Gazette*, 29 February 1968, 28 August 1972. A discussion of the role of blacks in state government during Rockefeller's governorship can be found in chapters 4 and 6.

18. Lottman, "The GOP and the South," 27.

19. *Arkansas Gazette*, 24 July 1970.

20. Congressman John Paul Hammerschmidt to author, 16 February 1988.

21. Interview with Marion Burton, 27 November 1987.

22. Ulysses A. Lovell to Odell Pollard, 12 August 1968, WR Papers, Record Group III, Box 524, Folder 6.

23. Odell Pollard to Ulysses A. Lovell, 27 August 1968, WR Papers,

Record Group III, Box 524, Folder 6.

24. Rockefeller had endorsed Bernard in 1968 but refused to press the Democrats for Rockefeller organization to do so. Bernard was more conservative than Rockefeller and therefore unacceptable to liberal Democrats who were willing to cross party lines to vote for the governor. The fight over the state chairmanship will be discussed in more detail later in the chapter.

25. *Arkansas Gazette*, 6 April 1969.

26. *Arkansas Gazette*, 2, 11 May 1969.

27. Memo from Judy Petty, 16 September 1969, WR Papers, Record Group IV, Box 53, Folder 2. The memo was Petty's account of the meeting and was not addressed to anyone. At the time, Petty was state chairperson of the Young Republicans.

28. Memo from Judy Petty, 16 September 1969, WR Papers, Record Group IV, Box 53, Folder 2; Van Rush to John Mitchell, 10 September 1969, WR Papers, Record Group III, Box 345, Folder 6.

29. Eisele was appointed in January 1970, evidence that Rockefeller was able to influence federal patronage decisions.

30. *Arkansas Gazette*, 3 October 1969.

31. *Arkansas Democrat*, 16 November 1969.

32. *Arkansas Gazette*, 10 December 1969.

33. Memo, Neal Sox Johnson to Winthrop Rockefeller, Odell Pollard and other distinguished Republicans, 25 March 1970, WR Papers, Record Group III, Box 345, Folder 5.

34. *Arkansas Gazette*, 18 May 1970.

35. *Arkansas Gazette*, 17, 18 May 1970.

36. *Arkansas Gazette*, 19 May 1970.

37. Neal Sox Johnson to Dr. Corliss C. Curry, 25 May 1970, WR Papers, Record Group III, Box 506, Folder 1.

38. Memo, John Ward to Governor Rockefeller, 20 March 1969, WR Papers, Record Group IV, Box 58, Folder 3.

39. Maurice "Footsie" Britt to author, 24 November 1989.

40. *Arkansas Democrat*, 24 April, 19 May 1969, 19 February, 8 March, 19 April 1970; *Arkansas Gazette*, 19 April 1970.

41. Ward, *The Arkansas Rockefeller*, 179–80.

42. Ward, *The Arkansas Rockefeller*, 182.

43. Unsigned memo to Winthrop Rockefeller *re* a meeting attended by Glen Jermstad, Truman Altenbaumer, Ray Cooper, Gene Young, Joe Gaspard, Lynn Blaylock, Lefty Hawkins, Harold Hughes, and Eddie Holland, 1 April 1970, WR Papers, Record Group IV, Box 58, Folder 3.

44. Winthrop Rockefeller to fellow Republicans, 9 April 1970, WR Papers, Record Group III, Box 95, Folder 4.

45. *Arkansas Gazette*, 17 May 1970.

46. *New York Times*, 10 June 1970; Ward, *The Arkansas Rockefeller*, 182–83.

47. *Arkansas Democrat*, 21 December 1969.

48. Interview with Robert Faulkner, 9 February 1988.

49. John Ward to Governor Rockefeller, 20 March 1969, WR Papers, Record Group IV, Box 58, Folder 3.

50. Ward, *The Arkansas Rockefeller*, 183.

51. Memo, Greg Simon to Bob Fisher and Charles Allbright, 5 August 1970, WR Papers, Record Group III, Box 640, Folder 3; *New York Times*, 28 July 1970.

52. In retrospect, Faubus recalled that "when I got Bumpers [in the runoff] I knew school was out." Interview with Orval E. Faubus, 14 March 1988; Bumpers, who had considered running in 1968 but decided "the time was not right," recalled: "I felt confident that if I could reach enough people, I could get into the run-off with Governor Faubus. I also felt that people would prefer to vote for someone relatively new on the scene than return a somewhat controversial former governor to office." Sen. Dale Bumpers to author, 13 October 1989; *Arkansas Gazette*, 26, 27 August, 1 September 1970; *New York Times*, 25, 26 August 1970; Hathorn, "The Republican Party in Arkansas, 1920–1982," 2: 332–33.

53. *Arkansas Gazette*, 2, 3, 4, 9 September 1970; *New York Times*, 6, 10 September 1970; *Arkansas Democrat*, 3 September 1970.

54. *New York Times*, 11 September 1970.

55. *Arkansas Democrat*, 24 October 1969; *New York Times*, 16 November 1969, 26 August 1970; *Arkansas Gazette*, 1 September 1968, 8, 11 November 1969, 17 June 1970; Faubus, *Down from the Hills Two*, 486.

56. *Memphis Commercial Appeal*, 10 June 1970.

57. *Arkansas Democrat*, 10 June, 4 August 1970; *Arkansas Gazette*, 28 July, 26 August 1970.

58. *Arkansas Gazette*, 22 June, 3 September 1970; *Blytheville Courier News*, 1 July 1970; Arkansas Republican State Headquarters, primary election county vote, WR Papers, Record Group III, Box 177, Folder 8.

59. Interview with Sterling Cockrill, 3 October 1989.

60. Interview with Sterling Cockrill, 3 October 1989.

61. Maurice "Footsie" Britt to author, 24 November 1989.

62. Telegram, John Ward to Winthrop Rockefeller, 16 April 1970, WR Papers, Record Group III, Box 571, Folder 3; *Arkansas Democrat*, 20 July 1969, 16, 19 April 1970; *Arkansas Gazette*, 17, 19 April, 14 June, 26 August, 3 September 1970.

63. *Arkansas Gazette*, 22 August 1969, 17, 18, 21 June 1970; *Arkansas Democrat*, 29 June 1970; *New York Times*, 21 June 1970.

64. Mid-South Opinion Surveys, 20 April 1970, 13 September 1970, WR Papers, Record Group IV, Box 82.

65. Winthrop Rockefeller to the editor of the *Arkansas Gazette*, 23 December 1969, WR Papers, Record Group IV, Box 51, Folder 1.

66. Reprinted in *Pine Bluff Commercial*, 24 April 1970.

67. *Arkansas Gazette*, 19 December 1969, 8, 20 March, 20, 24 June, 3 July 1970.

68. *Arkansas Gazette*, 28 December 1969.

69. Interview with John L. Ward, 8 September 1986.

70. Interview with John L. Ward, 8 September 1986, memo, M. E. "Pete" Thornton to Aretha Proctor, 21 November 1969, WR Papers, Record Group III, Box 332, Folder 2.

71. Interview with John L. Ward, 8 September 1986, memo, John Ward to The Group, 9 September 1966, WR Papers, Record Group IV, Box 56, Folder 7; memo, John Ward and Tom Eisele to Winthrop Rockefeller, 12 August 1968, WR Papers, Record Group III, Box 642, Folder 1; *Arkansas Gazette*, 23 February 1973; Ward, *The Arkansas Rockefeller*, 180.

72. *Memphis Commercial Appeal*, 31 December 1969.

73. Memo, Clark Evans to John Ward, 27 October 1970, memo, Richard Moore to Charles Allbright, 23 June 1970, WR Papers, Record Group III, Box 279, Folder 7.

74. *Arkansas Gazette*, 19, 20 September 1970.

75. *Arkansas Gazette*, 4 October 1970.

76. "Remarks by Governor Winthrop Rockefeller to the Arkansas State Republican Convention," 3 October 1970, WR Papers, Record Group III, Box 640, Folder 1; *Arkansas Gazette*, 4 October 1970.

77. *Arkansas Gazette*, 11 October 1970.

78. J. Bill Becker to Winthrop Rockefeller, 23 June 1969, Winthrop Rockefeller to J. Bill Becker, 3 July 1969, J. Bill Becker to Winthrop Rockefeller, 9 July 1969, WR Papers, Record Group III, Box 81, Folder 5; statement by Governor Rockefeller, no date, WR Papers, Record Group III, Box 640, Folder 1; *Arkansas Gazette*, 31 December 1969, 2 August, 15 October 1970; *Arkansas Democrat*, 11, 15 October, 3 November 1970.

79. Winthrop Rockefeller to Dale Bumpers, 29 September 1970, WR Papers, Record Group III, Box 428, Folder 4; memo, "Footsie" Britt to Winthrop Rockefeller, 5 October 1970, memo, John Ward to Winthrop Rockefeller, 16 October 1970, statement by Marion Burton, 26 October 1970, WR Papers, Record Group IV, Box 58, Folder 4; statement by Gov. Winthrop Rockefeller, 29 October 1970, WR Papers, Record Group III, Box 640, Folder 1; *Pine Bluff Commercial*, 8 October 1970.

80. *New York Times*, 17 October 1970.

81. *Arkansas Gazette*, 21 October 1970.

82. Ward, *The Arkansas Rockefeller*, 189; *New York Times*, 9, 17 October 1970; *Arkansas Gazette*, 11 October 1970.

83. Reprinted in *New York Times*, 17 October 1970; *Arkansas Gazette*, 28 October 1970. Rockefeller's post-election expense report showed that he spent $1,314,162 in the 1970 campaign. Bumpers' expenses totaled $293,676. *Memphis Commercial Appeal*, 1 January 1971.

84. *Arkansas Gazette*, 21 October, 1 November 1970.

85. *Arkansas Democrat*, 31 October 1970.

86. Mid-South Opinion Surveys, 6, 9, 31 October 1970, WR Papers, Record Group IV, Box 82.

87. *Arkansas Gazette*, 4, 5 November 1970; *Arkansas Democrat*, 4 November 1970; Hathorn, "The Republican Party in Arkansas, 1920–1982," 2: 345–47; Ranchino, *Faubus to Bumpers*, 70.

88. Unsigned memo, 5 November 1970, WR Papers, Record Group III, Box 639, Folder 3. In a September 8, 1986, interview, John Ward claimed authorship of the memo.

89. Ranchino, *Faubus to Bumpers*, 70.

90. Numan V. Bartley and Hugh D. Graham, *Southern Elections County and Precinct Data, 1950–1972* (Baton Rouge: Louisiana State University Press, 1978), 353.

91. Ranchino, *Faubus to Bumpers*, 71.

92. *New York Times*, 5 November 1970; *Arkansas Gazette*, 5 November 1970. The other Republican governor in the South was Virginia's Linwood Holton, elected in 1969.

93. *New York Times*, 13 September, 5 November 1970.

94. Daily Journal, Arkansas Constitutional Convention, Arkansas Constitutional Convention Records, University of Arkansas at Little Rock Archives and Special Collections, University of Arkansas at Little Rock Library (hereafter cited as ACC Records), Box 1, Folder 7; Arkansas Constitutional Convention Roll Call, ACC Records, Box 2, Folder 9; Calvin R. Ledbetter, Jr., George E. Dyer, Robert E. Johnston, Wayne R. Swanson, and Walter H. Nunn, *Politics in Arkansas: The Constitutional Experience* (Little Rock: Academic Press of Arkansas, 1972), 66.

95. "Text of Address by Governor Winthrop Rockefeller to the Delegates of the Seventh Constitutional Convention of the State of Arkansas," 10 July 1969, WR Papers, Record Group III, Box 85, Folder 1. Rockefeller had little contact with the Convention once it convened. But Marion Burton and G. Thomas Eisele were both delegates, so presumably the governor's ideas were represented. Interview with Robert Faulkner, 9 February 1988.

96. "Proposed Arkansas Constitution of 1970 with Comments," 10 February 1970, ACC Records, Box 2, Folder 6.

97. *Arkansas Democrat*, 5 November 1970.

98. Sidney S. McMath to Winthrop Rockefeller, 6 November 1970, WR Papers, Record Group III, Box 321, Folder 4; Executive Department Proclamation, 30 November 1970, WR Papers, Record Group III, Box 325, Folder 1; *Arkansas Gazette*, 28 April, 7, 26 June, 4, 31 October, 1, 5, 8 November 1970; *Arkansas Democrat*, 1, 5, 11 November 1970; Ledbetter, Dyer, Johnston, Swanson, and Nunn, *Politics in Arkansas*, 188–93.

99. Rev. J. F. Cooley to Winthrop Rockefeller, 17 November 1970, WR Papers, Record Group III, Box 443, Folder 2.

100. *New York Times*, 30 December 1970.

101. Robert Sarver to Winthrop Rockefeller and John Haley, 22 December 1970, WR Papers, Record Group III, Box 639, Folder 3; Anthony G. Amsterdam, professor of law, Stanford University Law School, to Winthrop Rockefeller, 22 December 1970, WR Papers, Record Group III, Box 646, Folder 6; statement by Winthrop Rockefeller, 11 January 1971, Commutation of Death Sentences—January 1971, Winthrop Rockefeller to Fred Oakley, chairman, Pardon and Parole Board, 11 January 1971, WR Papers, Record Group III, Box 646, Folder 1.

102. Ed Bethune to Winthrop Rockefeller, 30 December 1970, WR Papers, Record Group III, Box 339, Folder 4; memo, count of letters for and against governor's commutations, 21 January 1971, WR Papers, Record Group III, Box 646, Folder 1; *Arkansas Gazette*, 31 December 1970; *Arkansas Democrat*, 30 December 1970; *The National Observer*, 11 January 1971.

103. Winthrop Rockefeller, "Executive Clemency and the Death Penalty," *Catholic University Law Review* 21 (Fall 1971): 97–102.

104. *Arkansas Democrat*, 30 December 1970.

105. *Arkansas Gazette*, 6 September 1987. The other Southern state to conduct no executions was Tennessee. Between 1976 and September 1987, ninety people were executed in the United States—all but six in the South.

106. W. T. "Bill" Kelly to Dear Republican Co-Worker, 2 July 1970, Winthrop Rockefeller to Charles Bernard, 17 July 1970, WR Papers, Record Group IV, Box 53, Folder 2; *Arkansas Gazette*, 14 July, 5, 7 August, 12 September, 4 October 1970.

107. Unaddressed letter from Winthrop Rockefeller, 18 November 1970, WR Papers, Record Group III, Box 345, Folder 5; memo, Judy Petty to John Ward, 8 November 1970, WR Papers, Record Group IV, Box 53, Folder 2; *Arkansas Gazette*, 13, 15, 19 November 1970; Ward, *The Arkansas Rockefeller*, 186.

108. Ward, *The Arkansas Rockefeller*, 187; *Arkansas Gazette*, 22 November 1970.

109. *Arkansas Gazette*, 29 November 1970.

110. Interview with Robert Faulkner, 9 February 1988.

111. Reprinted in Ward, *The Arkansas Rockefeller*, 187; unaddressed memo from John Ward, 1 April 1971, WR Papers, Record Group III, Box 140, Folder 10; *Arkansas Gazette*, 8 May 1971.

112. *Arkansas Gazette*, 14, 15, 16, 17, 26 September, 27 October 1971, 16 February, 4 March, 5 April, 9, 16 July, 3 September, 9 November 1972; *Arkansas Democrat*, 15, 17 September 1971.

113. *Arkansas Gazette*, 20 February 1971; *New York Times*, 20 February, 23, 27 March, 30 April 1971; Moscow, *The Rockefeller Inheritance*, 293–94;

Collier and Horowitz, *The Rockefellers*, 444–45.

114. *New York Times*, 22 July 1971; Moscow, *The Rockefeller Inheritance*, 297.

115. *Arkansas Democrat*, 6 October 1972, 22 February 1973; *Arkansas Gazette*, 6 October 1972, 23 February 1973; *Pine Bluff Commercial*, 25 October 1972; *New York Times*, 23, 24 February 1973.

116. *Arkansas Gazette*, 5 March 1973; *New York Times*, 5 March 1973; Ward, *The Arkansas Rockefeller*, 200–06; Moscow, *The Rockefeller Inheritance*, 297–98; Collier and Horowitz, *The Rockefellers*, 446–47.

8. In Perspective

1. *Arkansas Gazette*, 21 June 1964; *WR Campaigner*, 16 September 1966.

2. Interview with Everett A. Ham, Jr., 27 November 1987.

3. Winthrop Rockefeller to Dr. Leslie E. Mack, 13 January 1967, WR Papers, Record Group III, Box 100, Folder 6.

4. Winthrop Rockefeller to R. Hugh Uhlmann, 26 October 1967, WR Papers, Record Group III, Box 604, Folder 3.

5. Interview with G. Thomas Eisele, Little Rock, Arkansas, 25 February 1988.

6. *Arkansas Gazette*, 23 August 1987.

7. *Arkansas Gazette*, 4 March 1973; "WR 70 Fact Sheet: Accomplishments during the Rockefeller Administration in the Area of Prison Reform," WR Papers, Record Group III, Box 640, Folder 2.

8. Interview with Cal Ledbetter, Jr., 15 September 1987. Ledbetter was in Arkansas's house of representatives during Rockefeller's governorship.

9. *Arkansas Gazette*, 27 September 1987.

10. Interview with John L. Ward, 8 September 1986.

11. Peirce, *The Deep South States of America*, 141.

12. *New York Times*, 22 February 1971; Peirce, *The Deep South States of America*, 142.

13. Interview with Cal Ledbetter, Jr., 15 September 1987.

14. Interview with Sterling Cockrill, 3 October 1989.

15. Memo, Charles Allbright to Winthrop Rockefeller, 24 May 1971, WR Papers, Record Group III, Box 639, Folder 2; *New York Times*, 9 May 1971; Williams, et al., *A Documentary History of Arkansas*, 246.

16. Interview with Cal Ledbetter, Jr., 15 September 1987; *New York Times*, 9 May 1971.

17. Sen. Dale Bumpers to author, 13 October 1989.

18. In 1966 Arkansas was one of only four states in the nation still electing their governor every two years. In 1984 Arkansas voters approved a constitutional amendment changing this to a four-year term. Cal Ledbetter, Jr.,

"The Office of Governor in Arkansas History," *Arkansas Historical Quarterly* 37 (Spring 1978): 69.

19. Interview with John L. Ward, 8 September 1986.

20. Interview with Robert Faulkner, 9 February 1988.

21. Ward, *The Arkansas Rockefeller,* 36.

22. Interview with Everett A. Ham, Jr., 27 November 1987.

23. Interview with Orval E. Faubus, 14 March 1988.

24. Nelson [Rockefeller] to Win [Rockefeller], 11 November 1970, WR Papers, Record Group III, Box 571, Folder 3.

25. Paul Meers to Winthrop Rockefeller, 14 December 1970, WR Papers, Record Group III, Box 538, Folder 3.

26. Interview with John L. Ward, 8 September 1986.

27. Interview with G. Thomas Eisele, 25 February 1988.

28. Sen. Dale Bumpers to author, 13 October 1989.

29. "Address by Governor Winthrop Rockefeller to the Arkansas General Assembly, 12 January 1971," WR Papers, Record Group IV, Box 196, Folder 9.

30. Everett Ham vehemently disagrees with this theory. He feels that it was possible to appoint more Republicans and that a two-party system may have been created had Rockefeller taken advantage of the opportunity that was there. Interview with Everett A. Ham, Jr., 27 November 1987.

31. Hathorn, "The Republican Party in Arkansas, 1920–1982," 2: 379–80.

32. Interview with Marion Burton, 27 November 1987.

33. Interview with Everett A. Ham, Jr., 27 November 1987.

34. Interview with John L. Ward, 8 September 1986.

35. The South encompasses the eleven states of the Confederacy. The Deep South includes Georgia, Alabama, Louisiana, South Carolina, and Mississippi, while the Outer, Upper, or Rim South refers to Virginia, Tennessee, North Carolina, Florida, Texas, and Arkansas. While Florida and Texas are historically part of the Deep South, most twentieth-century historians and political scientists place them in the Rim South because neither state fits the Deep South mold. Florida's politics have been tremendously influenced by mass northern migrations into the state, while Texas is as much western as it is southern. Arkansas is considered a swing state. Geographically it is in the Upper South, while philosophically it has much in common with the Deep South. Neil R. Peirce includes it in the latter in his book *The Deep South States of America.*

36. Strom Thurmond became a Republican in 1964. Alexander P. Lamis, *The Two-Party South,* (New York: Oxford University Press, 1984), 65–66.

37. Kevin P. Phillips, *The Emerging Republican Majority* (New Rochelle, N.Y.: Arlington House, 1969), 28, 54, 244.

38. Lamis, *The Two-Party South,* 3–4, 18–19; Charles P. Roland, *The Improbable Era: The South since World War II* (Lexington: University Press of

Kentucky, 1975), 81; Bass and DeVries, *The Transformation of Southern Politics*, 2, 7, 9.

39. George Brown Tindall, *The Disruption of the Solid South*, (Athens: University of Georgia Press, 1972), 55.

40. Tindall, *The Disruption of the Solid South*, 62.

41. Louis M. Seagull, *Southern Republicanism*, (New York: John Wiley and Sons, 1975), 93–104, 138; Lamis, *The Two-Party South*, 44, 65–66, 76–83, 113, 182; Lottman, "The GOP and the South," 19, 32, 36, 44, 61.

42. *Wall Street Journal*, 1 October 1970; Lamis, *The Two-Party South*, 134–35, 163–68; Seagull, *Southern Republicanism*, 118–24; Tindall, *The Disruption of the Solid South*, 66.

43. *Wall Street Journal*, 1 October 1970; Bass and DeVries, *The Transformation of Southern Politics*, 29; Lamis, *The Two-Party South*, 150.

44. Black, *Southern Governors and Civil Rights*, 342. The one state not mentioned, Texas, was an anomaly in the 1960s South in that race was not a dominant issue. The state remained solidly Democratic in this decade, but the economy was the primary reason. Lamis, *The Two-Party South*, 209; Lottman, "The GOP and the South," 78; Monroe Billington, *Southern Politics since the Civil War* (Malabar, Florida: Robert E. Krieger, 1984), 144–59.

45. Bass and DeVries, *The Transformation of Southern Politics*, 34–37.

46. The Ripon Society and Clifford W. Brown, Jr., *Jaws of Victory: The Game-Plan Politics of 1972, the Crisis of the Republican Party and the Future of the Constitution* (Boston: Little, Brown, 1973), 264.

47. *New York Times*, 9 May 1971.

48. Interview with Marion Burton, 27 November 1987.

Bibliography

Primary Sources

Manuscript Collections

Abilene, Kansas. Dwight D. Eisenhower Library.
    Dwight D. Eisenhower: Records as President. White House Central Files, 1953–61. Official File.
    Papers of Dwight D. Eisenhower as President of the United States (Ann Whitman File), 1953–61. Dwight D. Eisenhower Diaries Series.
Fayetteville, Arkansas. University of Arkansas.
    Orval Eugene Faubus Papers.
    J. William Fulbright Papers.
Little Rock, Arkansas. Arkansas History Commission. Legislative Records.
Little Rock, Arkansas. University of Arkansas at Little Rock.
    Arkansas Constitutional Convention Records.
    Arkansas Republican Party Archives.
    FBI–Little Rock Crisis Reports.
    Winthrop Rockefeller Collection.
    Wallace Townsend Papers.
North Tarrytown, New York. Rockefeller Archive Center.
    Audio Tapes. James Hudson Interview. 1 May 1973.
    Audio Tapes. Margaret Black Interview. 18 October 1973.
    Alvin Moscow Papers.
    Rockefeller Family Archives.

Interviews

Burton, Marion. Little Rock, Arkansas. 27 November 1987.
Cockrill, Sterling. Little Rock, Arkansas. 3 October 1989.
Eisele, G. Thomas. Little Rock, Arkansas. 25 February 1988.

Faubus, Orval E. Conway, Arkansas. 14 March 1988.
Faulkner, Robert. Little Rock, Arkansas. 9 February 1988.
Ham, Everett A., Jr. North Little Rock, Arkansas. 27 November 1987.
Ledbetter, Cal, Jr. Little Rock, Arkansas. 15 September 1987.
Ward, John L. Little Rock, Arkansas. 8 September 1986.

Correspondence

Britt, Maurice "Footsie." Little Rock, Arkansas. 24 November 1989.
Bumpers, Dale. Washington, D.C. 13 October 1989.
Hammerschmidt, John Paul. Washington, D.C. 16 February 1988.

Published Reports

Arkansas Department of Correction. *Annual Report to the Governor and the
    General Assembly Covering the Period March 1, 1968 to September 30,
    1970.* Little Rock: 1970.
Ewald, William R., Jr. *A Special Report for Winthrop Rockefeller: Development
    Program Recommendations for Arkansas.* Washington, D.C.: 1965.
National Council on Crime and Delinquency. *Probation and Parole in
    Arkansas: A Survey for the Arkansas Penitentiary Study Commission.* New
    York: 1967.
Penitentiary Study Commission Report. Little Rock: 1968.

First Person Accounts

Alford, Dale, and Alford, L'Moore. *The Case of the Sleeping People Finally
    Awakened by Little Rock School Frustrations.* Little Rock: 1959.
Bates, Daisy. *The Long Shadow of Little Rock, A Memoir.* New York: McKay,
    1962; Fayetteville: University of Arkansas Press, 1987.
Blossom, Virgil T. *It Has Happened Here.* New York: Harper and Brothers,
    1959.
Faubus, Orval Eugene. *Down from the Hills.* Little Rock: Pioneer, 1980.
———. *Down from the Hills Two.* Little Rock: Democrat Printing and
    Lithographing, 1986.
Hays, Brooks. *Politics is My Parish: An Autobiography.* Baton Rouge: Louisiana
    State University Press, 1981.
———. *A Southern Moderate Speaks.* Chapel Hill: University of North
    Carolina Press, 1959.
Jackson, Bruce. *Killing Time: Life in the Arkansas Penitentiary.* Ithaca, N.Y.:
    Cornell University Press, 1977.

Murton, Tom, and Hyams, Joe. *Accomplices to the Crime*. New York: Grove
    Press, 1969.
Rockefeller, Winthrop. "Development of Rural Areas through
    Industrialization." *The Arkansas Economist* 2 (Fall 1959): 1–7.
———. "Executive Clemency and the Death Penalty." *Catholic University Law
    Review* 21 (Fall 1971): 94–102.
———. "Philanthropy Faces a Change." *American Mercury*, February 1953,
    29–33.
Shannon, Karr. *Integration Decision Is Unconstitutional*. Little Rock: Democrat
    Printing and Lithographing, 1958.
Starr, John Robert. *Yellow Dogs and Dark Horses: Thirty Years on the Campaign
    Beat with John Robert Starr*. Little Rock: August House, 1987.
Ward, John L. *The Arkansas Rockefeller*. Baton Rouge: Louisiana State
    University Press, 1978.
Woodcock, Dale. *Ruled by the Whip: Hell Behind Bars in America's Devil's
    Island—The Arkansas State Penitentiary*. New York: Exposition Press,
    1958.

Contemporary Articles and Newspapers

Akron (Ohio) *Beacon Journal*, 15 November 1970.
Amsterdam News (New York), 1 January 1949.
Arizona Republic (Phoenix), 12 February 1968.
Arkansas Democrat (Little Rock), 1962–73.
Arkansas Gazette (Little Rock), 1953–73.
Arkansas Outlook: News of an Advancing Republican Party (Little Rock),
    December 1964–January 1971.
Ashmore, Harry S. "The Untold Story behind Little Rock." *Harper's*, June
    1958.
The Benton (Arkansas) *Courier*, 19 December 1968.
"Big Rock of Little Rock." *Reader's Digest*, March 1967, 111–15.
Blytheville (Arkansas) *Courier News*, 1 July 1970.
Business Week, 22 December 1956.
Chicago Daily News, 25 February 1970.
Christian Science Monitor, 22 September 1965; 11 November 1966; 5 February
    1968; 3 December 1969; 30 October, 3 November 1970.
The Cleveland Plain Dealer, 21 July 1968.
Dallas Morning News, 29 June 1969.
Dayton (Ohio) *Daily News*, 17 February 1968.
The Economist (London), 30 March 1968.
Fort Smith (Arkansas) *Times Record*, 28 February 1963; 19 January 1969.
"Here's What Happened in the Legislature." *Journal of Arkansas Education* 39
    (May 1967): 4–9.

Hollywood (Florida) *Sun Tattler,* 22 April 1965.
Hot Springs Sentinel Record, 22 February 1968.
Houston Chronicle, 31 January 1968.
Kansas City Star, 20 March 1968.
Kansas City Times, 9 May 1969.
Life, 23 February 1948; 6 September 1963.
Lomax, Louis E. "Two Millionaires, Two Senators, and a Faubus; The
     Curious Constellation of Arkansas Politics." *Harper's,* March 1960,
     73–76, 82–86.
Los Angeles Times, 4 February, 11 March 1968; 23 February 1973.
Lottman, Michael S. "The GOP and the South." *Ripon Forum* 6 (July–August
     1970).
Magnolia (Arkansas) *Daily Banner-News,* 7 November 1967; 7 February 1968.
Memphis Commercial Appeal, 1967–71.
Milwaukee (Wisconsin) *Sentinel,* 4 May 1967.
National Observer, 11 January 1971.
New Orleans Times-Picayune, 15 July 1968.
New Republic, 25 April 1964; 6 April 1968.
Newsweek, 23 February 1948; 1 June 1964; 24 May 1965; 12 February 1968.
New York Daily News, 16 October 1966.
New York Herald Tribune, 19 January–31 January 1958.
New York Times, 1931–73.
North Little Rock Times, 28 February 1963.
Pine Bluff Commercial, 1966–72.
Racine (Wisconsin) *Journal-Times,* 7 February 1968.
The Reporter, 22 October 1964; 5 October 1967.
Richmond Times-Dispatch, 17 April 1969.
St. Louis Post-Dispatch, 19 February 1967; 1 February, 23 April 1968.
San Francisco Chronicle, 1 January 1970.
Saturday Evening Post, 30 December 1950; 6, 13 January 1951; 29 September
     1956; 19 September 1964; 19 November 1966.
Shreveport Journal, 6 February 1968.
Smith, Adam. "Behold the Brothers Rockefeller, Bearing Gifts." *Esquire,*
     December 1983, 218–24.
Smith, Richard Austin. "The Rockefeller Brothers." *Fortune,* February 1955,
     138–50.
———. "The Rockefeller Brothers II." *Fortune,* March 1955, 114–18, 130–34.
Suffolk (New York) *Eagle,* 10 February 1968.
Time, 23 February 1948; 11 March 1957; 11 April 1960; 8 March 1963; 16
     October 1964; 2 December 1966; 21 July 1967.
Topeka State Journal, 8 May 1967.
Tulsa Tribune, 18 March 1965.
U.S. News and World Report, 20 June 1958; 1 February 1960; 4 May 1964.
Walker, John Hennessey. "2,000,000 Young Americans Get Boost to Aviation

Careers." *Popular Science*, March 1941, 49–53.
Wall Street Journal, 31 March 1964; 1 November 1966; 23 August 1967; 1 October 1970.
Washington, D. C., *Evening Star*, 21 April 1965; 12 July 1969; 29 October 1970.
Washington Post, 1 February 1948; 19 April 1965; 4 February 1966; 23 August 1969.
W. R. Campaigner: News of the Coming Victory in Arkansas, 15 August–24 October 1964; 4 August–1 November 1966; 16 August–1 November 1968.

Secondary Sources

Books and Articles

Ashmore, Harry S. *Arkansas: A History*. New York: W. W. Norton, 1978; reprint, 1984.
———. *An Epitaph for Dixie*. New York: W. W. Norton, 1957.
———. "This is Arkansas." *Center Magazine* 9 (November–December 1976): 2–7.
Bartley, Numan V. "Looking Back at Little Rock." *Arkansas Historical Quarterly* 25 (Summer 1966): 101–16.
———. *The Rise of Massive Resistance: Race and Politics in the South during the 1950's*. Baton Rouge: Louisiana State University Press, 1969.
Bartley, Numan V., and Graham, Hugh D. *Southern Elections County and Precinct Data, 1950–1972*. Baton Rouge: Louisiana State University Press, 1978.
———. *Southern Politics and the Second Reconstruction*. Baltimore: Johns Hopkins University Press, 1975.
Baskett, Tom, Jr., ed. *Persistence of the Spirit: The Black Experience in Arkansas*. Little Rock: Arkansas Endowment for the Humanities, 1986.
Bass, Jack, and DeVries, Walter. *The Transformation of Southern Politics: Social Change and Political Consequence since 1945*. New York: Basic Books, 1976.
Billington, Monroe Lee. *The American South: A Brief History*. New York: Scribner, 1971.
———. *The Political South in the Twentieth Century*. New York: Scribner, 1975.
———. *Southern Politics since the Civil War*. Malabar, Fla.: Robert E. Krieger, 1984.
Black, Earl. *Southern Governors and Civil Rights: Racial Segregation in the South as a Campaign Issue in the Second Reconstruction*. Cambridge, Mass.: Harvard University Press, 1976.

Blair, Diane D. *Arkansas Politics and Government: Do the People Rule?* Lincoln:
  University of Nebraska Press, 1988.
Boles, John B., and Nolen, Evelyn Thomas, eds. *Interpreting Southern History:
  Historiographical Essays in Honor of Sanford W. Higginbotham.* Baton
  Rouge: Louisiana State University Press, 1987.
Chase, Mary Ellen. *Abby Aldrich Rockefeller.* New York: Macmillan, 1950.
Clark, Thomas D., ed. *The South since Reconstruction.* Indianapolis: Bobbs-
  Merrill, 1973.
Collier, Peter, and Horowitz, David. *The Rockefellers: An American Dynasty.*
  New York: Holt, Rinehart and Winston, 1976.
Desmond, James. *Nelson Rockefeller: A Political Biography.* New York:
  Macmillan, 1964.
Dillard, Tom W., and Dougan, Michael B. *Arkansas History: A Selected Research
  Bibliography.* Little Rock: Department of Arkansas Natural and Cultural
  Heritage, 1984.
Dillard, Tom W., and Twing, Valerie. *Researching Arkansas History: A Beginners
  Guide.* Little Rock: Rose Publishing, 1979.
Donovan, Timothy P., and Gatewood, Willard B., Jr., eds. *The Governors of
  Arkansas: Essays in Political Biography.* Fayetteville: University of
  Arkansas Press, 1981.
Durning, Dan. "Arkansas 1954 to Present." In *Historical Report of the Secretary
  of State of Arkansas.* Vol. 3, *A History of Arkansas,* 186–202. Little Rock:
  1978.
Ferguson, John L., ed. *Arkansas Lives: The Opportunity Land Who's Who.*
  Hopkinsville, Ky.: Historical Record Association, 1965.
Freyer, Tony. *The Little Rock Crisis: A Constitutional Interpretation.* Westport,
  Conn.: Greenwood Press, 1984.
Gaston, Paul M. *The New South Creed: A Study in Southern Myth Making.*
  Baton Rouge: Louisiana State University Press, 1976.
Goldfield, David R. *Promised Land: The South since 1945.* Arlington Heights,
  Ill.: Harlan Davidson, 1987.
Grantham, Dewey W. *The Regional Imagination: The South and Recent American
  History.* Nashville: Vanderbilt University Press, 1979.
Harr, John Ensor, and Johnson, Peter J. *The Rockefeller Century.* New York:
  Charles Scribner's Sons, 1988.
Hathorn, Billy Burton. "Pratt Cates Remmel [b. 1915]: The Thrust towards
  Republicanism in Arkansas, 1951–1955." *Arkansas Historical Quarterly*
  43 (Winter 1984): 304–23.
Havard, William C., ed. *The Changing Politics of the South.* Baton Rouge:
  Louisiana State University Press, 1972.
Heard, Alexander. *A Two-Party South.* Chapel Hill: University of North
  Carolina Press, 1952.
Hess, Stephen, and Broder, David S. *The Republican Establishment: The Present
  and Future of the G. O. P.* New York: Harper and Row, 1967.

Hinshaw, Jerry E. *Call the Roll: The First One Hundred Fifty Years of the Arkansas Legislature*. Little Rock: Rose Publishing, 1987.

Hollinsworth, Harold M., ed. *Essays on Recent Southern Politics*. Austin: University of Texas Press, 1970.

Huckaby, Elizabeth. *Crisis at Central High, Little Rock, 1957–58*. Baton Rouge: Louisiana State University Press, 1980.

Huebner, Lee W., and Petri, Thomas E. *The Ripon Papers 1963–1968*. Washington, D.C.: National Press, 1968.

Jacoway, Elizabeth, and Colburn, David R., eds. *Southern Businessmen and Desegregation*. Baton Rouge: Louisiana State University Press, 1982.

Key, V. O., Jr. "Secular Realignment and the Party System." *Journal of Politics* 21 (May 1959): 198–212.

———. *Southern Politics in State and Nation*. New York: Alfred A. Knopf, 1949.

Kutz, Myer. *Rockefeller Power*. New York: Simon and Schuster, 1974.

Lamis, Alexander P. *The Two-Party South*. New York: Oxford University Press, 1984.

Ledbetter, Cal, Jr. "The Office of Governor in Arkansas History." *Arkansas Historical Quarterly* 37 (Spring 1978): 44–73.

Ledbetter, Calvin R., Jr.; Dyer, George E.; Johnston, Robert E.; Swanson, Wayne R.; and Nunn, Walter H. *Politics in Arkansas: The Constitutional Experience*. Little Rock: Academic Press of Arkansas, 1972.

Lester, Jim. *A Man for Arkansas: Sid McMath and the Southern Reform Tradition*. Little Rock: Rose Publishing, 1976.

Lisenby, Foy. "A Survey of Arkansas's Image Problem." *Arkansas Historical Quarterly* 30 (Spring 1971): 60–71.

———. "Winthrop Rockefeller and the Arkansas Image." *Arkansas Historical Quarterly* 43 (Summer 1984): 143–52.

Lundberg, Ferdinand. *The Rockefeller Syndrome*. Secaucus, N.J.: Lyle Stuart, 1975.

Manchester, William. *A Rockefeller Family Portrait: From John D. to Nelson*. Boston: Little, Brown, 1958.

Matthews, Donald R., and Protho, James W. *Negroes and the New Southern Politics*. New York: Harcourt, Brace and World, 1966.

Mayer, George H. *The Republican Party 1854–1966*. 2d ed. New York: Oxford University Press, 1967.

Moreland, Laurence W.; Baker, Tod A.; and Steed, Robert P., eds. *Contemporary Southern Political Attitudes and Behavior: Studies and Essays*. New York: Praeger, 1982.

Morris, Joe Alex. *Those Rockefeller Brothers: An Informal Biography of Five Extraordinary Young Men*. New York: Harper and Brothers, 1953.

Moscow, Alvin. *The Rockefeller Inheritance*. Garden City, N.Y.: Doubleday, 1977.

Murphy, Reg, and Gulliver, Hal. *The Southern Strategy*. New York: Charles Scribner's Sons, 1971.

Nunn, Walter, ed. *Readings in Arkansas Government*. Little Rock: Rose
    Publishing, 1973.
Nunn, Walter, and Collett, Kay G. *Political Paradox: Constitutional Revision in
    Arkansas* . New York: National Municipal League, 1973.
Oates, Stephen B. *Let the Trumpet Sound: The Life of Martin Luther King, Jr.*
    New York: Mentor, 1982.
Patterson, Thomas E. *History of the Arkansas Teachers Association*. Washington,
    D.C.: National Education Association, 1981.
Peirce, Neal R. *The Border South States of America: People, Politics, and Power in
    the Five Border States*. New York: W. W. Norton, 1975.
————. *The Deep South States of America: People, Politics, and Power in the Seven
    Deep South States*. New York: W. W. Norton, 1974.
Perry, James M. *The New Politics: The Expanding Technology of Political
    Manipulation*. New York: Clarkson N. Potter, 1968.
Phillips, Kevin P. *The Emerging Republican Majority*. New Rochelle, N.Y.:
    Arlington House, 1969.
Pyle, Tom. *Pocantico: Fifty Years on the Rockefeller Domain*. New York: Duell,
    Sloan and Pearce, 1964.
Ranchino, Jim. *Faubus to Bumpers: Arkansas Votes, 1960–1970*. Arkadelphia,
    Ark.: Action Research, 1972.
Reinhard, David W. *The Republican Right since 1945*. Lexington: University of
    Kentucky Press, 1983.
Ripon Society, and Brown, Clifford W., Jr. *Jaws of Victory: The Game-Plan
    Politics of 1972, the Crisis of the Republican Party and the Future of the
    Constitution*. Boston: Little, Brown, 1973.
Roland, Charles P. *The Improbable Era: The South since World War II*.
    Lexington: University of Kentucky Press, 1975.
Rubin, Louis D., Jr., ed. *The American South: Portrait of a Culture*. Baton
    Rouge: Louisiana State University Press, 1980.
Rusher, William A. *The Making of the New Majority Party*. New York: Sheed
    and Ward, 1975.
Seagull, Louis M. *Southern Republicanism*. New York: John Wiley and Sons,
    1975.
Sherrill, Robert. *Gothic Politics in the Deep South: Stars of the New Confederacy*.
    New York: Grossman, 1968.
Sindler, Allan P. *Change in the Contemporary South*. Durham, N.C.: Duke
    University Press, 1963.
Smith, C. Calvin. *War and Wartime Changes: The Transformation of Arkansas
    1940–1945*. Fayetteville: University of Arkansas Press, 1986.
Sobel, Lester A., ed. *Civil Rights 1960–66*. New York: Facts on File, 1967.
Strong, Donald S. *Issue Voting and Party Realignment*. University, Ala.:
    University of Alabama Press, 1977.
————. *Urban Republicanism in the South*. University, Ala.: University of
    Alabama Press, 1960.

Tindall, George Brown. *The Disruption of the Solid South*. Athens: University of Georgia Press, 1972.

Topping, John C., Jr.; Lazarek, John R.; and Linder, William H. *Southern Republicanism and the New South*. Cambridge, Mass.: Republicans for Progress and the Ripon Society, 1966.

Trover, Ellen Lloyd, and Swindler, William F., eds. *Arkansas: A Chronology and Documentary Handbook*. Dobbs Ferry, N.Y.: Oceana Publications, 1972.

Underwood, James E., and Daniels, William J. *Governor Rockefeller in New York: The Apex of Pragmatic Liberalism in the United States*. Westport, Conn.: Greenwood Press, 1982.

Watters, Pat. *The South and the Nation*. New York: Pantheon Books, 1969.

Wells, John F. *Time Bomb (The Faubus Revolt)*. Little Rock: General Publishers, 1962.

White, Theodore H. *America in Search of Itself: The Making of the President 1956–1980*. New York: Harper and Row, 1982.

Williams, C. Fred; Bolton, S. Charles; Moneyhon, Carl H.; Williams, LeRoy T., eds. *A Documentary History of Arkansas*. Fayetteville: University of Arkansas Press, 1984.

Woodward, C. Vann. *The Burden of Southern History*. Rev. ed. Baton Rouge: Louisiana State University Press, 1968.

———. *Origins of the New South*. Baton Rouge: Louisiana State University Press, 1951.

Unpublished Sources

Black, Robert Earl. "Southern Governors and the Negro: Race as a Campaign Issue since 1954." Ph.D. diss., Harvard University, 1968.

Drummond, Boyce Alexander, Jr. "Arkansas Politics: A Study of a One-Party System." Ph.D. diss., University of Chicago, 1957.

Hammons, Lyle W. "Campaign Communication Strategies and Techniques of Winthrop Rockefeller, A Study in Persuasion." M.A. thesis, University of Arkansas at Little Rock, 1985.

Hathorn, Billy Burton. "The Republican Party in Arkansas, 1920–1982." Vols. 1 and 2. Ph.D. diss., Texas A&M University, 1983.

Jones, Merrill Anway. "A Rhetorical Study of Winthrop Rockefeller's Political Speeches 1964–1971." Ph.D. diss., Louisiana State University, 1984.

Kielhorn, Thomas G. "Party Development and Partisan Change: An Analysis of Changing Patterns of Mass Supports for the Parties in Arkansas." Ph.D. diss., University of Illinois, 1973.

Index